What others a

She tells this secret ... who rarely spoke of their family's ... suddenly tell Bea, "Yes, I know what it is like, my child... my brother... my mother... or... has schizophrenia too." And in sharing there is a sense of relief. A sense of not being alone. Sense that would not be there had Bea not shared her story with them.

From *Canadian Entrepreneurial News*,
Spring/Summer 2008 issue, by **Xenia Stanford**,
CEN Feature Writer, Author, Editor and *The Writer's Guide*

You have truly turned your challenges into gifts! I look forward to your book. Put my name down for 3 copies. I know that my daughters would be eager to have their own copies. They always ask about you when we talk. They absolutely adore your spirited approach to life!

Maryanne Oxamitny
Educator, Colleague

I listened to Bea Weatherly speak at a conference in Red Deer in March 2008. Bea's message was heartfelt, personal, knowledgeable, and inspirational. She spoke about courage, her courage in the face of much adversity. Bea's presentation was touching and at the same time humorous. I laughed; I cried; I empathized. Bea is articulate; her speech was organized and logical, easy to follow, yet held incredible depth. There is no mistaking, she is one courageous woman! Now she is sharing her message in a larger way through her book and to a greater audience. Anyone anywhere who has a loved one with mental illness, multiple addictions or other challenges needs this book. Anyone anywhere who loves a good human interest story will want this book.

Marlene Nelson
Educator

Anyone with a non-neurotypical child knows how important it is to be blessed with a teacher who goes to the "nth" degree to make things work for your child and make the classroom a positive experience. Bea is one of those teachers. Bea Weatherly will always have a special place in my heart and now with her book she can help you understand your son, daughter, other relative, friend, student or anyone who faces challenges in life.

Linda Kellett
Parent

A Gift of Grace

Best wishes
Wendy

Bea Weatherly

A Mother's Journey Through Her Son's Schizophrenia

Bea Weatherly

A Gift of Grace

Copyright © 2008 by Bea Weatherly

Upside Publishing and Productions
www.beaweatherly.com

ISBN 978-0-9784547-0-8

All rights reserved. No part of this book may be reproduced or transmitted in any form without permission in writing from the author, except by a reviewer who may quote for review purposes. For more information, please write to the publisher at:

Upside Publishing and Productions
Suite A, 3639 Sierra Morena Road SW
Calgary, Alberta
T3H 3A7

e-mail: beaweatherly@shaw.ca
www.beaweatherly.com

The author speaks from her personal experience. Based on memory of events and journals; whenever necessary, she has recreated dialogue to tell her story and assist the readers in feeling they are experiencing the events firsthand. Names have been changed to protect the identity of certain individuals, except where permission was given or where quoted material or activities are in public record.

Credits: Dominique Petersen, cover design

PRINTED IN CANADA

Dedicated to my Parents,

Kristina Helena Gilbertson and
Edward (Ted) Hyslop Gilbertson

Mom and Dad had a huge influence on me. Mom modeled love and resourcefulness, Dad taught me to dream big, and both of them demonstrated the power and strength of a positive attitude. I have dealt with adversity in my life but, because of those struggles and the influence of my upbringing, there is that upside… I developed a free spirit and sense of courage.

Mom, you showed exemplary love and dedication to our family. You gave so much of yourself to raise six children in the house in the coulee. I still have the memory of you sitting in front of your Singer Sewing machine, cutting and sewing over second hand clothes and designing slippers lined with fleece ripped from the inside of a worn-out jacket. After school I walked across the meadows then stepped into the porch, coming home to the wonderful smell of freshly baked bread. I still make your famous oil and vinegar dressing for chopped green onions and leafy lettuce, which we pulled from your gigantic organic garden! It is your womanly love and strength that is a part of me and I share with my daughters, Nicole and Shelley.

I loved the way Dad would tell me, "Bea, you should write a book." At that time I wondered what he thought I knew enough about to warrant writing a book! Well, now I know!

My parents would drop by, visit and offer to look after the kids. Dad has passed away but is forever in my heart. Of course, I don't see him any more but it is as though he just hasn't dropped by for a while. Dad would be proud to know that I have written this book, even for the fact that it is somewhat of an open book, portraying the lives of family members.

When this book is published, Dad, let's dance around the kitchen just for old time's sake!

A Gift of Grace

*Kristina and Ted Gilbertson,
the author's parents, circa 1942*

Acknowledgements

Edward, you provided a license for me to write. When I asked you if it was okay for me to write this story, you would always say, "Mom, just write your book!" But...I knew it would impact your life! I tell what happened from my perspective. *A Gift of Grace* is a real story - an open book. Today you thank me for writing it because it gives your life credibility. You now have your "crazy" experiences acknowledged and accepted for the part they played in your life.

Nicole, thank you for being Edward's primary caregiver during the critical beginnings of his recovery, as your Dad and I were unable to do so since we lived so far away. You regularly communicated with Edward's healthcare team and *twice* you went to court to have Edward committed to hospital. You were the one who drove him to his appointments and did your best to ensure he was taking his medicine. While you were doing these things, you worked hard at building a relationship with Edward, and keeping Dad and me informed of his progress.

Although this might sound like a full-time job to most, you were also teaching part-time *and* taking classes at university to complete your engineering degree. And, as much more than simply your passion project, Edward's journey inspired you to create a company, *IDEGO Multimedia*, to help promote awareness and understanding of the diverse social issues that have impacted him. You had his artwork silk-screened onto T-shirts and now you are producing a 3D-animated documentary. I see much of myself in you, and I am so proud to be your mother.

Shelley, you have a compassionate soul. Your moral support uplifts me. You have a gift for listening, asking the right questions and helping me through difficult times. When I am down, you encourage me to realize I am making the right decisions. You're always just a phone call away. Thank you for offering moral support for your Dad, as well. I have always marvelled at your voracious reading habits. So, it wasn't surprising that I came across "Shelley

A Gift of Grace

will be my editor" in one of my old journals.

Marlene, my sister and best friend! You are the one whose consultation I respect and value. Your "positive vibes" have helped me get through tough times! Your generosities of time, money and spirit inspire me.

Xenia Stanford, my editor extraordinaire, thank you for your compassion and sincere interest in listening to my stories. You encouraged me to attach the emotion once again to painful experiences, so the reader could join me in the roller coaster ride with the will to hope for better days. I give you the credit for crafting my story; for your expertise and knowledge of plot. You are one of those puzzle pieces that fall in your lap and eventually is found. It's the one you've been looking for which helps complete a beautiful landscape! My book!

Foreword

My mother and I have a very special relationship. She is not only my Mom but is my best friend. Over the course of my lifetime, whether I was fully aware of it or not, she has been with me in spirit. She was with me when I first came into the world, taught me my first word, encouraged my first science project and now allows me to still dream BIG. The trials and tribulations of growing up and the unconditional love that my Mom gave me is what made me the man I am today.

Along the way, of course, I came into some hard and challenging times. I developed paranoid schizophrenia shortly after attending university although all along my life I have been somewhat of an eccentric. I admit that now. I was always encouraged to be myself and to explore the universe with excitement and a love for learning.

A Gift of Grace is a wonderful depiction of what it must have been like for my Mom to endure the years of torment that ensued due to my development of this debilitating and complex mental illness. I see my Mom's book truly is a "gift of grace" as the universal power of love has blessed us with coming out on the other side stronger and with the ability to accept some of life's more difficult realities.

I hope that anyone who has a loved one with any mental illness or concurrent disorder can read her book and find solace and hope that it is possible to recover even after the pain and agony. My Mom's book is a brilliant portrayal of our life together and apart, and now it is your turn to read the compelling and arduous journey that so often is hidden in secrecy and mystery.

May God bless you and keep you safe and free from the bondage of self and the horror of what lies beneath the broken shadows. The best is yet to come...

Edward K. Weatherly

1980

August 3, 1980

Edward, age 3, Czar

I nearly lost Edward today. We all went to the lake to enjoy the warm sun and cool waters.

My three children all were happily building sand castles while I was sunning and squishing my feet into the sand for a "natural pedicure." I let them wade in the water with me and urged them to stay within my protective reach. Now I sat back and watched them. I marvelled at my beautiful family and how lucky I am.

One of the other mothers came over to me and said, "What lovely children you have!"

I said, "Thank you" and thought to myself "It is so true!"

The three blond heads bobbed up and down as they ran around to gather more sand to build, "the biggest, bestest sandcastle ever, Mommy!" Their eyes shone in the sun and their perfect little bodies were a tanned contrast to their Nordic looks.

The perfect family: Nicole, the oldest at six, was clearly the leader of the pack. Never bossy, she managed to orchestrate the sand building while Shelley five and Edward three ran to gather the best sand in their pails to bring back to their oldest sister, the master builder.

"Did you know that a little girl drowned here a couple of weeks ago?" the other mother said.

"No, I hadn't heard that!" My heart skipped a beat, "How did it happen?"

A Gift of Grace

"I'm not sure, but I think she slipped on the wet pier," she said as she pointed to the wooden walkway beside me that ran out into the deeper water before it abruptly ended, "and drowned before anyone could reach her."

The goose bumps and hairs on my arms automatically reacted to the thought of someone's lovely child drowning in the very spot near where my children were so peacefully playing.

Then without warning Edward was running down the wooden planks of the pier.

"Stop Edward!" I called out, but his little legs continued running as I tried to catch up to him.

He reached the end of the pier and jumped in and my heart felt like it had stopped cold. The blood in my body seemed to drain as I reached the end of the pier and looked down. I couldn't imagine my life without Edward, my precious boy, the baby of the family, as I stared into the waters wondering if I would ever see him alive again. I tossed off my flip-flops in preparation to jump in to try to find him. Just then his blond head popped up and he was treading water as if he was a natural born swimmer.

"Look at me, Mommy," he called out. "Look at me."

I fished him out of the water and I just couldn't scold him even though I knew I should. I just wrapped his soaked body in a large beach towel and held him close. Maybe too close because he squirmed for me to let go.

Reluctantly I released my grip and said, "Edward, next time wait for me before you jump into the water. Wait for me."

"OK, Mommy!"

1981

June 21, 1981

Edward, age 4, Czar

It's Father's Day and we decided to make it special by driving to Shuswap Lake, BC yesterday for the weekend. Today we packed the blue metal cooler with a picnic lunch and made our way down the winding path to our blue and white boat with inboard motor. After everyone put on their lifejackets, we settled in our respective seats and enjoyed the ride around parts of the shoreline. The occasional splash from the spray of the waves was refreshing. The children and I giggled whenever the spray hit us.

Then we moored the boat and carried the cooler onto shore. After spreading the special blanket (which I sewed from squares of worn-out jeans) out on the hot sand, we opened the lid and enjoyed a wonderful buffet. After lunch we walked around the area looking for blueberries and the kids found some.

"Dad, you said you'd help us learn to water ski!"

Frank and I help Nicole put on her skis. Then Frank takes the other end of the rope and goes on shore. I lower Nicole into the water and hold her steady, while Frank walks until the rope is taut. He, slowly but with enough of a steady speed, runs and then, at the right moment, I give her a gentle push forward and she is skiing!

Yippee!

Then it's Shelley's turn and she is up and skiing. Now it's Edward's turn. They all make it up and away! Dad is a hero for Father's Day!

June 21, 1981 **3**

1986

April 1, 1986

Edward, age 9, grade 4, Czar

Today I was at the school entrance, supervising the last stragglers entering the school to return to their classrooms after morning recess. Suddenly, Edward burst into the school late. His khaki cargo pants and striped shirt with white cuff and collar were dirty from playing in the sandy schoolyard.

He was yelling, "Mom! Mom! There's biker leather men out there swearing at me and pulling my pants down."

Nearly out of breath, he continued, "They're on motorcycles and have leather jackets."

"How many were there?"

"A whole gang of them!"

My heart skipped a beat. As Edward's mother and the small school's principal, I was mortified and immediately concerned about all the students. Quickly I looked out the door and did not see anyone, but I could hear motorcycles in the distance. It was hard to tell if there were new tracks, but the ridges made by motorcycles were clearly evident in the sand.

Grasping Edward by the hand, I raced with him to my office to call the Provost Police Detachment, our nearest police office, and let them know what had just happened. As soon as I hung up, I immediately phoned the superintendent to let him know the events and convince him of the danger of these men lurking around other playgrounds, so he could warn other schools in the area of the danger. It then struck me that besides the approximately 30 children in the school, there were only three adults –

4 April 1, 1986

A Gift of Grace

all female: the secretary who had been a student of mine, the grade 4-6 teacher and me. So I put the school into lock down. The four outside doors were locked and I announced there would be no outdoor lunch or afternoon recess that day. The students would have to stay inside for board games or to play in the gym. Luckily there were only two classes to worry about. Besides being the principal, I teach grade 1-3. I taught Edward when he was in those grades, but this is his first year in the other teacher's class.

While waiting for the police, I returned Edward to his classroom and gave my students work to do. I tried to act as if everything was normal, so I would not frighten them. I kept calm on the outside to let them know everything was under control. Meanwhile I kept my eye on the road for a police cruiser. When the police officer arrived, for privacy, I took him and Edward to the gym change rooms just past the far side of the stage. He began to interview Edward, who answered the questions very matter-of-factly repeating the events exactly as he had told them to me. Then I told Edward to return to his class. The police officer said he would cruise around the small community of Czar, which has about 250 people, looking for any likely suspects.

After classes were dismissed for the day and I had watched the last student get picked up by the bus, I phoned Mom and Dad. I briefly told them about the events of the day and that I would meet them at my place. I locked up the school making sure everything was secure. I took Edward with me as I did not want him out of my sight. When everything had been double checked, we headed for home.

"There's Grandma Kristina and Grandpa Ted," said Edward as my parents' truck came rushing toward the house. I had never seen Dad drive so fast.

"What's going on," asked Frank, my husband.

I realized I had forgotten all about phoning him.

The bus from the high school had dropped off our daughters Shelley and Nicole across from the railroad tracks and they had already walked home. So with my family gathered around me, I let Edward repeat the frightening events of the day.

"Quit lying Edward," Frank said.

April 1, 1986 **5**

A Gift of Grace

"How can you say that?" my parents and I said at once.

"He's making it up," Frank replied.

This made me angry. After all, we raised our children not to lie. They told the truth at all times, even when it was painful or when they knew they would confess to something that would get them into trouble.

"Just tell the truth and we can deal with the rest," I would tell them.

Still Frank is refusing to believe this is not a lie, but tomorrow I am going to ask the school board to put up a fence around the school grounds.

Tonight I am close to tears because I imagine my little blond haired, blue-eyed boy running, trying to pull his pants up and tripping over the castles the children had made and falling into holes they had dug in the sandy ground that is typical of this part of Alberta, then scrambling to get out. I was relieved to know that he had outrun those bad people and had come into the school safely. You hear so many horror stories about children being molested and abducted. I had hoped living in the country and going to school in the village would protect my children from facing this risk. My goal is to be the best mother ever and protecting my children from harm is a huge part of this task.

> *The chatterbox starts to go off in my head. The little voice inside that questions me to try to throw me off balance. After all how could this be a lie? No nine year old could conjure up this scenario and then go through the drama of describing it to me, his mom, as well as to the police, then to recount the exact same details to his father and grandparents.*

I am thankful I had such a great upbringing by wonderful parents. My Mom was loving and my Dad kind with a great sense of humour. I remember him always laughing. On Saturday evening our family of three boys, three girls and our parents would sit around the kitchen table playing cards or board games like Monopoly or Crokinole. My Dad would get up and do a jig in the tiny floor space. Soon we would all be dancing and laughing. My older sister, Shari, would play *In the Mood* on the piano while my younger sister, Marlene, and I would dance together. Dad would continue his fancy jig while Mom would clap her hands in tune.

This love and laughter is what I want for my children. Now I fear some outside intruder will destroy our chance of having that.

August 20, 1986

Edward, age 9, soon grade 5, Czar

Today I cleaned the house and started getting things ready for the start of school. Next week I will have to prepare the school before it opens in September after Labour Day. While cleaning, I ran across the photo album of the kids when they were little and also the videotape of Edward singing when he was one and a half years old. I stopped and sat down to watch the video.

With my movie recorder, I had captured him, microphone in hand, humming and singing "Da, da, da da!" to the tune of our national anthem, *O Canada.* Such an early demonstration of musical ability! He most likely learned this tune from overhearing the hockey games on TV. Not knowing the words didn't matter, he had the tune so right. Later he memorized different commercials on TV and we would take delight in having him recite them over and over, as he stood in front of us, his first audience. On the video of his toddler tune, I saw him sway from side to side in perfect motion with the music. As it neared the end, we could see his entire body on the film, including his bottom half. He was wearing his sister Nicole's skirt that I had made for her to wear for her part in the Figure Skating Ice Carnival!

Now that vision came flooding back and I opened the album to flip through to see the photos where Edward was playing with his sisters and wearing their skirts. This upset Frank. He did not want his only son to be a sissy. I didn't think there was any particular harm, but I knew Frank was concerned and I wanted so much for

A Gift of Grace

him to have a great father/son relationship with Edward. Frank often spoke bitterly of his father and how he would avoid being around him, particularly when his father came home drunk, looking for a fight.

I also felt that the small red-necked village would have judged us if they saw Edward in girl's clothes and this would really hurt Frank's pride. So I would bribe Edward to remove his sister's clothes before Frank came home and especially before driving uptown to pick up a few things at the grocery store.

Since Edward's favourite outfit was Nicole's fringed skating skirt, I promptly went shopping to find something appropriate for a boy. I found a cowboy shirt with fringe on each side of the front. I hoped this would satisfy his wish to wear his sisters' clothes. I was sure the attraction was the fringe that moved as he swayed his body back and forth. He looked so cute in the fringed shirt. A real little cowboy!

But the fringed skirt wasn't the only girls' clothes he wore. Valerie, our neighbour's thirteen year old daughter, is an excellent baby-sitter because she enjoys playing with the kids. She even does a few chores around the house, like folding the towels in the laundry basket! I knew she dressed Edward in the girls' clothes and put wigs on his head. Edward loved it. What else could we expect? Girls were everywhere around him. He has two older sisters. Nicole, the oldest, is one year and five months older than Shelley, who is two years and eight months older than Edward. The three of them are very close and I am not just referring to age. Also when I taught Edward in grades one, two and three, he had only three classmates in his grade and they were all females. This past school year he was not in my classroom, so I am not sure to whom he relates during school time, but most of his non-school time is spent with sisters, his mother and a female baby-sitter. I wish he'd spend more time with his dad.

I encourage Edward to go out to the garage to be around his dad and maybe pick up some handyman abilities, but he would rather stay inside and bake cookies with me or play house with his sisters. When he was younger, he enjoyed stirring up cakes and baking them in Nicole's Easy Bake Oven. I am sure it is harmless and he will eventually grow out of the desire to hang around girls so much.

August 22, 1986

Edward, age 9, soon grade 5, Czar

Edward has always been my darling son and just so adorable when he was very young. I remember how he used to stand on a wooden chair beside me at the kitchen counter watching me fix the lunches for Dad, his sisters and me. He had just had his bath, was dressed in light blue printed pyjamas, with bare feet, his blond hair slicked down to the side and his face scrubbed super clean. I loved the fresh smell of my pure Ivory soap child beside me. What could be any better than that!

There was a time when Edward was very picky with his eating and I was worried he wasn't eating enough to grow. I made a chart out of cardboard and we agreed that he'd get to put a coloured star in the appropriate spot after he finished each meal. Soon the stars started filling in the chart. He was so easily pleased.

Edward started to experience bad dreams at an early age and would ask to crawl into bed with us. I remember the warmth of my parents' bed when I had those "boogeyman" dreams. I remember the night my youngest sister and I got to snuggle up in bed with Mom because Dad was away. She taught us to say our prayers: "Now I lay me down to sleep... God bless Mommy, Daddy..." I was glad Edward felt the same comfort, even though Frank complained.

A piano was the first purchase I made after I started teaching in September 1969. I faithfully made twelve payments of one hundred dollars each until it was all paid off. I was so proud of my piano.

One afternoon I was playing the country song, *Ashes of Love*, on the piano when Edward sidled up beside me and demanded, "I want to play that!" I was playing simple cords with my left hand and picking out the melody with my right. So, I showed him how I played it and he picked it up quickly. It was then that I decided the kids should have piano lessons.

A Gift of Grace

I asked my friend's mom if she would be able to teach the kids, but she was too busy. Then I heard about a very competent teacher, named Martha, who lived in Provost. One Saturday the children and I piled into the car and drove to Provost. We knocked on her door. She answered but said she was busy with a student. She agreed to check her schedule and at the very least interview the kids. She gave us her phone number and promised to call me soon. As we said our goodbyes at the door, Martha scolded Edward for touching one of her ornaments. I hope he now minds his manners when he's taking lessons!

Nicole was in grade four then, Shelley in grade three and Edward in grade one. Martha found time for all three to take lessons. So I drive them to her house every Tuesday evening for piano lessons. Most of the time they convince me that we should drive by the Burger Baron to pick up some burgers and fries for the 35-minute ride home. We usually sing rounds to pass the time and the time flies. I really enjoy these rides and we are all building those wonderful family memories I want my children to have of their childhood.

I do it all! I am a Super Mom. Every night after I do the dishes and clean up the kitchen, I gather all five lunch kits, clean out the dirty Tupperware and wrappers, and wipe the lunch kits out with a dishcloth. I line the lunch boxes up on the island counter and start loading them with a banana and an orange, a small tub of yogurt, slices of cold hamburger with dill pickle on whole wheat bread and a juice box. Then a treat... homemade chocolate cake or maybe a piece of homemade pumpkin pie with whipped cream.

I enjoy my life. I love teaching. I love my kids and think it is important to take them to piano lessons, dance lessons, Cubs and Brownies. I wonder if they will always remember the Downhill Toboggan Tournament I organized for them and the neighbour kids. I gave out mini trophies as awards. Will they forever remember when I helped them set up the Lemonade Stand in front of the house by the side of the road, so they could catch the farmers as they sat in their grain trucks waiting for their turn at the elevator? I supplied the beverage made with "real" lemons while Grandpa Ted constructed the stand, similar in design to the lemonade stand of Charles M. Schulz's Peanuts' gang.

I wonder if they'll remember all the gingerbread houses we make each Christmas and then invite the neighbour kids over to have

A Gift of Grace

tea and nibble on the gingerbread until there are only crumbs left. I hope they will always remember fondly when I played nurse with them and pretended to be the nurse by wearing a pair of white panties on my head to imitate the white caps nurses used to wear. Then I gave them Smarties for medicine! We also play house and pretend school. We have such fun!

Sometimes though, when I stand at that counter and pack lunches "day in and day out," buy the groceries, take out the garbage and do the same thing the next week, I wonder... is this what my life is all about? What will I do when the kids leave home?

Enough reminiscences, I must cut Edward's hair tomorrow. I shave it during the summer and the blond spikes go perfectly with his wonderful tan and large blue eyes. I wash and braid the girls' hair. Then when we take the braids out, the girls instantly have long, curly blonde hair. I guess I like to see them in curls as it reminds me of the way Shari would give Marlene and me a Toni to curl our hair. Braids are just a much easier way! They look gorgeous with their naturally blonde hair. Shelley has brown eyes like her dad and Nicole has blue eyes like Edward and me. I have a beautiful family. I count my blessings.

I'm glad a fence has been put around the school. No more bikers riding into the sandy soil in the schoolyard.

August 22, 1986 **11**

1987

September 1, 1987

Edward, age 10, grade 6, Czar

How fast the last two years seemed to fly by. My life was so busy at school and at home: driving the kids to Girl Guides, dance lessons in Wainwright, music lessons, Cubs and hockey. Now at last I am taking a year off!

I taught in Czar without much of a break since I received my teaching certificate. Then the superintendent asked me to accept the position of principal and I did. I worked very hard both teaching and being principal at the same time. A new school was built and I helped with moving into the new facility. Now my own kids are all pretty much teenagers and I feel like I need to take a year's leave of absence. So I asked and was told yes!

Yes! I have the leave and I'm staying at home this year!

I took time off when Edward was born and I went back teaching in September 1979, when Edward was just under a year old. Mom (Grandma Kristina, as my children call her) offered to care for Edward, which was great for me, because I was able to go back teaching, which I love. This babysitting lasted until June 30, 1982, the summer before Edward started grade one. Edward loved being with them so much he refers to it as the time "I lived with Grandma Kristina and Grandpa Ted."

It tugs at my heart that he felt he lived there full time, when I was the one who dressed him in the morning and packed up what he would need for the day. Then I would give him a big hug and kiss when Dad picked him up. After school I would drive to my parents' house to get him and bring him home. Then we would all have dinner together, he would play with his sisters and I would join in when the chores were done. Before bed I bathed him, got him

A Gift of Grace

ready for bed, tucked him in, read to him and gave him lots of kisses before I turned out the light. Then the weekends were spent at home when I devoted my time to my children. How had he forgotten that?

I can understand why he flourished under my parents' care. Mom loved looking after him and when she asked him what he wanted to eat he invariably answered, "Pancakes, Grandma!" Pancakes are a favourite in my family and my Mom makes the best Swedish pancakes!

Edward was named after both of his grandfathers, my Dad (who goes by Ted) and Frank's father. Edward is a favoured grandchild, especially by my parents. Dad took an active part with my Mom in caring for him. When Edward asked one of his many questions about many far flung topics, Dad would take it upon himself to give him the most thorough of answers.

Mom and Dad took him along to a variety of places to teach him about the world around him. They traveled to the courthouse, airport, community events and the Hutterite Colony. Then they dropped in for coffee with friends and relatives all over the countryside. Dad could strike up a conversation with anyone! Mom would tell him, "Teddy, you meet up with the darndest people!"

Finally with the school year coming to an end, a few days were set aside for "Beginner Days" when the children who would be entering school in the fall would have first exposure to school.

Since I was teaching grade one and two that year, I anticipated an easy adjustment for Edward. Mom and Dad were sad to let Edward go because he had become such a part of their everyday life.

On the first of the Beginner Days, it was a rainy spring day, so the kids stayed in and were skipping rope in the gym. I am not sure what happened exactly, but the other teacher, who was supervising the gym class, said Edward tripped over one of the ropes and ended up falling into the garbage can. It must have been full of leftover lunches, because Edward was brought to me so stinky and smelly that he was feeling sick. I took him to the teacher's washroom to clean him up, but he started throwing up. He was so sick, he couldn't stay in school. I called Mom to pick him up and

September 1, 1987 **13**

A Gift of Grace

take him to the doctor. He ended up staying in the hospital overnight.

What a traumatic introduction to school! This incident must be way past him, because he now excels at school and everything he does.

Take piano for example. At the kids' first piano recital in June 1984 when he was seven, Edward played Ludwig Van Beethoven's, *Ode to Joy*, a difficult number for his age. His teacher scolded him though, because, "Edward, it was technically correct, but you played it way too fast!"

> *I think Edward probably thought... the faster the better... but he soon learned to follow her direction and is already an excellent pianist. Music is an important part of Edward's life and he seems very attracted to Beethoven. I read up on him and concluded that he was one of the greatest and most radical composers of all time. History claims he was a tormented genius who went deaf later in life. "Ode to Joy" was adopted as Europe's anthem in 1972, just four years before Edward was born.*

December 1, 1987

Edward, age 11, grade 6, Czar

It feels great to have a year off, take a mental break and have fewer responsibilities outside my own family. Thankfully, Frank's management job affords us to do that.

Nicole is in grade ten, Shelley in grade nine and Edward in grade six. The girls take the bus to school in Hughenden, a village ten kilometres away. Edward walks up the hill and over the railroad tracks to the school in our home village of Czar. Since the motor-cyclists have not been seen around for the past two years and he is older, I am confident Edward has no trouble going to school on his own and, so far, so good.

A Gift of Grace

Nicole seemed bored with Math and was indifferent about doing her homework, so I study each chapter and review with her. I love to hear what she gets on each quiz because she's happy now and getting top grades.

Shelley is excelling in her school work and demonstrating an exceptional love for reading. I recall a day when she was younger and I thought I should be checking the content of the books she was reading, but it had become a moot point because she had become such an avid reader that she developed the skills to choose books that were appropriate for her level of interest and understanding, yet challenge her to increase her reading ability.

I remember one time at Mom's home in Hughenden when I was there with Shelley, who was four years old at the time. My brother, Ron was at home visiting. Shelley was on a chair reading the book, *Seven with One Blow* by Walt Disney and, all the while Shelley was reading, she twisted around on the chair, positioning herself in all the ways possible to imitate all the actions in the book! Obviously, there's no need to worry about Shelley.

Ron exclaimed, "Bea, she's actually reading that book?" I laughed, "I think Grandma and I have read that book to her so many times that she has memorized the words and knows when to turn the pages!"

Mr. Foster is Edward's teacher and he has a way of helping Edward focus his high energy, along with increasing his appreciation for politics, ancient history, astronomy and the world beyond the small village of Czar!

It's off to a good year.

December 1, 1987

A Gift of Grace

CHRISTMAS GREETINGS 1987
From Martha Halzelton, music teacher

The greatest waste of our natural resources is the number of people who never achieve their potential. Get out of the slow lane. Shift into the fast lane. If you think you can't, you won't. If you think you can, there's a good chance you will. Even making the effort will make you feel like a new person. Reputations are made by searching for things that can't be done and doing them. Aim low: boring. Aim high: soaring!

Charles Swindoll

*I asked for strength that I might achieve
I was made weak that I might learn humbly to obey.*

*I asked God for health that I might do greater things
I was given infirmity that I might do better things.*

*I asked for riches that I might be happy
I was given poverty that I might be wise.*

*I asked for power that I might have the praise of men
I was given weakness that I might feel the need of God.*

*I asked for all things that I might enjoy life
I was given life that I might enjoy all things.*

*I got nothing that I asked for ---
But everything I had hoped for...*

*Almost despite myself, my unspoken prayers were answered
I am among all men most richly blessed.*

Unknown Confederate Soldier

Dear Nicole, Shelley, Edward and Beatrice,

You are really having a busy year in your family this year with lots of things happening.

A Gift of Grace

Nicole, your work is progressing quite well. You just need to develop more self confidence in what you are doing. One big requirement – please read extra music every day – pop, hymns, and some classic. The more you do the easier it all becomes and observe while reading. See how your theory is being applied in your pieces. Do some theory every day – that is much better than long stretches at a time with big gaps in between.

Shelley, you are moving much better lately. The biggest thing to remember is the relaxed feelings across the shoulders. Never try to put a piece together too quickly if you are inclined to tense up so. Work hands separately and together. Listen to what you are playing so that your ear can help you. Try to see a completed piece in your mind. Pick up lots of extra things to play. The more you read the better you become.

Edward, you are a busy little beaver this year. Don't lose that enthusiasm. But remember slow work is necessary to put on a good finish. Listen to lots of good music, absorb, and watch other people who are good performers for ideas. But most of all, listen closely to yourself when you practise, think in sentences and do work slowly.

Beatrice, your children are very musical, and with your help and concern should move along nicely. I'm glad to see you doing the theory as well. It helps when two can discuss it.

Have a wonderful holiday.

Love,
Martha

Thank you for the baking. It was greatly appreciated.

I appreciate Martha's letter because she talks about each child's qualities and what is required for each to take it to the next level. This doesn't happen that often. The girls tell me they are tired of hearing from everyone how talented Edward is.

December 1, 1987

1988

June 15, 1988

Edward, age 11, grade 6, Czar

Edward is still the high achiever in all he does. Besides his collections of hockey cards, rocks, stamps and coins at home, in school he turns in amazing assignments and is the top of his class.

He has always been full of energy and drama. One warm, sunny morning he stood on the balcony of the second floor of our home in Czar and recited Alfred Noyes', *The Highway Man*, verbatim, demonstrating great love for the genre as he dramatized his unique recitation of poetic verses. Without his knowledge, we sat quietly on the patio below and watched him act out the poem with great flair and recite the words with exaggerated drama. It appeared as though he was honouring the branches of the Laurel Leaf Willow!

Besides reciting poetry, he loves singing, playing the piano and performing musical theatre at the Music Festivals held in Provost, something Edward and his sisters have been doing for the last seven years. Grandma takes the kids to the daytime performances, because most times Frank and I are at work.

Edward and I belong to the local Drama Club and we have so much fun performing! From February 25-27 of this year, Edward was in his first performance, *The Titanic*, as Harold Goodwin, one of the children who died on the ship. Since then I have joined the Club to enjoy the camaraderie.

Edward's father is not the drama type. He is practical and realistic. Instead of sitting around indoors, he prefers to hunt and fish. Frank also takes so much pride in renovating our houses. I enjoy this as well, because I too want to have a lovely home.

A Gift of Grace

When the kids were about four, six and eight years old, we renovated the home Ken and I bought just before our children were born. We tore off the roof, added a second storey and changed the plan of the main floor. I love our house! Right after our marriage, we lived just up the hill from this one. I looked at it longingly from up the hill and across the railroad tracks. For a year and a half I hoped the people who owned the house would sell it to us. Then they did. It was always my dream to own this home and this proves dreams can come true!

While we were renovating, I played games with the kids to keep them occupied and teach them the fun of helping out. Since there were so many shingle nails to pick up, I invented the "Nail Game." I gave them a penny for each nail they picked up around the house and outside. I kept a running tally on the stairs inside the house.

We all slept in the basement during reno time. As we were getting into bed, Frank would put on a stack of long play records for us to listen to as we fell asleep. These included Charlie Pride, The Statler Brothers, Fats Domino, Johnny Cash, Waylon Jennings, Jimmy Reeves, and the one and only – Hank Williams!

It seems that Frank can do anything he puts his mind to. When Nicole was about eight years old, she "wrapped" the score of her Ms. Pac-Man. Frank heard the special music indicating that she had beat the game and he was motivated to try his skill at it. He sat in his big sofa chair a few evenings until he, too, could wrap Ms. Pac-Man! He is an intelligent and analytical man. In my opinion, he is a self-taught chemical engineer since he manages a sulphate plant where formally trained engineers are contracted to work for him.

> *I admire him, but do I really love him? I don't think about it that often. My life is what it is and I am focused on my children. I believe I am a good wife.*

I am generous with my time and money, love to teach, keep a garden and indulge my children. I also enjoy drama, music, art, watercolour painting, cooking, baking and dancing.

June 15, 1988 **19**

A Gift of Grace

I still drive Nicole, Shelley and Edward to Provost for piano lessons every Tuesday evening. The girls still complain that Edward hogs the piano stool and does more than his share of practicing, a concept that is difficult to share with parents of other children taking lessons. They have to coax and cajole to get their children to play even an hour a night. Edward practices after dinner until bedtime and, in fact, would play through the entire night, if we let him. My children say they learn discipline and the power of expression from taking music lessons. I never have to coax, only settle the arguments over the piano stool and then go about our evening chores with beautiful music playing in the background.

I know my children are off to a good start.

1989

February 23, 1989

Edward, age 12, grade 7, Hughenden

My left breast has been itchy and weepy, so I went to see the doctor.

He said, "It's probably caused by the seam on your bra."

"No, I don't have a seam there."

Ignoring my response, he filled out a prescription for cortisone cream with instructions to apply when needed. At school I try to hold out until recess or noon, but in class it becomes too itchy to bear. I can't leave the room, so I give the children some work to do at their desks. Then I go to my desk and bend down far enough that the children can't see. I lift up my blouse and apply some cream. I get about 30 seconds of relief, but I have to go back to teaching a lesson.

In less than a couple of days, it was beyond bearing. No matter how much of the cream I applied, it wasn't enough. I would be in the middle of teaching a Math lesson and a sensation of itchiness would overwhelm me. I couldn't keep applying more cream often enough or soon enough. The urge to scratch made me extremely irritable. I felt bitchy.

I went back to the doctor and practically threatened not to leave his office until he referred me to a specialist. He sent me to a doctor in Edmonton, who referred me to an oncologist. The oncologist scraped some tissue from my nipple. Talk about a sudden and such intense pain! It still hurt as I drove the two and a half hours back home.

I went back to work the next morning. That was two weeks ago. Today the school secretary appeared at my classroom door and

A Gift of Grace

announced, so loud I'm sure the entire class heard, "Dr. Hepburn is on the phone for you."

I left her supervising the class and went to the phone expecting to hear it was time to go see him for the biopsy results.

"Hello?"

"Mrs. Weatherly?"

"Yes."

"Your results are in from the biopsy."

"Oh, okay."

"You have breast cancer."

Just like that! How would I get through the rest of the day? Did he even think about that?

I did get through the day. I am resilient. I am Superwoman!

February 26, 1989

Sunday morning
Edward, age 12, grade 7, Hughenden

Our local Drama Club gets together in January and produces a play on the last Thursday, Friday and Saturday of the month of February. These three nights are always very successful and well-received by the audience. An extremely talented woman writes the scripts and lyrics to the songs, as well as composes the music. Also she plans the costumes and decorations for each special performance. She even chooses the menu for our dinner, which always magically complements the theatre. Tour buses come from

A Gift of Grace

different parts of Alberta bringing people to watch our amateur dinner theatre.

I did get through that day – the day the doctor gave me the news – which just so happened to be the opening day of this year's play, *Garden Party Royale*. My role was a funky photographer and I danced onto the stage to the music of Dire Straits' *The Walk of Life*. The special effects fellow built a bra of extraordinary dimensions and he trimmed the perimeter with white mini Christmas lights. It was a bit bizarre because I am keeping the fact that I have breast cancer from my family until the play is over.

> *Before the last performance on Saturday night and before taking my steps onto the stage, I looked down at my left breast and whispered, "This may be the last time you're on stage, honey!"*

Afterwards I told my younger sister, Marlene, and we wept.

February 26, 1989

Sunday evening
Edward, age 12, grade 7, Hughenden

I told Frank the news. He didn't show much reaction other than to inquire when surgery is scheduled.

This afternoon, I asked the children to come sit on the couch with me. They started to tear up before I even spoke. Perhaps the seriousness of my face or an ominous tone in my voice sparked fear in them. Perhaps it was that I had told them I had something important to tell them.

I told them I had breast cancer and I will be going to Edmonton for surgery. Then I supposed there would be some treatment after that. We sat hugging and crying.

April 23, 1989

Edward, age 12, grade 7, Hughenden

I made lesson plans and hired a substitute for two days. I drove myself to Edmonton on the morning the surgery had been booked. The female surgeon advised me that she probably will not have to remove the entire breast. I signed the consent forms to agree to whatever they decided had to be done would be done.

I woke up from surgery to find what the doctor had advised was what happened. She says I can have cosmetic surgery to make my breast look more normal. Cosmetic surgery! That's so vain!

I opted out. After a one day recovery, I drove myself home.

What does the future hold for us? Only time will tell.

One day at a time.

June 12, 1989

Edward, age 12, grade 7, Hughenden

I was scheduled for six weeks of radiation at Foothills Hospital in Calgary. This was most of May and June. I made lesson plans for the entire time I would be gone and contacted the substitute teacher to take my place until the end of this school year.

I drove myself the five hours to get to Calgary and I am staying with my sister Marlene here. I drive back and forth from Mar's house to the treatment and back to her house again. After almost

A Gift of Grace

six weeks of radiation, the skin of my breast is raw and burned, like severe sunburn. My breast is not pleasing to the eye as it looks as though it was tarred and feathered... dissed! A vision of nasty... likened to having the middle of potato chips adhering to my breast, while the edges of the chip, curl. I'm braless, but remain hopeful!

At first I felt guilty because the treatment takes only minutes. Then I have the rest of the day to do what I want. Suddenly I realized I had a gift of time, me time, free time from the responsibilities of the daily life of wife, mother, teacher and Superwoman.

I deserve it, especially this year. After my year off I wasn't given a class in Czar or nearby. I was rejected! The superintendent and principal informed me that I was not wanted in Czar because a set of parents considered me to be the "dregs" of teachers. It was a slap in the face that I was turned down after my years of unblemished service to the school district, all because they believed some parents of students I never even taught. Instead I have been a Resource Teacher driving to Amisk, Metiskow and Bodo teaching students with special needs. I burned a lot of kilometres up and down Highway 13, and was finding no satisfaction in my teaching assignment. I didn't think I was seeing the students often enough to make a difference in their learning.

So in this time of reprieve, this down time, I cook the meals for Mar, Blaine (her son), and me. I try new gourmet recipes. I shop. I cook. I bake. I read. I organize the kids' photos and award certificates. I take watercolour and calligraphy courses accompanied by Frank's sister, Nora. We have lots of fun! This is such a healing time.

Meanwhile Frank drives the children to piano lessons. Somehow they are surviving. Someone cooks. Someone cleans. Someone does the dishes. Someone does the laundry. Someone does the lunches. Shelley is 14 and Nicole 16. Probably a lot falls on their shoulders.

Still I don't feel guilty. I feel I am owed this time.

A Gift of Grace

August 1, 1989

Edward, age 12, soon grade 8, Hughenden

After my year's leave, I was not given a teaching position in Czar because I was the dregs of all teachers according to some parents whose children I had never taught! Amazing! But even more amazing is that the superintendent and principal believed them instead of having faith in me after my years of teaching and even as principal of the very same school from which I was rejected.

I spent the school year on the road assigned to no particular school and being spread very thin. So thin that the students I saw did not have enough of my time to make a difference and I seemed to spend most of my time in the car. The only bonding was between me and the road! Then I got cancer.

Alrighty then... the universe must have something else in store for me...

I spoke with the superintendent in June to let him know I just want to be given a fulltime position with a regular grade. I told him the travelling resource teaching position was not benefiting students and was not acceptable for me. He just informed me he has found an opening for me in Provost to teach grade five.

Yippee!!!

A Gift of Grace

September 30, 1989

Edward, age 12, grade 8, Hughenden

After two years of study, Edward was confirmed in the Lutheran Church. He achieved his goal right on time, even though he joined the group late and one kid said Edward wouldn't pass because he had missed so much. Well Edward showed him and any others who doubted his ability by passing the test with a mark in the nineties. That's my Edward!

Edward showed how much he connected with the spirituality because he has been doodling with the abbreviation X. He learned in his studies that X stands for Christ and Xian for Christian. I find his drawings everywhere, all based around the letter X.

I have concerns about the pastor though. He smokes and the kids come out smelling like smoke and alcohol. I believe he encourages the kids to smoke and drink. I refuse to let Edward stay overnight with the pastor at his home because of one particular kid I would rather Edward avoid. Now that confirmation is over, I want to keep Edward away from the pastor as well. I just have weird vibes about him.

My parents can't understand my sense of foreboding.

"The pastor is wonderful and a very good friend of ours," Dad tells me.

Mom says, "Bea, I can't understand what you think he might do!"

Still I can't shake the feelings that the pastor's intentions and influence are not the best.

"He's married, Bea, with two babies," Mom says.

If he is so holy why does he do and say these things that cause such an icy feeling to grip my heart?

December 11, 1989

Edward, age 13, grade 8, Hughenden

Right back to the routine! After cancer treatments in Calgary and summer at home, I am back to my life as I know it – wife, mother, teacher and Superwoman!

We are still living in Czar and now all three kids go to school in Hughenden. Frank took a turn driving the children to piano lessons, while I was receiving cancer treatments in May and June. Martha Hazelton is an exceptional teacher, who offers advice and encouragement to do their best work. Many lessons go over time and Frank or I wait in the vehicle. At the annual Music Festivals, Edward won many awards for piano playing, poetry recitation, singing and musical theatre.

Edward quit playing on the hockey team. Frank was disappointed. Edward always seemed to be teased when he was in hockey and reacted by withdrawing, trying not to be noticed. Quite the opposite to when he is on stage reciting poetry, playing the piano or acting in a play!

Yet, he seems to be very different now. I know my cancer scare and treatment caused the children great stress. The girls told me they cried a lot. Edward tells me he felt like there was a hole in his life when I was gone. He is more secretive. He spends time in his bedroom reading Hardy Boy books. He hangs out with Chris and David. He loves horror movies. He tells me how after reading the Hardy Boy book *Face* he and Chris saw the Face in an abandoned building in town. I hope he is joking and not delusional. Maybe it is the make-believe of the poetry he loves to recite and act out with great exaggeration when not observed. Maybe it is the drama, the stage and the enthused audiences that he has come to love.

I think he is drinking and smoking pot with his friends. He comes in smelling of alcohol and his clothes have the scent of pot. Should I confront him or hope it passes? I thought I had instilled

A Gift of Grace

better values in my children. Was it because I was gone for so long?

Our big brown and white dog Max trails after him, even as he pedals his way down the gravel road to Shorncliffe Lake. Edward doesn't seem to mind. At least he has someone following him. I wish I knew for sure what he is up to, but even then what could I do?

1990

February 9, 1990

Edward, age 13, grade 8, Hughenden

My Dad, "Grandpa Ted" to Edward, is in Calgary in the Tom Baker Cancer Centre, part of the Foothills Hospital. We drive to Calgary to visit him whenever we can. Mom (Grandma Kristina to Edward) has a cot in his room. She is spending every day and night with him and, knowing Mom, she will not leave his side until he goes home. The doctors do not give him much hope, but he is a fighter and determined to survive. Our last visit really impacted Edward, because he showed me his Ethics Assignment on which he received a well-deserved A.

Title: "A Hero I Know"

My Hero: My Grandpa
by Edward Weatherly

> In my life there have been many, many people I look up to and could be considered my heroes. All these people contributed to the ideas and values I believe and practice today. One of my heroes, my favourite, is my grandfather. His name is Edward Hyslop Gilbertson. He is a very level-headed, responsible, mature, loyal, ethical and humorous person. He is my one and only grandpa.
>
> Grandpa is about five feet twelve inches in height, sixty-nine years of age, has grey hair, and usually wears jeans and an oxford shirt. His voice is kind, pleasing to the ear and good for telling interesting stories.
>
> I have known him for a very long time. When I was about three, he and Grandma took care of me until I could go

30 February 9, 1990

to school. During that time I traveled all over Alberta and Saskatchewan with them. He worked, so Grandma and I tagged along. He is very knowledgeable about agriculture and machinery. He has taught me a lot with his patience.

My Grandpa has traveled to many places. He has been to Europe, the United States and Mexico, and to most parts of Canada. He gained a lot of his knowledge from his traveling and from his reading. I think that his love for learning new things helped him to tell all his many interesting stories.

For the past twenty years my grandpa has been a Cat operator, farmer and repairman for this area. When I lived with him I learned from his experience. Because of this, each day he worked, he gained new information about many things. I admired his ability to learn and to be curious.

I think I have gotten different characteristics that are part of his personality. He is very friendly, kind, cheerful, and his "visit and have coffee" habits make him well liked. When I see and talk with him I learn about his great determination, the importance of getting a task done without delay and his belief to never be disloyal to a friend.

My grandpa is very special to me. He has been a main figure in my life and has influenced me tremendously. I have learned honesty, determination, friendliness and a love for music. I love him dearly. Unfortunately he has picked up a fatal disease called cancer. Before this he was strong, had a bit of a belly and was always cheerful; always laughing and having fun. Now most of these things have been taken away from him. But his determination to get well still stands out.

At this moment he is suffering in a hospital in Calgary. He is frail and is slowly slipping through the hands of medicine. I hate to say it but he could pass away very soon. But even though the type of cancer he has is fatal, I feel his never-ending determination and pride shine through his sickness, and will overpower and kill the cancer.

A Gift of Grace

When I visited him last, he told me, "Don't lose faith in me." He continues to hold on to his vast storage of courage, pride and dignity. I will not let Grandpa down. I will become what I want to be and will be the very best I can be. He has been a vital part of my growing up and his spirit shall always be with me.

Edward K. Weatherly

Portrait of Dad/Grandpa: Edward (Ted) Hyslop Gilbertson

Bea Weatherly, 1992

February 21, 1990

Edward, age 13, grade 8, Hughenden

My Dad has been my strength and my greatest supporter. He never appeared weak to me. So it was frightening when he started getting dizzy at times. Finally we convinced him to go to the doctor. When that doctor could not diagnose it, Dad tried several different doctors. Dad had stopped smoking ten years ago, so we were unprepared for the diagnosis that finally came – lung cancer! He had surgery to remove a lump on his neck where the cancer had spread, but the cancer in his lungs was too advanced. He faced gruelling treatments he was told may not work. He faced the future with hope and his positive spirit.

He said to me, "Bea, if you can go through treatment, I can too!"

Mom was there at his side day and night, and was still there with him when he passed away. We were coming up to the first Family Day holiday on Monday February 19, 1990, but Dad would not be with us that day. He passed away on February 16 and on February 19 we held his funeral. What a way to celebrate the first Family Day!

My grief is too deep to even fathom. I try to submerge it. I have no choice but go on. I must follow in my Dad's footsteps.

> *Dad, I will go forward with your shining example and be the very best parent for my children.*

No time to grieve. The annual play opens tomorrow night and Edward has a major role in it.

A Gift of Grace

February 27, 1990

Edward, age 13, grade 8, Hughenden

Edward turned in another stellar performance in this year's play *Dogfather*. He played the part of a journalist and Poodle-Aire.

Although we are relative newcomers to Provost, Edward is already making quite an impression. When we go to community events, we are often greeted with, "Oh, so you are Ed's Mom, Ed's Dad and Ed's sister!" This may be what contributed to some underlying sibling rivalry. They say he is the favourite at home and in the community!

June 5, 1990

Edward, age 13, grade 8, Hughenden

A time of promise and heartbreak! Adam, my brother-in-law died of a heart attack at age 38. We are rallying around my sister-in-law to give her support.

Yet, this is a time to be very proud as a parent.

Edward entered the Science Fair at the local level and qualified for the regional. From there he was off to the Canada Wide Science Fair in Windsor, Ontario and I went with him. His project was called *Wave Velocity Analysis.*

Proudly we brought home his plaque and certificate of participation.

Edward also was awarded "The Most Promising Student Award" at the Music Festival's prestigious *Colour Night* held last Saturday. I took a photo of him with his two proud Grandmas with their

A Gift of Grace

arms around him. It doesn't stop there. He received the top points in Track and Field for boys his age again! He has done this every year from grade one to now grade eight! This award is for the best athlete from four different schools in the western part of the Provost School Division.

My Mom cuts out clippings from *The Provost News* of Edward's achievements. She has collected a lot now! Edward's only 13!

I also have a tub of medals, certificates and other awards from his piano, speech (especially his poetry recitations), track and field, musical theatre, schoolwork; first national science fair, drama club, singing (voice), Cubs, hockey, baseball, volleyball and the list goes on. What great achievements will the rest of his life bring?

Anyway his accomplishments earned him a treat. Shelley and Nicole offered to take him to Wainwright for the day. I was happy to let him go. They are very responsible older sisters.

June 6, 1990

Edward, age 13, grade 8, Hughenden

I waited up, but it was late when they came home that night, so we all went straight to bed. When I went to wake Edward in the morning, he rolled over and I was shocked! He had a tattoo on the top of his right arm! I can tell it is a real tattoo not a fake wash off. I am so furious! I lash out at Shelley and Nicole for allowing him to do this.

"But Mom, it wasn't our fault! He met some guys and took off. When he caught up to us again he had this tattoo."

"Edward, where did you get the money for the tattoo?"

"Oh, I didn't have to pay anything. They did it for free!"

"Were they real tattoo artists," I asked, fearing the worst.

June 6, 1990 **35**

A Gift of Grace

"No, Mom. They just did it. Isn't it cool?"

"But Edward, you can get very sick from dirty needles!"

He seemed to feel I was making much ado about nothing, but I was mortified. How could he sully his body like this? It will be forever permanent, a scar on his young body. After all I had done to protect the perfect skin he had at birth, now it is marred!

Now knowing this happened, I have to somehow inform Frank without him going through the roof. I should force Edward to tell his father. Or maybe I should just let him find out on his own... God! I was ready to let Edward "have it!" Why was this happening? A tattoo wasn't something you could just erase the next day!

Even worse, the one he got was not a symbol to be proud of! It was a sword with a drop of blood, which to me represented a violation of all that was pure in a young boy.

It really annoyed me that this had happened, because I took pride in raising my family and he didn't even consult me on something that was going to stay with him for a lifetime. He had acted so impulsively!

November 18, 1990

Edward, age 14, grade 9, Hughenden

Edward took a hunter's education course in September and did very well. He could not hunt until he turned 14 this month. Frank could hardly wait to introduce his son to the thrill of the hunt. Yesterday Edward went hunting with his dad, shot a whitetail deer and has a photo to document it. The look on Edward's face in the photo told me all I needed to know about that trip. I don't think he enjoyed it much. I wonder if the rifle will suffer the same fate as the pellet gun Frank gave him when he was much younger. I took Edward out and we shot a few pop cans off the

A Gift of Grace

fence posts, but other than that he has not used it. It is no longer around.

Previously, I had heard from Edward how hunting for birds, which he could do since age 12, was pretty scary. He hasn't gone into much detail. He hasn't said much about the deer hunt either.

Are the annual fishing trips we take enjoyable? The children don't seem to complain, but what difference would it make if they did. There are never any questions or options when summer comes around. We go fishing. The whole family is together, doing family things, which is important to me in spite of the work of packing up the motor home, gear and food we need, as well as closing up our house for the summer.

Of course, sometimes I wonder how Edward ever survived childhood. He was always taking risks. Edward tells me that when he was very young about six or seven, he and Alex straddled a big log to cross a rushing river and reach their Dads' favourite fishing hole.

> *He could have drowned! Frank thinks I baby Edward. I just want Edward to be able to grow safely. Perhaps my worry does hold him back.*

The summer I was recovering from my cancer treatments, Edward went to Cranberry River in Northern BC, one of our favourite spots, with Frank, Edward's Uncle John, his cousin Harold and the Thompsons (Alex, the son, who is five months younger than Edward, and Stephen, the father, who went to school with Frank). It was good for him to get out with his Dad and the "boys."

The girls and I stayed home, which was nice for us too. It gave me more chance to heal. The house was quiet with just the girls and me. They are more like young women now.

Edward has been showing more interest in doing things with his Dad lately. They seem to be bonding, not just with the fishing and hunting trips, but also painting the jeep together.

Edward does hang out with some boys that are of questionable character, but he has a big crush on Ashley and Taylor, both girls his own age. When he is with them, I feel he is safer.

November 18, 1990 **37**

1991

May 5, 1991

Edward, age 14, grade 9, Hughenden

This spring has been a difficult one. Frank lost his job because the plant where he was manager shut down. He received an offer from the owner of a plant in Slave Lake. Edward, Frank and I drove there to check out the community. We decided it wasn't for us. The manager said he would have some consulting work for Frank. Still it may mean depending upon my salary for awhile. I'm sure this will not sit well with Frank. It will affect his pride.

Then on April 8 my brother Ronnie died at 47 years of age from arrhythmia. His heart went out of sync and couldn't right itself. My brother-in-law Stephen died two weeks later from emphysema at age 45. Frank and I were born in the same month of the same year. So at 43, we are close to the age of family members that just passed away.

I'm still optimistic that my cancer is cured and I have no other health issues. But I worry about Frank. When he was only 26, we were on our way home from Calgary on snow-covered roads with the two girls who were toddlers at the time. Frank was extremely thirsty and we stopped frequently along the way so he could use the washroom and buy some root beer. He remarked about having the strange sensation of a "dry tongue." Immediately after he was diagnosed with diabetes, I started cooking and baking according to the recommended diet for diabetics. It's a very sensible food plan and a great choice for the whole family. I remove fat from meat and make sure we don't consume too much sugar, even if it's natural sugar.

> *I am doing everything I can for my family, but I think I am beginning to feel numb. I also am mad at myself, but I am not sure why. Maybe it's my low expectations.*

A Gift of Grace

May 18, 1991

Edward, age 14, grade 9, Hughenden

Edward talked non-stop last night after returning from the Canada Wide Science Fair in Vancouver. His project was chosen at the Alberta Regional level to go to the Canada Wide Science Fair in Vancouver, British Columbia.

Unlike the one in 1990 in Windsor, Ontario, I didn't attend with him. Since his science teacher, who was his mentor and a very dedicated teacher, was going, I didn't need to go. Nor was I asked. Not that I mind because he gets to enjoy some independence while still having adult supervision.

The project received honourable mention, but when he came home all he could talk about was the United World College and how he "must" apply. One of the tours offered to participants in the Science Fair was a trip to the Lester B. Pearson College, United World College of the Pacific, on Vancouver Island near Victoria, the capital of BC. It is one of about seven institutions in different parts of the world, called United World Colleges. Edward went on and on about how the program was such high quality and that he simply must go! As he continued to explain the advantages of the education at United World Colleges, Frank seemed bored and left the room. Frank listens to enough to know what is going on, but he isn't always one for the fine details.

The college's main curriculum is the International Baccalaureate Diploma Programme for gifted students.

Edward and I sat at the kitchen table and talked until late. I looked through the brochure with him and it explained:

> *The UWC select students from around the globe at a pre-university level, selected on merit, regardless of their financial, ethnic, religious or educational background and regardless of their ability to pay. A UWC Scholarship is highly prestigious as it gives the students a chance to develop a global and tolerant mind combined with strong*

A Gift of Grace

academic skills. The schools are known as some of the most high-status high schools in the world and UWC graduates are very interesting for major universities and companies.

"See Mom," he said, "I apply for the scholarship and it doesn't cost you anything!"

I'm sure there will be some costs, such as clothing and perhaps spending money, but what an opportunity! A United World College education seems just what he needs to challenge him and remove him from bad influences. Surrounded by high achievers, like him, can keep him striving to reach even higher goals than he could achieve locally, no matter how good our schools are.

I am excited that he is excited. I am impressed by what he tells me about the program. I am happy to have my precious son back to normal. No guns, no dope, no fooling around with the wrong crowd. I just hope the students there are more tolerant than some are here.

"Mom, I have the application forms and guide. Will you help me pick out the best college?"

"Of course, I will, but let's do it tomorrow. It's late now."

We said our good nights and I had such a good sleep. Things are falling into place.

May 19, 1991

Edward, age 14, grade 9, Hughenden

Even though he's over two years away from entry into a United World College, Edward came down after breakfast with his application filled out. He even had marked his top five preferences of the seven locations.

A Gift of Grace

"I bet you did this last night after we went to bed."

"I couldn't sleep, Mom. I had to get it ready to mail right away."

I looked it over, gave him some suggestions and told him I would drop it off at the post office tomorrow morning on my drive to school. He seemed like he wanted to run the ten miles to the post office to get it in right away, but I managed to convince him it wouldn't go anywhere from the post office on Sunday. Besides, I reminded him, the earliest he could get in is 1993-1994 year and, if successful that term, he can continue in the 1994-1995 year. It would be the equivalent of grade 12 and first year university.

"I know, Mom, but I want to be sure to have my application in as soon as possible."

He is so excited. I am so relieved and grateful he went on this trip and found out about this college system.

Once again I feel such hope for the future.

June 9, 1991

Edward, age 14, grade 9, Hughenden

Edward has another accomplishment to add to his ever-growing list! He entered the Oddfellows' Speaking Competition. Just back from the Science Fair in Vancouver and the visit to the United World College on Vancouver Island, Edward spoke about "Global Federalism."

He said, "Evil and good portray the dilemma in which our present international leaders are in. They are struggling for the balance between the existing principals (sic) of democracy and totalitarianism."

His notes for the speech continue, "The world is a much different place than what it was at the beginning of the 20th century.

A Gift of Grace

Wars, revolutions, hot and cold wars, and the growth of man's knowledge have resulted in the creation of vast technology which has and is continuing to bring each person, community and country closer together. This also has consummated an air of immediacy among nations where it had not existed before. As our population, technology and knowledge increases, the world and its people will become exposed to different societies, religions, cultures and socio-economic facets. This closeness will force the world to become smaller. It will force everyone to interact more. As they interact and are exposed to one another, the barriers of history will crumble, resulting in a global evolution. Ignorance and intolerance will eventually disperse."

This led him to the belief that, "With a changing world with changing perspectives, it is now possible, where 40 years ago it was not, to have a World Federalistic Regime. This Global Government would operate similarly to the United Nations..."

This was fitting since the competition was to be on a United Nations' topic and first prize was a trip to the UN in New York. Edward placed second and received a briefcase.

He can't always be first but, perhaps this is a mother's biased perspective, I thought his speech was the best.

I reminisce about the fear I experienced when I was growing up... news of The Cold War coming from the small light blue radio sitting in the corner of the kitchen cupboard. I had visions of the Russians bombing us and all my family dying. The fall of the Berlin Wall on November 9, 1989 is a symbol of getting rid of that war and providing many people with hope and happiness.

December 8, 1991

Edward, age 15, grade 10, Hughenden

Life is tumultuous.

The good news first!

42 December 8, 1991

A Gift of Grace

I love teaching in Provost! The school has about twenty-five teachers for students in kindergarten to grade twelve. I drive for a half hour, teach one class of grade five and work with a large staff. This is a gift for me!

I received a phone call from a colleague who had taught in Czar with me and she apologized for spreading rumours about me. Moot point... I'm teaching in Provost now!

Frank has a contract in Slave Lake, consulting for a sulphate company.

Both girls are in university. Shelley started school when she was five years old. Her birthday was just a day before the cut off date of February 28th. This means that she is in her first year at the University of Calgary while Nicole is in her second.

Shelley has often expressed appreciation for letting her start school the year after Nicole started. This scenario reminds me of my own childhood. My younger sister and I were very close and when it came time for me to begin school, she was jealous and didn't think it was very fair I got to go and she didn't. For me it just meant that I had her and my younger brother to play school and "teach" when I came home!

I am so glad my daughters are doing well.

Edward on the other hand is causing me concern. He is in grade ten and I worry about him a lot. He has lost his high energy and amazing exuberance. I don't know what it is with him this year. Frank and I took Edward to Lloydminster and he played his piece on the piano at the College and won the music competition. Edward was neither enthused about going to this competition nor elated about winning. It is a wonder he won in spite of this attitude. His behaviour is extremely unusual because he has always thrived on performing.

I am really worried about him. He appears extremely disturbed and confused. This is not like him. He is usually upbeat, very talkative and always telling us what he wants. But now his behaviour seems suicidal. Will he attempt to take his own life? How can I respond to these warning signs? I know I must, but I also must be cautious about how to do this without pushing him over the edge.

December 8, 1991 **43**

A Gift of Grace

December 10, 1991

Edward, age 15, grade 10, Hughenden

During parent teacher interviews, Mr. Bolton, Edward's English teacher, tells me how very impressed he is with Edward. Mr. Bolton explains he is helping students build speaking skills this year. He praises Edward's ability to speak. It is not a surprise to me after his recitations, drama, Science Fair and Oddfellows' entry.

Of more concern to me were the topics Edward chose to speak about. One was on "Why Adolescents Run Away from Home." Edward received 90%. The next one was "Should 'television violence' come under a new rigid code of censorship?" Edward's mark was 95%. The teacher told me the gist of each speech. Immediately I was worried. Why is he writing about running away and television violence? Are these topics close to his heart?

"It is a pleasure to have Edward in my class," Mr. Bolton said.

> *Meanwhile there is a lump in my throat and a pain in the pit of my stomach. I feel like I am going to faint.*

"Are you OK?"

"Yes, yes. I just didn't eat before I came," I lied.

I moved on to the next teacher, but Edward's high marks in those subjects were no comfort to me. I managed to get through the interviews and as soon as I came home, I headed for the desk in his room and found the 3 ½ x 5 cards on which he had written out his speeches.

His television censorship speech starts:

> Society's once strong moral foundation has now in the last twenty years deteriorated due to the extensive harm and damage that television has had on children, adolescents

44 December 10, 1991

A Gift of Grace

and society as a whole. I strongly feel that there must now be a new rigid code of censorship to shelter children of the future...

So far not too much to worry about, especially since we do not watch much television, but he continues,

> When children are exposed to shows which are violent and obscene, the child unconsciously creates an image of how he or she should react in a similar situation. These graphic pictures of how society operates cause the child to behave in a manner which is far from normal... Many different shows on television are violent... If the messages aren't violent they are sexist or deal with sexual issues... Children and adolescents cannot truly understand and differentiate between reality and fantasy... Many violent shows, even cartoons, such as Teenage Mutant Ninja Turtles, cause children to grow up believing weapons and force are the answer to any problem they may have...

At least Edward is advocating against violence. So this is good. Does he have first hand knowledge that it is difficult knowing the difference between reality and fantasy?

December 11, 1991

Edward, age 15, grade 10, Hughenden

I ran out of time last night to read the cards for the speech on why adolescents run away. This title is the one that worried me the most of the two speeches his teacher mentioned to me. Maybe I did not want to face it last night after a long day.

Here are the key parts:

> "In today's society there is much pressure upon individuals to perform, beginning at a very early age... Adolescents respond to this excessive pressure by simply running away.

A Gift of Grace

"They are unable to cope with the expectations that are placed before them... perhaps they are afraid and feel inadequate when trying to cope with the pressure of modern society... they are usually tired of the demands made of them to achieve. Parents expect them to do well scholastically and socially. They must receive awards, make teams and stay out of trouble... Runaways often are lonely and feel depressed because they think that others aren't accepting them for that they are. They rebel against authority because they find it difficult to understand its relevance.

"... most runaways have a low self-esteem and sometimes feel they are merely just a nuisance to their parents. Somehow they perceive themselves to be unwanted... these unfortunate fragments of society may lack guidance from parents for one or more reasons. Their parents may be divorced or perhaps one of them has died, or maybe they both are working all the time. In other words, their parents just don't have that time to spend with them.

"... it has been found that many runaways have been in some way or another abused physically or sexually by someone close or by a stranger. This usually adds to the feelings of depression and guilt of being used and useless in the community or society as a whole.

"These are the causes. Adolescents want to escape and relieve themselves of all their problems. They don't see any solution, only to run away. They search for an answer to their dilemma, often turning to drugs, prostitution, crime and even joining cults or gangs which are likely involved in illegal activities that contribute to the confusion the adolescent feels.

"After a period of time acting irresponsibly, the youth perhaps discovers that the security he thought he had found has just been a short term solution. At this point, the runaway realizes that he has compounded his original problem and, unless he gets immediate help from someone who cares, he is destined to a life on the streets."

Wow! I wrote out almost the entire speech from the cards. Is this how Edward feels or does he know other teens who have this dilemma?

I put the cards back, but I wonder if he would be upset if he knew I took them. Would that be another incident to chalk up for a reason to run away?

Still I feel justified. I need to know what is happening in his life that he is not talking to me about. We always talked about everything. Now he seems off in his own world. I suppose running away is better than suicide. Less final! Is he depressed because he feels too much pressure to perform?

December 20, 1991

Edward, age 15, grade 10, Hughenden

This evening I eavesdropped on a telephone conversation between Edward and Chris, a boy Edward always told me was his one and only "best friend." This boy had moved to Czar for a few years and then he had moved to Fort McMurray when he was about ten years old. They must have kept in touch by telephone. The conversation I heard was unnerving because he was talking to Edward about gaining access to guns and mushrooms – stuffing the dope down the legs of a pool table so that his enemies would not catch him with it. Edward was speaking as though he might even like to get hold of the odd gun and some dope.

I started hyperventilating and nearly had a heart attack.

When he was off the phone I let him know that I was listening to his telephone conversation. He was not impressed with my intrusion, yet he did not show much emotion.

A Gift of Grace

"Why are you having such a conversation with him?"

"I talked the way I did because it is fun and then he tells me more."

> God! I wonder what is going on in this kid's mind. Will he really buy guns and dope and go on a doped up shooting rampage?

I know he is already smoking cigarettes and marijuana with a young boy who just moved into town. Is this what is making him so crazy?

1992

January 22, 1992

Edward, age 15, grade 10, Hughenden

He obtained letters of reference for his application to United World College as required. He just received the two glowing ones I copied to tuck into this journal.

I am hoping this is just what he needs to get him back on track.

Hughenden Public School
Hughenden, Alberta
Computer Department

January 19, 1992

TO WHOM IT MAY CONCERN

Edward Weatherly attended Hughenden Public School in grades 7 to 10 where he was an outstanding student. I taught him some classes in each grade but came to know him best by being mentor for his science fair projects in grades 8 and 9.

The grade 8 project studied the effect of density and viscosity of liquids on wave motion. The grade 9 project used a multiple reflected laser beam, photo-diode and home-made computer program to very accurately measure and analyze the acceleration of steel balls down a ramp. As well as learning about the science topics, he learned much about materials and the significance of various sources of error. He was able to explain to science fair judges, the principles of mathematics and physics that are taught in courses from grades 11 to first year university. Both projects

A Gift of Grace

took him to Canada Wide Science Fairs. In grade 9 this was in Vancouver in May, 1991 where he received honourable mention.

One of the tours at the Vancouver fair allowed Edward to visit the Lester B. Pearson College of the Pacific near Victoria, British Columbia. He was impressed by the quality of the program and determined then to apply there as soon as possible. As he explained the advantages of an education there, I also was impressed and encouraged him in his determination.

Edward has developed a mature set of ethics that is more firmly established in his character than one would expect of a young person. The enthusiasm, diligence and quality of work that Edward displayed in his science projects were the same as what he brings to each of the many activities he undertakes. His school grades have been consistently excellent. For several years he has rated highly in Music Festival, in piano and in voice at provincial level in both Alberta and Saskatchewan. He is a valued member of a local theatre group whose quality of work is well established. He becomes involved in more different things at the same time than anyone I have ever known.

His energy, enthusiasm and interest appear to be without bound. After quickly establishing that a taxi driver in Vancouver had his mind firmly set upon an unusual track, I was at a loss for conversation. Edward was not; he was truly interested in the driver, maintained a lively conversation, and learned about another style of thinking.

Any educational institution will find itself proud to list Edward Weatherly as one of its graduates.

Sincerely,

Teacher
(Name withheld)
B.Ed., Physics
M.Ed., Computer Applications

A Gift of Grace

Hughenden Public School
"A Place Where Futures Begin"
Hughenden, Alberta

To Whom It May Concern

Edward Weatherly has informed me that he is applying to attend United World Colleges. I am aware of the goals of United World Colleges and can unequivocally state that Edward is worthy of your consideration and would be an excellent student at UWC.

As Vice-Principal and social studies teacher in Hughenden, I feel I am qualified to comment on Edward's academic qualifications. Since Hughenden is a small community, I am also aware of Edward's out-of-school accomplishments.

Edward was a student in Hughenden Public School for Grades 7, 8, 9, and 10. I had the privilege of having Edward as a student in my Grade 10 social studies class. Edward was an extraordinary student and consistently scored in the 90's on examinations. Edward exhibited a natural flair for writing and was willing to take risks and experiment with various writing styles in order to produce work that was interesting and that commanded attention. Through his writing, Edward demonstrated critical thinking skills and an open-minded approach. Edward always carefully considered all sides of any issue he was dealing with and also showed that he understood that there are inherent dilemmas in most issues.

Although I did not teach Edward in any other subjects, I know from looking at his results and talking to his teachers that Edward was an excellent student in all disciplines. In science, Edward put many hours into science fair and always advanced from the local level of competition to the regional level. Twice at the regional, Edward advanced to the national level of competition. In the National Science Fair of 1991 held in Vancouver, BC, Edward placed fourth.

Edward made many valuable contributions in extra-curricular activities. He put a great deal of time and effort into the school newspaper and served with distinction on the Youth Services Board, a Board made up of student representatives and representatives from various local authorities. This board is charged with

January 22, 1992 **51**

A Gift of Grace

the responsibility of providing student counselling services and arranging for life-skills presentations for young people.

In community activities, Edward also made many significant contributions. He was a dedicated performer with a local theatre guild and received favourable comment from the Edmonton Journal's theatre critic. Edward is also enrolled in the piano program of the Royal Conservatory of Toronto and was the winner for three years in a row of a community award annually given to the student who accomplished the most in music.

Edward very definitely has a global outlook as evidenced by his participation in a public-speaking contest sponsored by the Oddfellows. This contest is held annually and is designed to foster greater awareness and appreciation of the efforts of the United Nations by requiring participants to speak on a topic pertaining to the United Nations.

Edward's global outlook was also evidenced by his enthusiastic participation in the "Stepping into the Global Community Symposium" which was held in a neighbouring community to celebrate Canada's ethnic, racial and cultural diversity, and also to focus on the benefits of multiculturalism.

In conclusion, I would like to reiterate my belief that Edward would be an ideal student of United World Colleges.

Yours sincerely,

Vice-Principal
Name Withheld
Hughenden Public School

March 26, 1992

Edward, age 15, grade 10, Hughenden

I was Edward's manager backstage for his part of Glenn Gould in *Remembering Gould*. He played the adult years of Gould's life from ages 18 to his death at age 50. I didn't take a role on stage for the performance in February of this year.

The Edmonton Journal ran the following article by Alan Kellogg, Arts and Entertainment columnist, in his column entitled "Gould would have appreciated Czar's remembrance," re "Czar Theatre Guild sells out every night (quadrupling the hamlet's population) for the annual Marion Kelch production – written, composed, produced, designed, worried through and promoted by the Lloyd Webber of Battle River Country..."

> And although one hesitates to mention individual actors in amateur productions for a variety of reasons, the wonderful performance of the adult Gould by (15 year old) Edward Weatherly (his dog played Gould's dog Nick) demands special note. Perhaps he will favor us with another role in next year's production, based on the sinking in 1914 of CP's Empress of Ireland in the St. Lawrence.

Someone in the cast contributed a wooden chair with its legs sawed off, just like was done to the famous Glenn Gould's piano chair. Gould's father had cut a bit of the legs off and put in "jacks" so the height of the chair could be changed. For years Gould used this chair at his piano and he wouldn't part with it or even repair it long after it was worn out. The wooden chair donated for our play was painted black with splashes of different hues to colourfully represent Gould's no longer stylish (if it ever was) piano chair.

> *After the play I brought the chair home and placed it in front of my Lesage. It will remind me of the joyful times we had at our off the beaten track, yet popular, dinner theatre.*

A Gift of Grace

The best thing about this year's play is the enthusiastic and serious actor is back on top of his game!

May 30, 1992

Edward, age 15, grade 10, Hughenden

Tonight I asked Edward why he didn't enter this year's Science Fair.

He just shrugged. Within the last two months he seems to have lost interest in many things. He won the competition in Provost at their annual Music Festival and was selected to go the Festival in Lloydminster. We had to practically drag him kicking and screaming to go. Before this year, all the king's horses and all the king's men would not have kept him from going to a competition. He loved to prepare and perform.

I have been so anxious this school year. I drive to Provost to teach and phone home every night just to hear his voice. I secretly have an overwhelming anxiety about whether he will be safe until I get home. I still suspect that he is depressed and possibly suicidal. I don't want to verbalize the word for fear that it would "be out there" and would actually be realized in the universe.

Before I leave to drive home after my day of teaching, I always phone home to check if he is okay so I can have a peaceful mind on my drive home. Sometimes he is not at home, so I phone around for him and most often I reach him at the new boy's place. Not one I want him to be around, but at least I have the peace of mind that he is alive and I can go home and find him okay.

Many days while driving home I am so distraught about his whereabouts and what he is doing that tears well up and flood my face. To ease the agony I stop by the Burger Baron and order some fries. They help to settle my stomach but aren't enough to take the hurt away.

A Gift of Grace

News about yet another war, this time the third Balkan Wars, is on the CBC radio station as I drive home each evening.

Maybe I'll get lucky and a world war will break out and I won't have to deal with this family matter – it will be inconsequential –- yes, an Armageddon would be timely.

I saved two of his messages on my phone, just so I have his voice to listen to in case something should happen to him.

I had such hope when he was working on the UWC application and the play. It hasn't lasted.

August 5, 1992

Edward, age 15, grade 11, Provost

We sold the house in Czar. It broke my heart. Over the summer we have been moving and unpacking to set up our new house, but it was so difficult moving from our home in Czar. We had gone to great lengths to renovate that house and I loved it!

When we were in the house in which we started our married life, the one I called the "honeymoon house," we were directly up the hill from what I started to call the "dream home!"

We lived south of the railroad tracks and the "dream home" was north of us on the other side of the tracks. I longed for this house as I looked out at it from the kitchen window while washing dishes. I would dream of living in it, enjoying all the trees and bushes it had in the huge yard. There would be room for a garden, too!

When I drove by I would see how the yard and trees were so well groomed. Spruce and lodge pole pine grew around the perimeter. Five mountain ash trees lined the front of the property. The yard was huge… almost an acre. My dreams included planting a garden,

A Gift of Grace

serving my family crisp fresh vegetables and cutting colourful, fragrant flowers to brighten the rooms inside the house.

When we heard from Frank's grandmother that the house was up for sale, I was so excited! Could it really be that the dream home could be ours? My heart warmed to think we could live in this beautiful mansion with its huge yard.

We arranged a viewing of the property and as we inspected the yard, I noticed yet more flowers, such as pink flowering spirea and cranberry bushes along the west wall. There was even an apple tree growing in the middle of the front yard. I imagined standing at the kitchen sink in the dream home, admiring the blossoms and, with the window wide open, inhaling the intoxicating fragrance. I could sit on the back porch and smell the Lily of the Valley that was tucked into the corner beside the steps. Talk of a natural high! My dream was fulfilled when we bought the house. I loved living there. It was all I had imagined and more.

Now Frank decided on his own we would sell the dream home and move to Middleton's farm near Provost and rent from them. Edna Middleton went to school with Frank. She and her husband lived in a trailer on the farm, while the mother-in-law lived in the original homestead house right next to the trailer. The mother-in-law just recently moved to a house in Provost, leaving the farmhouse empty.

Frank said it would be closer for me to drive to school. Why didn't he ask me? I didn't mind the 60 minute return trip to school each day because I could look forward to the dream home in Czar. The round trip now is 40 minutes less, but my first teaching job was further from our honeymoon house where we lived at the time and never did I complain. In the morning I eagerly look forward to my day and the drive home clears my head as I shake off any school thoughts and start to mentally drift into the comfort of my home and my family. Maybe Frank is protecting us from community gossip because I'm not teaching there anymore.

He says we will buy an acreage near Provost and build a house there. I will hold him to it, but gone is my dream house to some other family.

Dreams can come true and true dreams can be shattered.

August 30, 1992

Edward age 15, going into grade 11, Provost

I drove Edward to a few parties this summer and when I picked him up there would be a stench of smoke coming from his clothes. One of the parties was at a trailer on the south side of town.

I enrolled Edward in Driver's Education and then helped him practice for his license. He passed his test first try and was given permission to take the car one evening to attend a party at a neighbour's home. The next day I found a dent in the back side of the car near the rear end. Edward claimed it got there from some boys who had been fighting and slammed one another into our car. I asked him how the party went and if he had fun. He said it was all right.

A few days later, I discovered he was missing his ball cap with the NYC logo. I had recently purchased it and it was thirty bucks! I asked Edward where it was.

"Some guy at the party took it off my head, ripped the beak off and tossed it into a corner."

"What did you do after the guy did that to your cap?"

"Nothing, Mom, I knew I'd get pounded if I said anything. I just laughed it off."

Then last night he asked me for permission to take the car to a party on a neighbouring farm.

"It's OK, I'll drive you," I said.

"Why can't I take the car?"

"Don't worry, I have the time," I said and left the room, not wanting a verbal confrontation.

A Gift of Grace

During dinner he was very quiet and looked down most of the time. I avoided eye contact, but I knew he would not kick up a fuss with Frank there.

"I'll do the dishes later," I said to Frank, "I'm driving Edward to the Smith place."

Frank just shrugged and went into the living room to read. I went upstairs to grab my keys and driver's licence. When I came down to the garage, the car door was already open and Edward was waiting by the driver's side door.

"Why can't I take the car? Don't you trust me?"

"Actually Edward, it's not you, but how will I know the car won't get damaged at the party like it did last time?"

"It's me you don't trust! Admit it," he said trying to grab the keys out of my hand.

"Edward, stop that or you can walk!"

He said nothing, but turned around and went back into the house. I closed the car door and entered the house too.

"I thought you were driving Edward someplace," Frank said.

"He changed his mind," I replied and went to the kitchen to clean up the dishes.

I allow Edward to manipulate me a lot of the time and although he backed down, I don't feel good about what happened. I know he didn't come with a manual and I am doing the best I can with what I know.

September 15, 1992

Edward age 15, grade 11, Provost

I don't know what to make of his writing. A prolific and already noted writer according to his teachers, Edward turns in assignments to do with mystery and drama. Not so bad, but the English 20 teacher alerts me to his writings that deal with the dark side of life, gender identity issues and weird fantasies.

Here are some excerpts from his latest essay for English 20, called "A 'Fantasy' Assignment: Haven," due September 10, 1992:

It was the summer of '63... I turned eleven that summer... In Haven, a slow picturesque town of less than a thousand, up until that summer, there weren't many boys for me to hang around with. There were boys my age that lived on the other side of town, but, as always it seemed, I didn't fit well...

So I wandered around by myself, feeling out of place and without a purpose. Although through time, I began to read into myself very well. I grew all the more thirsty for someone to share my thoughts with and dreams... the passions which burned in my mind. But, there were no friends to be mine.

So, after eleven years of not having a best friend and feeling I had not experienced the real wonders of boyish childhood, someone or something answered my prayers. In from another county, there moved three families to Haven, each having children... all having a son my age. I wanted to feel as though they would treat me as their equal, I wanted to release the boy inside me which needed to be let out...

"Antoinette... Antoinette! Please, come to the piano for your lesson! I am behind schedule already because of your absentmindedness!" A fat scrag of a lady lisped these words with a taunt lip... This very ugly lady sat belittled

A Gift of Grace

in a large fur chair, beside her Steinway grand...

Startled, Antoinette (Tony as she loved to be called) slowly withdrew from her dream and came to just as her teacher announced her thoughts... She always seemed to find herself wandering into wild places and into other bodies...

... Antoinette, in her tight tube skirt and with her hair in a honeycomb, was confused with her sexuality. She had feelings she felt were unnatural and unusual. She constantly compared herself to the opposite sex, trying to find answers to questions of why she was the way she was. She felt she was different from the rest of the girls and she knew she had to decide what she had to do. She knew there was another side of the human being which she wanted to feel, a side that was so forbidden, that only her dreams could step so far as to take her there. [The story drifts off to the group of boys smoking and playing cards.]

... "Hello, Antoinette," whispered Mrs. Haplord derogatorily. She whispered "Hello" to her several times over, but then one scream leapt from her throat and literally shocked Antoinette out of her daze.

"I'm sorry, Mrs. Haplord, I didn't mean to go off again like that..." Antoinette didn't know what to say, for she wasn't aware of how long she had been out.

"I don't think I can handle this any longer, Antoinette, I think we must stop your lessons as they stand now, for you obviously are not motivated. And, you cannot concentrate. I think you better think over what you want to do with your musical career."

"I know what I want to do with my musical career," answered Tony. "I want to give it to you! This isn't where I want to be at all. I want to be outside, with nature and with people. I want to do things that are not on the list of things for young ladies to do..."

...Antoinette put on her shoes and ran out the door. She ran all the way home, sobbing uncontrollably. She felt angry and confused. She didn't know what to think, nor

A Gift of Grace

what to do. When she got home, she was completely drenched...

She closed the door... The gray motionless haze from the sky filled the room with a strange feeling. Forbidden thoughts were erupting from her mind. She took off all her clothes and laid them in a pile in the middle of her room... she lay down on her bed naked, and listened to the rain. She listened to her thoughts.

That summer we met the Devil. We saw Him when we were all together, so it wasn't a fragment of our imagination. We saw his hissing tail and the black ominous snakes exiting from his skull. We were in the forest, we thought we would be safe, but He is everywhere, He Who Walks Behind is always watching. He knew our thoughts, he felt our desire to be together, but he also knew we had strength.

... I did the deed that saved us all. I was the one to sacrifice my soul. I remember that summer. I will be locked in hell so friends can be together, so people can have memories, I am a boy, a creature with a tail that hisses, but from my skull there are no snakes...

I wrote down what I could of the story. The parts I found most disturbing, because there could be a deeper meaning. Is this why he is less interested in the piano than he used to be? Is he feeling differently from others his age? What dark forbidden thoughts does he have?

The teacher wrote "A very unique story – you have a way of expressing yourself which is unusual."

Yet the teacher told me about the story because she feels there could be this deeper meaning.

Is Edward just particularly sensitive to other people's problems or is this something to do with him?

September 15, 1992 **61**

A Gift of Grace

December 21, 1992

Edward, age 16, grade 11, Provost

At the parent teacher interview, Edward's grade eleven Math teacher told me that Edward wore his heart on his sleeve and suggested that he shouldn't be quite so open. Obviously he is not being open with me. He used to share everything with me. How I miss that little boy.

Edward just completed a very thorough autobiography of his life as his school project assigned by Mr. Dudley at his high school in Provost. It is a real treasure, which I will make sure never leaves the house. It includes many of his awards, certificates, photos and writing, and documents his life up to this year. I doubt the teacher meant for such effort to go into the assignment. But this is typical Edward. For many of his school assignments, he does much more than is asked of him.

> *Thank you, teacher for this assignment. I hold onto it knowing that if anything happened to Edward, I would at least have this autobiography to keep and pore over in his memory.*

I think there are things though that he is telling no one. Things I have begun to suspect.

> *As I write this, I rationalize his openness this way. He probably feels free to share every last thing about his life, other than a secret that he must not expose unless he wants to risk getting hurt. After all we are living in the heart of Redneck Alberta.*

On the cover of his autobiography, Edward has written "Open and read... these stories came from the heart... affecting me profoundly!" Inside, one of his statements is "I feel like the man

A Gift of Grace

in the mirror…my soul is searching for something greater!" It reminds me of Michael Jackson's song *The Man in the Mirror.*

Willow Deeply Scarred,
Somebody's Broken Heart
And A Washed-Out Dream
(Washed-Out Dream)
They Follow The Pattern Of
The Wind, Ya' See
Cause They Got No Place
To Be
That's Why I'm Starting With
Me
(Starting With Me!)

I'm Starting With The Man In
The Mirror
(Ooh!)
I'm Asking Him To Change
His Ways
(Ooh!)
And No Message Could Have
Been Any Clearer
If You Wanna Make The World
A Better Place
(If You Wanna Make The
World A Better Place)
Take A Look At Yourself And
Then Make A Change
(Take A Look At Yourself And
Then Make A Change)

Edward is committed to being different, having a unique style and personality. He also wants to make a difference,

He writes, "The path leading to my FUTURE is but a series of STEPS… I have my destiny in my hands. I ALONE, with the help of my CREATOR, can make a difference!"

December 21, 1992 **63**

1993

January 5, 1993

Edward, age 16, grade 11, Provost

When we were living in Czar and Edward was 15, I avoided approaching Edward over his drug use, hoping it would stop, but finally I decided we had to confront him. So I arranged a meeting with Frank and Edward. The three of us talked about smoking pot and its consequences. Frank was very helpful and it made me feel great that I had chosen to share what Edward had been doing instead of bearing all that stress alone. For some reason, I have difficulty discussing with Frank the hot issues of child-rearing.

There is another issue though that I am keeping from Frank and not confronting Edward about. Edward often asks to stay overnight with a young boy, who is a friend of his, but I always decline.

He doesn't know that I have heard from Lena and Matthew what he told Pat. Edward played Cher and Pat played Sonny at a community celebration in Provost and the crowd really enjoyed their singing and dramatization. They were a hit! Pat had a big crush on Edward and it was pretty obvious. Girls flocked to him so this was not unusual.

Edward had said to me earlier this year, "Mom, maybe I should take Pat to a movie." He didn't sound convinced.

Lena said Pat told her that Edward stated he can't date her because he is gay. Was this just a joke because he did Cher in drag? Or was this just his response, so she would understand that he wasn't trying to lead her on, but treasured her friendship? Pat told Lena she thought Edward was either joking or said it because he didn't like her enough to want to date her. In any case, I think Pat was crushed.

A Gift of Grace

But is it true? This is the big secret I was wondering if he was keeping. Well if so, I guess the secret is out. He shared it with Pat. Did he think she would not tell anyone or doesn't he care anymore?

Still he is not telling me and regardless of whether it is true or not, am I going to permit him to stay over at a boy's house if there is a possibility he is gay?

I just find it inappropriate to respond, "Sure, Edward, you can stay overnight, just make sure you get your chores done first." After all, would any parent consent to letting their fifteen or sixteen year old son sleep overnight with another parent's fifteen or sixteen year old daughter or vice versa?

Should I ask him and risk hurting his feelings or angering him? Perhaps I'll wait to see if I am wrong.

April 27, 1993

Edward age 16, grade 11, Provost

Edward just returned from the *Forum for Young Canadians*. Like so many other things he decides he can do, he won the scholarship and trip to go to Ottawa to join with students between the ages of 16-19 from all over the country and learn how government works. There were about 150 students chosen for the week long session Edward attended.

The students were put up at a hotel in downtown Ottawa and every day they went to the Parliament Buildings where they attend sessions and were joined by Members of Parliament and other government officials at the banquet. A teacher usually accompanies his or her students. Edward, however, was sent off on his own.

A Gift of Grace

Another accomplishment, another scholarship win, another certificate of achievement to add to the still growing clear plastic bins of medals, plaques and documents that detail a wonderful part of his life. I don't allow these bins out of the house. He loses keys, his driver's license, books and many more items. So if something happens to Edward, I still have these bins full of accomplishments.

Of course, nothing substitutes for Edward being around and the memories we share together. Still looking in the plastic bins, feeling and reading his winning submissions is comforting. It makes me feel like I am a good parent. Whatever else he is going through cannot all be our fault.

Edward has every chance of doing something great with his life.

May 23, 1993

Edward age 16, grade 11, Provost

Edward just returned from his third Science Fair. He competed at the regional levels and once again was chosen to go the nationals, Canada Wide Science Fair, in Riviere-du-Loup, Quebec. His partner for the science fair project was a classmate named Victoria.

The project was entitled "Up, Up and Away." It had to do with designing a modified Dobson spectrophotometer. Again I did not attend this one or the one in 1991. I only attended the one in Windsor in 1990. This year Miss Venus supervised two students with a project representing Hughenden and so she agreed to supervise Victoria and Edward with their project as well. I felt they would be safe.

See Edward, it is just as I always told you: you can do anything you set your mind to. I hope you set it for beyond the sky's limit!

A Gift of Grace

He returned satisfied with their entry, but now all his focus is on finishing grade eleven and getting into a United World College.

June 3, 1993

Edward, age 16, grade 11, Provost

One my way home today, I picked up an envelope for Edward. It had the logo of the UWC, so I was anxious for Edward to open it. I could hardly wait to see if he was accepted. I don't see why not, but it is like opening a report card at the end of the year to see if you've passed, even if you're an honours student. You still have that sense of anticipation.

I waved the envelope as I drove down the driveway and Edward could hardly wait until I stopped the car to get it and rip it open.

"Mom, I've been accepted for an interview!"

"That's great! Well, no doubt you will blow them away. You have honed your speaking skills for making your case in front of the Science Fair judges."

"Yes, I'm sure I'll get in."

Edward always makes a good impression on people, especially adults. I'm sure his prediction is correct.

"The date for the interview is for the 11th in the afternoon."

"OK, I'll take the day off and I'm sure Dad will want to go too. Guess I better get your suit dry cleaned."

I am in a Mom and teacher get ready mode, thinking of all the things we need to do before the 11th. This is so exciting. Scary too! It just dawned on me. My son would be leaving home sooner than the usual grade 12 graduation. Only two more months…

A Gift of Grace

*I knew he would be accepted and I secretly dreaded the
thought of having none of my kids at home.*

June 11, 1993

Edward, age 16, grade 11, Provost

I expected Edward to be more nervous than he was this morning.
I should have known with all the public speaking and drama he
has done, this to him is a walk in the park. I am the one who is
nervous. I'm not sure why.

He looked so good in his black suit with a blue tie to match his
eyes. His blond hair was carefully combed and with some last
minute grooming tools to take along, we set off for Edmonton.

Frank drove us the 230 kilometres to Alberta's capital city for the
interview. We waited for Edward in the reception area as he went
in to be interviewed.

He came out looking very confident, shaking the hands of the
interviewers.

"OK, let's go," Edward said.

I think he wanted it to appear he was in charge!

August 15, 1993

Edward, age 16, going into UWC (grade 12)

A week later after his interview for UWC, Edward received a letter of acceptance for a two year scholarship and was selected to go to his first choice at Armand Hammer United World College of the American West in Montezuma, New Mexico. Frank and I are so proud!

It's August and in a few weeks, Edward will be off to New Mexico. Last week I took him shopping for clothes and other essentials. I bought him a laptop computer for his studies. It was an expensive week, but I am elated that Edward has this opportunity. Of course, my heart feels like it is going to break from the pain of knowing he will be far away. I hope he will be OK.

Today we held a party for him in the garage and invited some of the friends he had made from grade eleven in Provost. The Middletons and both Grandmas helped celebrate, too. I made most of the food, including potato salad, Grandma's famous green jelly salad, a vegetable tray and other side dishes. Frank made hamburgers on the BBQ. It was a very low key affair. We just sat and talked about the great future Edward has in front of him. He shared the exciting things he would experience at the college.

I wonder if his heart is also aching at the thought of separation, like mine is. My last child at home... Empty nest... my beautiful, intelligent son... I won't be able to see him every day to make sure he is safe.

We promise to stay in touch by phone.

A Gift of Grace

August 20, 1993

Edward, age 16, going into UWC (grade 12)

We drove Edward to Edmonton so he could participate in his orientation of the United World College campus. He met Taj, who also would be attending UWC for the first time.

Nicole had just finished teaching for two months on a tall ship called Concordia, belonging to a special program called Class Afloat. She was home and did not have a job yet, so she agreed to accompany Edward and me to Montezuma, New Mexico. I am so proud of Nicole. My oldest child has grown into such an independent young woman now. She has her Bachelor of Education degree and her Practicum teacher promoted her as a great candidate to fill in for a math teacher who wasn't able to finish the trip on the tall ship. She was bubbling with exciting details of how much she enjoyed the opportunity of participating in the last leg of the journey, sailing along the eastern coast of North America from the island of St. Martin to Newfoundland.

This ship acted as a floating school for grade eleven and twelve students learning curriculum while sailing around the world. She taught math while out at sea and enjoyed the field trips while docked in various harbours. Nicole marvelled at all the wonders of New York City! Only there briefly, she had packed in so many sights, sounds and tastes to last a lifetime. I am so proud of her.

August 27, 1993

Edward, age 16, going into UWC (grade 12)

After packing what we needed with Edward trying to fit everything for a full year into a couple of suitcases, the three of us drove the 230 kilometres northwest to Edmonton to catch the plane to Sante Fe, New Mexico. We landed and right at the airport rented a car to take us to Montezuma.

The weather was hot and dry, hotter than our hottest prairie summer day back home. It seemed so stifling, it was hard to breathe. So were we ever glad for the air conditioning in the car.

Just as we turned into Montezuma, Edward asked if we could stop so he could check things in the trunk. I pulled over and handed him the keys. I watched him through the rear view mirror as he opened the trunk with the keys and fixed his hair, which didn't even have a strand out of place. Still he wanted to be perfect.

As the trunk closed, I winked at Nicole because she too had noticed him primping. He got back into the car as I sat and waited.

"Mom, let's go! I don't want to be late!"

"Well, give me the keys!"

Edward scrambled, searching his pockets and digging into the back seat.

"Oh, Mom! I must've dropped them in the trunk!"

He looked mortified.

"Well, that's just great! Now what will we do?" I asked.

Silence.

"Just kidding! I have a second pair."

"Oh Mom! You scared me half to death!"

Laughter ensued and we were back on our journey. We arrived at the campus and helped Edward carry his luggage to Meredith House, the residence he would be living in for the next two years.

We met Edward's roommate Carlos, as he was already in the room. It seemed a little awkward since we weren't sure of what to say. He seems like a very nice young man. Well groomed and polite.

A Gift of Grace

We went down to look around the campus. We wanted to find the cafeteria, library and music room. A picturesque castle stood high on a hill just beyond the college buildings. Edward was excited with the anticipation of making lots of friends with students representing seventy different countries around the world!

Students are assigned a host family who will let the student stay with them on weekends and holidays. This is to help them transition to the new life, since almost all of the students were away from home, many for the first time. At least we know Edward will enjoy some homemade meals and help retain the sense of a family presence. We met Edward's host family and the father happens to be a psychiatrist at the mental hospital in Montezuma.

After a busy day of Edward orienting himself to his new surroundings, Nicole and I drove back to Sante Fe leaving my only son by himself. I know the roommate, the host family and the many positive people we met that day will be a great help in settling him in for his new adventure.

Who is going to help me get used to my son not being at home? Not being able to assure myself he is OK just through a simple phone call before I arrive home and then see him when I walk in the door. I have much to reflect upon as I look out the plane window as we take off from Sante Fe to Edmonton. What had seemed an adventure on the way there was now a sense of loss as Nicole and I leave without Edward.

November 10, 1993

Edward, age 17, going into UWC (grade 12)

I baked a chocolate cake last night, iced it this morning with butter icing and brought it to school to share with my students. It's Edward's birthday but he isn't here and Frank shouldn't eat too many sweets.

A Gift of Grace

I cry tears and I am enveloped with sadness. I phoned to wish him a happy birthday but he wasn't in his residence at Meredith House when I called…

Happy Birthday, Edward!

ᐰovember 23, 1993

Edward, age 17, UWC (grade 12)

I get phone calls from Edward to let me know how he is doing. I also call Meredith House and usually I have to do some phoning around to get hold of him. I found out he sometimes stays in the room where he practices piano and ends up sleeping there all night.

This concerns me, thinking of him sleeping on the floor and wondering if anyone would come across him and harm him.

He tells me he goes out at night with his friends and they spend time by the bridge… wherever that is!

Edward called me one night and sounded like he was high on life.

"Mom, you won't believe how wonderful it was tonight! We were all standing out in the rain and were soaking wet, singing at the top of our lungs, the song, *We Are the Champions.* It was so absolutely fantastic!"

Soaking wet is not an image to comfort a mother. I picture him being ill because of it.

A Gift of Grace

During one conversation with Edward, he told me he went into Santa Fe with a young man he had probably met in a bar and they were riding in a convertible with the roof up because it had been raining, but they had the windows rolled down. They parked at a 7 Eleven, his friend went into the convenience store and Edward stayed in the vehicle. While Edward waited, a biker saw him and said, "Quit staring!" Then he approached the car and shoved his knife through the canvas top of the convertible. He cut Edward's hand as he put it up to protect himself. He says he has a big scar. What is it about bikers!

He tells me about other times he and a friend take a bus into Santa Fe and they study at a woman's place. He plays the piano for this older woman and they swim in her pool. She even lets them use her car to drive around the city and then they stay overnight with her.

How did they meet her? Why does she want these young men around? Why does she allow them such privileges? Should I be worried?

In another conversation he told me about hitchhiking into Santa Fe, then riding in the back of a half ton and getting a bad sunburn on the way home. Oh, yeah, they smoked a bit of pot with friends and their parents.

What is he getting into? Who are these parents that they smoke pot with these young people? Should I call the host family to ask them to watch out for him?

December 23, 1993

Edward, age 17, UWC (grade 12)

Edward complains about his Outdoor Pursuits instructor. He says he is arrogant and chauvinistic. For some reason the two of them do not hit it off, but Edward needs to see it through to get his credits for the course.

He told me the father, the psychiatrist, in the host family thinks I am controlling. What gives him the right to say such a thing? He barely even knows me!

Edward phoned a few days ago to tell me he has written me a letter and that he made some kind of confession in it.

"Is it good or bad?"

"A bit of both."

Oh, no! My long time fear is going to become a reality: he will probably tell me in this letter that he is gay. The past several years I feared he was gay and what it would be like for him to live his teen years in our redneck community.

The letter came and his confession turned out to be one of only lying... I can handle that. It wouldn't be the first time Edward had lied...

Every kid lies to some extent at some time in his life. Right?

Now, after nine years, Edward informs me the biker story at Czar School was all a fabrication. I had fallen for it. I witnessed the police questioning him and heard him telling them the exact

A Gift of Grace

details that he told me. Frank never believed him and insisted that Edward was making it up. I had been so angry that Frank gave him a hard time. Now Edward tells me he made it up.

Some day I will ask him, "Why would you make up such a story?"

Edward told me before he left for UWC that, when he was younger, he would secretly wish someone would come and take him away. God, I am so happy that didn't happen! It would have destroyed me to think that some stranger had made off with my son. Why would he wish such a thing? I thought I had given him the best upbringing. I tried my best.

Oh, did I mention? ...he didn't mention the bad thing... I guess I get to learn about that when he comes home. God, he causes me a lot of anxiety.

1994

Provost, Alberta
March 1, 1994

Dear Mr. Hainsworth,

We would like to thank you for the scholarship that you are providing for our son. It is because of this financial aid that he has the opportunity of attending The Armand Hammer United World College in Montezuma, New Mexico. Its mission statement expresses an ideal education.

In January Edward was experiencing some problems with his jaw. He saw the college nurse and she helped him arrange for an appointment with a dentist in Las Vegas. The dentist was able to provide a splint for him on the same day as his appointment. I understand that the college paid for these expenses. We really appreciate this and that he received such prompt attention.

Edward is enjoying the college very much. He enjoys working with the students and comments on how all the teachers are so willing to help him learn.

We believe that Edward is receiving a great education. He is becoming a responsible young man committed to the ideals of the college. We hope that you will be able to support future Albertan students. It is a wonderful opportunity for them to attend such a fine college.

Thanks again.

Yours truly,

Beatrice Weatherly
Frank Weatherly

c.c. President AHUWC

June 20, 1994

Edward, age 17, UWC (finished grade 12)

Edward came home from his first year at UWC. His yearbook is full of autographs and best wishes from his friends. He had obviously made lots of friends and I was happy for him. He showed me a letter from Whitney Soo, his Literature teacher from UWC.

June 16, 1994

Dear Ed,

I'm heading out today --- hope your summer is going fine and you are working hard on your EE! Here are some old papers for you – some prairie news – they're really outdated but thought you'd enjoy reading them. You're welcome to stay here at my parents throughout the summer – if you can get your hands on a car to drive back and forth... have fun at the orientation - you'll meet Taj's parents. So adios – take care – be responsible! Hope Provost doesn't get you down. I'll see you in August.

Whitney

> Hope Provost doesn't get you down? What does that mean?

I asked Edward what EE stands for and he said it's the Extended Essay he has to write for his IB points. He is writing on Ukrainian Canadian Communists during World War II, how they were put in concentration camps. We are not even Ukrainian! It seems Edward always is interested in the plight of the underdog.

A Gift of Grace

His report marks and comments ranged from exceptional to satisfactory.

Satisfactory? When had Edward ever had a mark of satis-factory?

July 21, 1994

Edward, age 17, UWC (finished grade 12)

Today Edward wanted to rent and watch a film from the National Film Board of Canada. It is called: *Out: Stories of Lesbian and Gay Youth*. I put it on my MasterCard and we watched it together.

Frank had no interest in seeing the film. I guess this is just another case of Edward's sympathy for the underdogs in our society. He said he wanted to shed some light on the topic for me. I really didn't know too much about gays and lesbians and he was aware of that. I do remember the boys teasing the girls when I was growing up. They claimed that the girls had a code: if a girl wore green on Thursday, she was a "lesbo" and that was a sign for other lesbians. How did boys come up with that one?

From the film I gathered a sense that gay people were nice and normal, just like the rest of us in most respects.

Edward has been going into Edmonton on the bus to visit his teacher Whitney Soo. She is staying at her parents' house and Edward says he is welcome there. He doesn't have the use of a car but says when he is ready to go to their house for the night he phones Whitney and arranges for her to pick him up at the farthest transit stop at the edge of the city. Then she takes him a ways out in the country to where her parents live.

Edward tells me Whitney is a lesbian. So at least there's nothing to worry about him being with her.

But what all does he do during his frequent visits to Edmonton?

A Gift of Grace

August 16, 1994

Edward, age 17, UWC (finished grade 12)

I decided I just had to ask him the big question, "Are you straight?"

"No, Mom. That was the bad thing I was going to tell you when I came home. I guess you beat me to it."

"Edward, it's not a bad thing. Besides, I've pretty much suspected it since you were a little guy."

"You never said anything."

"I didn't know when to say something until now. Anyway, you better go tell Dad."

"I don't want to."

"You better. He's out fencing behind the house."

While Edward was out sharing his truth with his father, I am having a conversation with myself about what role I played in all of this. My chatterbox has verbal diarrhea...

I did everything right. When I was pregnant with each of the kids I followed the doctor's suggestions and took no aspirin, drank no alcohol, no cold medicine, not even second-hand smoke, as I was adamant that Frank not light up in the cab of the vehicle. I measured the exact amount of fluoride to put in the kids' apple juice and I satisfied every craving possible when I was pregnant. Oh, no, maybe it was the tender stalk of rhubarb with hints of poison left before its leaves unfurled... or the result of feeding him chicken raised in long, sun-starved barns that caused him to be gay!

A Gift of Grace

I did push him to do things with his Dad. He did do some things with his father, like fishing and hunting, especially the deer thing. I guess he did those things just to get approval from his father, because he has never picked up a rifle since.

Edward half-heartedly walked out to where Frank was fencing and was gone only a short while. He came back into the kitchen.

"How did it go?"

"He says I've got my head stuck up my ass."

Before he could say anything more, Frank stormed into the house and arguments between him and his only son ensued. The girls, home for the summer, came from their room to see what was going on. Well, I guess his secret is out now, as the girls were hearing for the first time their brother is gay. The girls became upset. Frank was still on a rant. "Get real!" were the main words I heard over and over. That and swearing! How could this be happening to our family?

I want to run away!

All the while I wanted to tell Edward, I still loved him, no matter what. I knew I couldn't get a word in edgewise, so I kept quiet. I would not have been heard over the din anyway.

Edward had enough and took off on his bike. I took off in the car to follow him. He must have taken shortcuts because I didn't see him on the roads. I headed to the Provost bus depot as that is where I took him when he wanted to go to Edmonton to see Whitney. I guessed that is probably where he would want to go now.

I spotted his bike just lying against the bus depot at the Esso Gas Station along Highway 13. The Greyhound had just taken off to Edmonton. Edward was nowhere around. He must have taken that bus. How convenient that it left when it did.

I returned home not knowing what to do. Frank was still fuming. I looked in on the girls. Their faces told it all – red and tear-stained. I couldn't deal with them then. I had to be with Edward.

August 16, 1994

A Gift of Grace

I was anxious about his safety. I hopped back in the car and headed for Edmonton.

I drove straight to West Edmonton Mall where the kids and I shopped many times over the years. I headed for Fantasyland Hotel. I had always wanted to stay there. I booked a room, just a regular room. There was no theme room that exactly befitted my tormented mother state. I phoned home and told them where I was staying. I was glad it was one of the girls that answered and not Frank. I didn't know what to say to him and he was probably still spitting nails. I think he was blaming me. That I was too soft on Edward... That I babied him... That I let him manipulate me...

After locating the yellow pages listing night clubs, I tried to figure out which ones would be gay. It was an exercise in futility. Instead Edward phoned me.

He had called home and got my hotel phone number from one of the girls. Thank goodness!

I gave him my room number and he came over. I agreed to go to a bar called The Raven. It was an opportunity to investigate the life of a gay son, to see his hangouts. I had always imagined gay bars as full of people dressed in leather, chains and tattoos, pornography on the walls and people openly having sex.

I was pleasantly surprised! We were greeted with a big hug as we stepped into the entrance.

We're in! I am going into a nightclub with my seventeen year old son (underage) and encouraging him to lie about his age so I can check out his haunt. We sat at a small table by the wall and he bought me a bottle of Corona beer with a slice of lime shoved down the neck.

"Is it okay if you sit by yourself? I want to speak with someone I just met."

"Yeah, it's okay. Go ahead!" Many people were dancing, so he probably also wanted to dance.

A Gift of Grace

Yeah! I can relate to that because music and dancing soothes my soul.

Later, a young man came and asked, "Do you mind if I sit down with you?"

"I don't mind." He sat and lit up a cigarette.

"Do you care to dance?"

What the heck! He is young enough to be my son and I didn't relish the thoughts of sitting on this stool all night.

As we danced, another young man tapped me on the shoulder, asking me something but the music was so loud I was unable to hear clearly what he had said.

"What did you say?"

"I said," pointing to Edward, "Is he your son?"

"Yes!" I replied, nodding my head.

"Wow! I just didn't believe that his Mom would actually go out dancing at a gay club!"

As I glanced around, I saw mostly young men. Two young girls were sitting at a small table and I noticed a couple of older men.

After some dancing, Edward phoned a taxi for me and I went back to my hotel room. When Edward arrived somewhat later, he was on a high, as he confided that he had kissed a guy and he enjoyed it.

I just smiled...and held back a tear.

August 16, 1994

August 17, 1994

Edward, age 17, UWC (finished grade 12)

Edward and I had a good chat this morning. He told me that Whitney Soo introduced him to many of the haunts for gays in Edmonton. When he went to Edmonton on his own this summer he would hang out at the Gay Coffee Shop or the Gay and Lesbian Drop-In Centre. If Whitney wasn't with him, she would pick him up from the last transit stop – often in the wee hours of the morning – and take him to her parents' place where she was staying for the summer.

"Do you remember Taj that we met at orientation in Edmonton?"

"Yes, I do."

"He was my first gay friend."

"Oh."

What is a mother supposed to say? Oh, that's good, but the moment had passed.

Edward had extremely long conversations with Sam and Fred, young men he introduced me to at the dance.

"We have so much in common, Mom."

He told me he also stayed overnight with Fred, who worked at a retail clothing store.

Edward told me he needs to get "primary resources" from Edmonton Archives because these materials are not available in New Mexico. He said it is for his Extended Essay on Ukrainians in Canada during World War II.

"Will you drive me there?"

Of course, he knows I'll do it.

> ---what a sucker I am... I'll do anything for him in the name of education and he recognizes that...

At least he is trying to accomplish something of value this summer.

August 20, 1994

Edward, age 17, UWC (finished grade 12)

Since we will be staying for maybe a week, we checked into the Holiday Inn. It is cheaper here.

During the day we check out the Archives and at night we check out the bar scene.

Now that he is out to his family and left home in a hurry, I followed him to try to understand how he feels, what he thinks, how is it appropriate for me to act so I can support him? So yesterday he took me to a bookstore on Whyte Avenue and showed me the shelf of gay and lesbian resources. One shelf, that's all...

I purchased two books. One is *Now That You Know* written by Betty Fairchild and Nancy Hayward, and the other by Eric Marcus *Is It a Choice?*

I started reading them last night. Actually skimming to the most important parts... opening my eyes to my son's world.

> Yes! Sexual orientation is determined at birth... it is neither changeable nor a matter of choice... it's in the genes...

A Gift of Grace

I am reminded of the time Vince phoned and asked Edward if he would like to watch the movie *Philadelphia* starring Tom Hanks. Vince, who lived on a ranch just down the hill from us on the way to Provost, was a young man the same age as Edward.

I had seen the movie and when Edward came home from watching it, I asked him what Vince had said about it.

He responded, "Vince just made a comment at the end saying, 'I guess we just have to keep an open mind, right, Ed?'"

How true. Yet as far as I knew Vince didn't know Edward was gay.

I really respected Vince's family. They seemed to have a very loving relationship and exuded happiness. Vince's mom was my nurse during the delivery of the girls. How peaceful and hopeful my life was then.

I remember the time when Edward asked me to accompany him to an information night in Provost about HIV and AIDS. I assumed the same interest in other people who had problems and whom Edward wanted to help. Now I know there was a deeper reason why he wanted this information. Going with his Mom was probably a good cover.

I weep... I visualize that sometime in the future quite likely I will experience this same kind of sadness... my own son living with HIV... I pray that my research will provide a kind of backup plan.

August 25, 1994

Edward, age 17, UWC (finished grade 12)

Back home now, I remember how Edward asked me if I could get the Superintendent of Provost School Division to write a letter of reference for him before he left for the second year of UWC

A Gift of Grace

because he would have to start applying to universities. The letter was there, addressed to me, probably because I was the one who requested it.

When I opened it, I find the Superintendent has listed all Edward's past accomplishments. Reading it makes me very sad.

Will Edward be able to fulfill his dreams? Will he surmount his challenges and be the star he was destined to be?

I cried as I read.

PROVOST SCHOOL DIVISION NO. 33
Provost, Alberta
August 12, 1994

To Whom It May Concern
Re: Edward Weatherly

I met Edward in 1984; I was a new superintendent while Edward was a precocious student entering Grade 3. Edward has since grown into a mature, confident, and versatile young man. I am pleased to describe some of the attributes which will allow Edward to make his way into a challenging career of his choice.

Edward is a very strong academic student. He has always attained excellence in all his grades and subjects. During his Grade 11 year he applied for and was selected as a Canadian representative to Armand Hammer United World College of the American West. This selection included the awarding of a Prince of Wales Scholarship from the Alberta government. Edward entered the United World College program with a sound basic education. He has prospered in this enriched program which includes college as well as those in the International Baccalaureate program.

Edward's strengths extend beyond academic excellence. Edward is a volunteer in his community; in a local museum, schools and nursing homes. As an accomplished musician, actor and vocalist, he has competed locally, regionally and provincially. With the Royal Conservatory of Music, Edward's Grade 10 diploma was

August 25, 1994 **87**

A Gift of Grace

"First Class Honours with Distinction." As a young science enthusiast, Edward was selected to represent our region in three National Science Fairs. His project on the analysis of ozone won national honours, a first in his section and third overall. As Chair of the Young Scientists of Canada, Edward helped prepare students for their attendance at the 90th Nobel Prize Ceremonies. As a young man with a social conscience, he has participated in provincial forums on human rights. For one presentation he interviewed the leader of an American racist group, the Church of Aryan Nations, keeping him online for over an hour while revealing things he ought not to say publicly. He has spoken in our parliament buildings in Ottawa and was selected to attend a United Nations youth Pilgrimage in New York. These are the skills I see Edward using to advantage in a future career, a career of potential social significance.

A personal incident illustrates Edward's skills as a 13 year old. As a competitor in our regional science fair, I observed Edward from several vantage points. As a judge, Edward's project and defence were obviously a cut above his peers. His resource sources had extended beyond the usual-literature reviews, teachers and parents; Edward's sources also included professors from far off universities. Probes assured me this was still Edward's project; I was impressed with his tenacity and confidence. As a bus driver, I saw Edward in action with his peers. He was known by all and liked by everyone. He was the person to be seen with, pleasant and respectful to all. I have never encountered similar academic and social skills in any other young man or woman.

Edward Weatherly has all the attributes of a fine family; care, sensitivity, and talents and interests in a variety of personal and professional areas. His balance of academic and personal skills, merit development and refinement in a challenging environment of study and interaction-your institution. I recommend him as an outstanding young man.

Yours truly,
Name Withheld
Superintendent of Schools

# September 5, 1994

Edward, age 17, UWC (2nd year)

Edward is back at UWC for his second year there. The girls are doing fine.

Finally, a home of our own again! Frank bought us an acreage north of Provost. We had to buy a house from North Battleford and move it to the acreage on a brand new wooden basement with a heated cement floor. I had no part in the decisions.

He promised we will put up a wall to divide the dining and living room, and lay beautiful hardwood flooring in the kitchen, dining room, living room and hallway. Somehow though, I don't feel much enthusiasm.

Frank always says, "Get real," but right now, I don't know what is real. Have I sold myself short?

Do I have low expectations for my life right now? Have I settled for whatever it brings? Who can I blame but me?

September 20, 1994

Edward, age 17, UWC (2nd year)

I read voraciously any article I come across about gays and lesbians. I took my two newly purchased books to school. After teaching a lesson, I take one of these books out from under my lesson plan book and read words that validate my stand on the matter, all the while my students are working on their assignments.
I am trying so hard to understand.

I continue to read the words and empathize with Edward, realizing that in my class of 31 students there is a good chance that I have three gay children. Statistics show that 10% of the population are gay. So... then... that means Provost Public School has approximately 25-28 gay students.

How are we as teachers and administrators providing for all our students' health and wellness? Are we all on the same page?

~November 15, 1994~

EDWARD IN ACTION

Edward, age, 18, UWC (2nd year)

UWC student first in competition

Ed Weatherly, second-year United World College Student from Alberta, Canada, won district first place in the New Mexico Music Teacher's honors competition in Los Alamos. Weatherly performed a solo piece on the piano, "Elegie" by Rachmaninoff.

Others who competed in the district were 11th and 12th graders from Las Vegas, Santa Fe and Los Alamos. Weatherly is now eligible to perform in state competition to be held Nov. 12 in Farmington. His piano teacher, Linda King will accompany him. King works with about 12 UWC students at the school.

Credit: *Daily Optic*, Las Vegas, New Mexico, Thursday, November 3, 1994

Edward won first place in the New Mexico Music Teacher's Honors Competition at the district level in Las Alamos on November 3. He even had his picture in the paper playing Rachmaninoff's *Elegie*. This is an amazing achievement, something the "old" Edward takes in stride. Another clipping for his bin of accomplishments and for Grandma Kristina's scrapbook, we are so proud of him.

The "old" Edward is in action. It is so wonderful that he has his enthusiasm for music back and that he is showing others what a fine piano player he truly is. He was disappointed he didn't win at the state level, but that is his competitive spirit back in full gear. The district win shows that he can exceed at a higher level than offered in our local area at home. I am so proud showing the other staff at school the clipping of my son.

A Gift of Grace

Edward Weatherly III   STUDENT REPORT

English A
I can't decide what it is that keeps Ed from a consistently first-rate performance in this class, whether it's that his mind works faster that his words or that his creativity produces too much simultaneous material. Whatever the cause, sometimes he has difficulty making things clear. In writing, I think a careful re-reading of his prose will help his communication. In speaking, a little pre-planning as well as persevering in making himself understood. Whatever remedies he undertakes should certainly not get in the way of his wonderful idiosyncratic approach to ideas or the enthusiasm he has to express them.

Music Higher Level
Edward has a very solid background in music, so I think he will do very well with his music curriculum. He is also a very gifted pianist; I am hopeful he will do well on the concerto competitions next semester. He is very energetic and this boosts the pace of the class. With consistent and creative work I can easily predict a '7' on his IB exams next year.

French B Subsidiary Level
Ed appears to be more at ease with both oral and written French. He must still guard against occasional basic grammatical errors in composition and expand the range of his vocabulary. I am pleased with Edward's attitude and progress so far.

Math Methods
Edward's performance in class is good. His ability to grasp and apply mathematical principles has improved since the beginning of the semester. If he practices enough he will excel in the subject.

Chemistry Higher Level
Although this has not been an easy course for Edward, he has worked very hard toward understanding the material as well as he can, and his last exam showed significant improvement. He needs to continue to keep current in his study of the course material, but potential for doing satisfactory work in the future is present.

Advisor
Edward has made a positive first impression at the college during his first semester. Indeed, he has managed his time well, so far,

between academics and activities. Edward is certainly an asset to our community.

Resident Tutor
Edward's very great talent has made many demands upon his time. That he is able to find time to handle these priorities, and still keep up academically and socially speaks well for his maturity. He is a welcome asset to the dormitory.

Vice President
Edward has made good academic progress this semester, enjoys the UWC experience, and interacts well with peers and adults. Edward is a cooperative and contributing member of our college community, and we enjoy having him at the college.

The Armand Hammer United World College's Service Program requires all students to participate in a Wilderness Service and a Community Service. Therefore, Edward was on a team that hiked in the Grand Canyon and participated in the successful search for a lost hunter. He also tutored students in piano.

He will be successful only if he is able to focus his energy in the right direction.

December 19, 1994

Edward, age 18, UWC (2nd year)

Edward's 18th birthday came and went last month. Trying to reach him at school and wondering what he is doing, is torturous.

Then I received his first semester report card. His marks are not what I expected he would make. It's good that he excels in music, but to receive a comment of "potential for doing satisfactory work in the future is present" is not like him. The teachers' comments range from positive to hints of problems that Edward had rarely displayed in school in the past. Yet the English teacher's comments evoke the ghosts of Edward's "idiosyncratic" thoughts. I am worried sick and it is doing no one any good, especially me.

A Gift of Grace

So I finally had to seek help from the Family Services Program, which is affiliated with the Alberta Teachers' Association. Through this program teachers can find psychologists and the cost is partially covered. They suggested I meet with a psychologist in Lloydminster, which I did. I poured out my heart to her yesterday. All the while she kept this smile on her face indicating to me she had no idea what trauma I was experiencing.

She suggested that I go home and make two lists: one of all Edward's strengths and the other of all his weaknesses. I did this exercise but I am never returning for her services. I figure that I probably can sit on a lawn chair in front of the caraganas in the backyard in the spring and talk to the bushes. That way I will get as much feedback as I received from the professional.

STRENGTHS

- intelligent, does well in school
- athletic, does well in Track and Field
- ambitious, sets high personal standards
- friendly, people seem to be attracted to him
- determined, gets the job finished
- Frank and I raised him with integrity, our values and beliefs, and strong work ethic
- raised in an environment where family is important
- has shown that he can work to fulfill a long-term goal (science fairs, music, drama productions)

A Gift of Grace

The process of writing this down on paper was supposed to help me realize that I most likely had nothing to fear about Edward and his gayness, or, that I had every right to be concerned about his direction in life. I am not sure.

The Vice-President's comments are certainly true and the last sentence issues the challenge Edward must meet and conquer: "He will be successful only if he is able to focus his energy in the right direction."

WEAKNESSES

- idolizes power, money and fame
- overly ambitious, might do anything to attain his personal goals
- young and vulnerable
- people may take advantage of his friendliness
- no money
- stubborn, has a big ego
- trusts others too much and shares his thoughts too openly
- seeks immediate gratification

You can do it Eddie! Where is the bright boy who wowed everyone with his intellect, talent and hard work?

1995

January 27, 1995

Edward, age 18, UWC (2nd year)

I am concerned Edward is acting strangely or maybe just acting...
like he has done on the stage so many times. He told me that he
had painted his body completely white to assist a classmate with
an art installation for an Art Exhibit.

*Now I acknowledge it is just fine for me to be geograph-
ically distant.*

He joined in the Gay Pride Parade.

At least Edward has been proactive in collecting reference letters
to support his applications for entry into university. He has
applied to the University of Toronto, McGill, Queens, Trent,
Williams College, Stanford University, University of Harvard,
University of Princeton, and others. Each application meant a
cheque of money to be sent along in the envelope.

At least it is for his future, so we don't mind doing this. I hope he
is accepted with a scholarship as that will help reduce the amount
of money we need to give him. There may be living expenses that
the scholarship won't be enough to cover. Most of them cover
tuition, fees and books. Still with his bright mind, it is a great
investment to support him in going to the best college he can.

He can apply for loans as well once he is accepted at a university.

Letter of reference for application to the University of Williams
College:

A Gift of Grace

Director of Admission
Williams College, Williamstown
Massachusetts

Dear Williams Admissions Committee:

I have known Edward for approximately a year and a half. We are classmates at the Armand Hammer United World College of the American West. First of all, I would like to congratulate you for receiving Ed's application to attend your prestigious institution. Ed is one of my closest and dearest comrades. I have had the privilege to become very close to this talented and extremely sensitive man through our active involvement with our socialist club. He is an excellent student in terms of academics, but his genius is demonstrated best through his incredible sense of social responsibility and musical ability. He is truly a sincere and creative person. He is a person who crosses many of the social barriers that seem to define us all. I have seen his acute ability to communicate his ideas with verbal respect, eloquence and lucidity. Edward is both articulate and dramatic. I have complete and utter respect for Ed and this is reflected in his popularity with many people on campus. But, beyond these seemingly superficial descriptions, I would like to define exactly what makes me feel proud to know him.

Last year during Spring Break, I had the chance to accompany Ed on a "service project" in Saltillo, a city situated in northern Mexico about an hour from Monterrey. This service project enabled me to work with Ed outside the confines of our small international community. At this time, the presidential election campaigns were taking place. Contrary to our school's acknowledge-ment of our activities, we assisted as much as we could with the campaign for the candidate of the Socialist Party of Mexico against Colosio. This was my chance to get to know Ed as a political revolutionary and market socialist. I believe that this experience enabled us to become very close; it gave us the opportunity to see ourselves as active members of the socialist movement.

Ed has a true revolutionary spirit. He uses his language and creativity to his advantage. He has an amazing talent for helping people without any hint of selfishness. He belongs to that special category of humanity that truly makes an impact on their world. As one of his peers, I can state unequivocally that he will make

January 27, 1995 97

A Gift of Grace

waves wherever he goes. For the sense of brevity, I believe that he can succeed at whatever he chooses. It would be a mistake for you not to accept Ed as one of your future graduates.

Yours faithfully,

Sven

Classmate at AHUWC

Reference Letter for Edward for college applications

Santa Fe Chamber Music Festival
Young Musicians Program
Las Vegas, New Mexico

To Whom It May Concern

Ed Weatherly has been taking piano lessons from me for one and a half years. During this time he has matured rapidly from being a roughly exuberant and technical pianist into an expressive and musical player. He can communicate line and phrasing, delicacy and power. He has a strong technique, is a good sight reader, has a steady sense of rhythm, and has a good ear. He is familiar with much music literature and is becoming more and more aware of how to communicate different styles and tone colors. He learns new music quickly. He is a good performer, doing his best when he has an audience.

Sincerely,

Name Withheld
Nationally Certified Teacher of Music

Reference Letter for Edward for his college applications

The Armand Hammer
United World College of the American West
Music Faculty

Scholarship Committee
Santa Fe Chamber Music Festival

Dear Scholarship Committee:

I am writing in support of my student Edward Weatherly. Over the two years that I have known him, he has shown incredible growth. He has developed from an intelligent, but awkwardly naïve music student, into one who is focussed, concise and sensitive.

This is most apparent in applied music. He has become a very accomplished pianist. In November he won the New Mexico Honors Piano competition.

He carries this ability into the classroom where his comments are challenging and insightful. I am convinced that his continued growth will enable him, come May, 1995, to receive highest marks on his International Baccalaureate music assessment.

Edward deserves to continue growing at the most challenging level possible. This chamber music program would be a great opportunity for Ed to expand his musical horizons. Thank you and good luck with the selections process.

Sincerely,

Name Withheld
UWC Music Instructor

A Gift of Grace

University of Toronto
Admissions and Awards

February 15, 1995

Mr. Edward Kenneth Weatherly III
Armand Hammer United World College of the
American West
P.O. Box 248
Montezuma, New Mexico

Dear Mr. Weatherly,

Congratulations! I am delighted to tell you that you have been chosen as one of the University of Toronto National Scholarship finalists for 1995.

As you know, each of the students who entered the National Scholarship competition had been chosen by their school as being truly outstanding. Each application has been evaluated by at least three separate adjudicators; the final decisions represent a consensus of opinion that your submission and academic achievements are among the very best we received. You can be very proud of being recognized in this way.

I am pleased to invite you to participate in the interviews which will result in the selection of approximately six National Scholars. The selection interviews will be held on the university campus on April 10th to April 12th; you should plan to travel on April 9th and 13th. The university will cover your travel expenses equivalent to economy-class air fare from your home in Canada. If you wish, we shall also arrange your travel for you. As soon as you confirm that you wish to participate, we shall make arrangements for housing in a university residence.

The National Scholarship Selection Committee is chaired by the Provost of the University. Each student will have two interviews, one with about four members of the Committee and a second with a faculty member in the field relevant to the student's original work.

During the three days, we shall also be showing you the campuses and facilities of the University of Toronto. Although there is a serious purpose for your visit to the University, we hope that the experience will be enjoyable and interesting...

All students chosen as National Scholarship finalists are assured of receiving admissions scholarships if they attend the University of Toronto. Those who are not designated as National Scholars receive Arbour Scholarships, valued at $2,200 per year for four years. As you probably know already, the National Scholarships are valued at $5,000 per year for four years plus free residence in the first year.

You are to be congratulated, as well, on being the recipient of a University of Toronto National Book Award. This honour is in recognition of your exceptional abilities, in the eyes of your school and of the University. The National Book Award will be sent to your school for presentation.

I am looking forward to having the opportunity to meet you in April. If, in the meantime, you have any questions, you are welcome to call my office. If you have access to email, you are welcome to use it instead.

Sincerely,

Name Withheld
Associate University Registrar
University of Toronto
Admissions and Awards

A Gift of Grace

April 24, 1995

Mr. Edward Kenneth Weatherly III
Armand Hammer United World College of the
American West
P.O. Box 248
Montezuma, New Mexico

Dear Mr. Weatherly:

I am delighted to congratulate you on your selection as a
University of Toronto National Scholar.

This letter is intended to provide you with the details of the
University's offer to you. These include:

- Admission to the undergraduate faculty and, if relevant, college, of your choice;
- Admission to the residence most appropriate to your faculty/ college choice and payment of all residence costs during your first year of study;
- A scholarship of $5000 per year, tenable for four years. An outline of the terms and conditions of the scholarship is enclosed.

There will also be a number of special opportunities arranged by
the University. Each student will be linked with a faculty member
who will act as a mentor. Regular gatherings will be organized;
these will range from purely social events to academic symposia.
We shall plan an initial get-together early in the fall term.

In order that we may issue an official offer of admission, we would
be grateful if you could return the enclosed forms confirming
your choice of faculty and college, and also providing us with
information to help us select your mentor. If you have any   questions, you are welcome to call us at...

I look forward to hearing from you.

With my best wishes,
Name Withheld
Associate University Registrar
Admissions and Awards

May 1, 1995

Edward, age 18, UWC (2nd year)

Double Wow!! Edward has been selected for University of Toronto not only as an applicant, but also for the four year full scholarship. He went to Toronto for the final interview and now he excitedly faxed the letter accepting him as a University of Toronto National Scholar!

He also received a letter of congratulations from the University of Toronto, Office of the Vice-President and Provost, on being chosen as a University of Toronto National Scholar: "You can be proud of this very special recognition of your abilities and accomplishments."

We also received a copy of a letter sent to Edward from the Buffalo Trail Regional Division #28, Wainwright, Alberta. It congratulates him on completing his studies at United World College saying, "The Board of Trustees of the new Buffalo Trail Regional Division, which includes the former Provost School Division, are very proud of your accomplishment."

Definitely, we are so proud of him!

A Gift of Grace

Edward Weatherly III   **STUDENT REPORT**

May 1995 United World College of the American West
House: Meredith

Higher Level: History
Edward's academic performance this term has been erratic. He has missed far too many classes and did rather poorly on the trial exam. I don't think that he studied for it. If Edward studies, he should do well on the IB exam, but if he does not apply himself, I am not optimistic about his chances of passing.

Higher Level: Music
Ed is easily the strongest musician in his class. I am convinced he received highest marks on the performance component of his music IB. His compositions were strong as well, so he has a great opportunity to receive highest marks on his overall music IB grade. This will be guaranteed by diligent preparation and acute musical reactions on his two IB music exams. Ed's sensitivity to this subject will only grow as he moves on to greater challenges in his life.

Higher Level: English A1
Ed firmly aspires to do well in his final IB result and I sincerely hope that he will. He has worked very diligently at improving his writing; the breadth and depth of his ideas sometimes make it difficult for him to provide appropriate expression in writing. He has been a stimulating person to have in the class discussions; I hope the future will bring him fine adventures and great successes.

Subsidiary Level: Applied Chemistry
The quality of Edward's work in Applied Chemistry has varied over the past year. If he can remain calm and focussed when answering exam questions and be aware of time allotments, he should be able to improve his exam performance sufficiently to assure a comfortable passing grade. I wish him much success in this effort.

Subsidiary Level: French B
Ed worked steadily during the first semester but failed to sustain his effort. This has compromised his chances of significantly improving his 1994 IB grade. It was a pleasure teaching Ed. I wish him every success at university.

A Gift of Grace

Subsidiary Level: Math Studies
Though he did write a very good and interesting Math Studies Project on mathematics and music, Ed has not done the work he is capable of doing in mathematics this year. His good sense of humour has made the class fun to teach. He will be missed at our school next year.

Advisor's Report:
It has been a pleasure to serve as Ed's advisor. He is a talented, sensitive, and creative young man. We will certainly miss Ed, his talents, and sense of humour. I wish him all the best in the future.

Resident Tutor:
Some of Ed's enthusiasms almost got the best of his self-discipline this term. He is certainly a very talented young man. I have had many serious conversations with him and do not doubt his ability to achieve all he wants out of life. Hopefully, he can find that necessary sense of perspective to help him with future endeavours. Our best wishes to him for the future.

Community Service:
Ed appears to have enjoyed his service, Performing Arts for Children, although his commitment could have been a little stronger. He spent a good deal of time making up missed service days. Ed has the ability and skills to be a strong leader. I hope he uses them in the future. I wish him well.

Activity Report:
Edward participated in a Model UN conference in Los Angeles last January. Even though he had just joined the activity, he did a most credible job. The college team did very well at the Conference and won several prizes.

Vice President's Report:
Ed has enjoyed his experiences at the college and has contributed to many aspects of college life. Hopefully, there will continue to be improvement in self-discipline and other areas of responsibility in meeting academic and personal commitments. These attributes will be necessary for success in tertiary education and meeting the challenges of adulthood.

May 1, 1995

A Gift of Grace

June 29, 1995

Edward, age 18, UWC (end of 2nd year)

It was interesting to read all the letters and reports. I could see him from other people's eyes. I am definitely proud that Edward received the scholarship and all the awards. I have almost become used to him being away, but I do worry because his behaviour is troubling. He just doesn't seem to be himself. He is not the Edward I know. Yet all the awards and accolades are given to the young man who is my Edward. Obviously, he can still impress when he wants to.

I also worried after I read of his erratic marks noted in his May Student Report, but Edward must have studied because he was successful in achieving an IB Diploma. He received a seven out of seven in Music and a four out of seven in French. The four in French was enough to pass and the seven in Music shows his greatest talent.

This phrase from his report sticks in my mind: "Improvement in self-discipline and other areas of responsibility in meeting academic and personal commitments are attributes necessary for success in meeting challenges of adulthood."

Mom (Grandma Kristina), my sister Shari and I flew to Montezuma, New Mexico, to attend Edward's special graduation ceremony. We enjoyed a variety program of very talented students one evening and the next day we watched the graduation ceremony, which was set up on the soccer field with flags from seventy different countries flying proudly. They provided a colourful backdrop behind the bleachers where the students were seated. Afterward, there was cake, champagne and a mariachi band playing in the shade of the trees along the field.

UWC makes education a force to unite people, nations and cultures for peace and a sustainable future.

Just what Edward wrote in his Oddfellows' speech when he was still in high school! Probably explains his socialist leanings. UWC obviously was the perfect education for a person of this mindset. I hope he does all he can to achieve success at UofT. There is no limit to what he can do, if he puts in the effort.

June 30, 1995

Edward, age 18, UWC (end of 2nd year)

Edward received a letter from his yearlong roommate asking him to read it after he boarded the plane back to Canada. Edward had replied right away and received a response back. Edward was very excited about the letters and gave them to me to read. He said the roommate was from a strict Catholic family in South America and at first was awkward being around a gay person. This letter shows how far the roommate progressed in his views over the year and how caring he has become toward Edward.

Dear Roomildo:

You kind of know already what you mean for me. O.K. I accept that it has been hard for me to live with you. But it is not because you are explosive, or whatever, it's just because I care a lot about you and I always feel stressed about your problems. I always wanted to help in a subtle way, without you noticing that I was helping, but it was difficult because I did not want to intrude on your private life or make you aware of many things.

You have got a difficult path. You have to start thinking about changing some parts of you, so that you can improve to your maximum. I'll be always praying for you. Don't doubt it.

It was fun to know you, to discover you, although I don't think I understand you.

A Gift of Grace

Well, roomi now I'm leaving. I feel bad about letting you go. Who will take care of you? I really appreciate your friendship. Remember to go and visit me in Venezuela. The doors of my house are open whenever you need a hand.

Please, take care of yourself. Don't let people move you around. You need to look after yourself more carefully. Thank you for being in the other side of the room. Thank you for sharing with me. I will miss you a lot.

Good luck, you will be fine. (hope)

Carlos

Roomildo:

Thank you very much for your note! It was very important to hear that you liked me. Sometimes I was unsure of that. If sometimes I act severe towards you it is just because I care for you and I'm trying to do what is best for you.

Although you are "different and difficult" sometimes (but not much) you mean a lot for me and that's why I care about what you think of me.

Once again thank you very much for your support and for being such a good friend and roomie.

Thanks a lot.

Carlos ....

July 25, 1995

Edward, age 18, summer between UWC & UofT

Frank stepped on a nail and ended up in the Provost Hospital.

Nicole and I painted kids' faces at the July 1st celebration in Provost and when we went to visit him at 11:00 p.m., he was not in the hospital! He had been taken to Edmonton in an ambulance because he had complications with his breathing and heart, and he became very sick. It was suggested that he had possibly suffered from a heart attack. Frank's chronic illness of diabetes in the hospital! He had been taken to Edmonton in an ambulance because he had complications with his breathing and heart, and he became very sick. It was suggested that he had possibly suffered from a heart attack. Frank's chronic illness of diabetes was causing pain and suffering as it slowly affects his overall health and well being.

Shelley, Nicole, Edward and I drove to Edmonton to be with Frank. He was very ill because of the effects of the blood poisoning, so we got a room in a nearby motel and stayed in the city until he was starting to get better.

Edward displayed very self-centred behaviour and wanted to go out after supper each night and the girls and I couldn't fathom this kind of behaviour when his father was in the hospital. Edward did not seem worried about his Dad and he was not compassionate at all for the trauma the girls and I felt.

What was going through this kid's head?

He had not visited his Dad yet, so I suggested that Edward do so. He finally went to the hospital and had only been in his Dad's hospital room for a few minutes before they were arguing. Frank yelled at him saying that it was evident that Edward was behaving similar to one of his brothers, who lived off the avails of others.

A Gift of Grace

This was obviously not helping Frank recover so I took Edward out of the room and decided I would just take him home with me to do the chores. I had the garden to weed, lawn to mow, mail to get and bills to pay. Perhaps this way Frank would feel Edward was being more responsible.

On the way out of the city, Edward and I had supper with my sister, Marlene, at her friend's home. Edward behaved badly saying he didn't want to just sit there all evening and "just visit." He wanted to go to a movie, walk up and down Whyte Avenue, and check out the coffee shops.

Obviously I had to take him out of there and started on my way home.

In the car Edward continued to be very demanding. At that point I decided to stay over in Wainwright, go to the bank in the morning, apply for a student loan for him

and he could darn well take the Greyhound back to Edmonton and I don't care what happens to him!

Oh, if it was only that easy!!

After sleeping in a cheap motel, we headed for the bank and were able to get his first five thousand dollar student loan. Then he asked if he could use my suitcase.

Yeah, right, I'll just empty my clothes on the back seat so that you can fold your clothes nicely for your escapade in the city lights.

No, you're not getting my suitcase; I was pissed! I was gripped in a turmoil of negative emotions and hopelessness.

I asked him what he wanted to do about his clothes.

A Gift of Grace

"Take me to Co-op and I'll buy some garbage bags."

I parked outside the store and he came out with a box of large orange bags. He stuffed his clothes in and tied it up. I drove to the bus terminal and he went in to purchase his ticket. He came back out and informed me that the bus would arrive in half an hour.

God, am I crazy? I don't know what to do with him! He breaks my heart time and time again. He shows no appreciation for anything I do for him.

We hear the air brakes of the Greyhound as it stops in front of the small building. Edward jumps out of the car. We say little to each other. I don't ask for a hug and he doesn't offer one.

I grit my teeth, seething with anger and disgust for what I have done in response to my teenage son who shows absolutely no empathy for anyone and focuses only on his self-centred wants. As I watch him walking deliberately toward the bus carrying his orange "suitcase," I die a little bit more inside. He goes up the steps of the bus and disappears.

He's officially off on a week exploring his identity. I cry and weep all the way home, wallowing in my sadness and sense of failure. I hate my life...

I consider myself an innately good person. I raised my children to be good people. Why is this happening?

I drove home to our acreage, weeded and watered the garden, and paid the bills. Then I drove back up to Edmonton to see Frank and the girls.

A Gift of Grace

August 5, 1995

Edward, age 18, summer between UWC and UofT

Edward phoned one evening from the Hotel MacDonald and wove a tale about dining with the Prince of Cathay.

"He wants to give me a ring, Mom!"

"What! Why?"

"To be engaged to him, but I told him I couldn't accept it."

Well, good for you!

"He gave me a painting instead. He said it was worth a lot of money."

Yeah right! I'm glad he couldn't hear my thoughts!

Later that week, Edward came home on the Greyhound carrying a hefty suitcase and a trunk full of clothes and memorabilia from his prince. Tailor made suits, tuxedo, jackets and vests, black patent leather shoes, elaborate belts, along with various Chinese pottery items, numb chucks, flying stars, decorative coat pins embedded with gems, a swastika pennant and an old painting. Edward was extremely excited when he got home and laid out all his new belongings onto his bed to show me. He was speaking a "mile a minute" describing his adventures with this Prince of Cathay.

"I didn't spend any money, Mom! I still have my loan money."

How did I feel knowing my son had been a kept man? Surreal!

Then Edward handed me an envelope addressed to me from his Prince.

112 August 5, 1995

A Gift of Grace

August 1, 1995

Dear Mrs. Weatherly,

On behalf of your son Edward I am writing to you in the hope that you might gain a better understanding of my friendship with him.

Edward came into my life by chance. In those early instances at the prelude of our relationship, my life long sense of intense loneliness became diluted. Within moments our sense of appreciation for each other grew with profound rapidity. The rest as they say is history.

Both of us are now on route to commence a significant chapter in our lives. We have agreed to keep in contact with each other in the hope of a better future.

As a gesture of my fondness and appreciation for your son I extend him the liberty of free access to my wardrobe and my general circumstance in life.

I give to you my word of honour that I will always hold Edward in the highest esteem without pride or reserve. I shall not in any event take him for granted nor will I allow myself to take advantage of his person. Edward means the world to me as he does to you. I extend to you my respect for raising such a fine young gentleman.

I am yours truly,

Lee X. Choy
Edmonton, Alberta, Canada

Apparently the parents of the prince had exiled their gay son to Edmonton, Alberta, Canada. How sad for him! This escapade will never be shared with Edward's father.

A Gift of Grace

September 11, 1995

Edward, age 18, University of Toronto

That wasn't all the acknowledgements Edward received toward his education. He received the Alexander Rutherford Scholarship of $1500 from Alberta Heritage Scholarship Fund, Students Finance Board, Edmonton, Alberta.

Then the University of Toronto, Admissions and Awards had notified Edward that he has been assigned a mentor. She is the Acting Co-ordinator of the Ethics, Society and Law Program. With Edward's interest in world affairs, culture and ethics as evidenced in his school and UWC assignments; this should be an interesting mentor for him.

The letter says, "We believe that the mentorship opportunity is an important feature of the National/Arbor Scholarship Program. Depending on interests and needs, you will probably develop a somewhat unique relationship with your mentor. Some of the mentors are within the same college or faculty as the students; others are not, but have been chosen on the basis of a mutual academic interest. All are prominent members of the faculty who have expressed real enthusiasm for this role."

October 20, 1995

Edward, age 18, 1st year at UofT

So Edward is at the University of Toronto, Trinity College on a full scholarship. He phones and often mentions Galen Rogers, a dignitary at the University of Toronto that he met when he was flown there for the National Scholar interviews.

114 October 20, 1995

A Gift of Grace

Galen already seems to be a big part of Edward's life. He tells me Galen took photos of him and entered them in competitions. What kind of photos? I asked him that but Edward ignored the question and went on to tell me that Galen likes "making conversations with him" and that flattered him.

What kind of photos? What kind of competitions? This drives me crazy not knowing!

Edward sends me a copy of a poem Galen wrote to him.

Dearest Edward,

Silence is often more expressive
Than a jumble of words:
But...
Edward, darling, let us dream
That we, in love, are an endless seam,
Cloth disparate, old and young
Bound together with the eye's intent.
You all beauty, blond and slim,
I, the ancient, sage and mentor;
Yet our moods, and shared expressions
Slay the myths of age and shame.

GAR

Accept my gift of "good fortune"
You will walk where Hadrian walked

Much Love

"Much love"! What the hell is going on? What gift of "good fortune?"

On the phone and in his letters it appears Edward is visibly excited and flattered about this person's attention. I am invisibly dreading what is happening to Edward! It sounds like Galen is a "dirty old man" preying on a young man's innocence.

October 20, 1995 **115**

A Gift of Grace

November 1, 1995

Edward, soon age 19, 1st year UofT

Dear Edward,

I'm writing this letter because I feel a few things need to be 'cleared up'.

I received your $1500 award from Edmonton. I will be filling in the amount of $315 on the blank cheque you signed for me in August. (Remember, you left it for me.) It cost $15 to handle the transaction with this letter. I won't cash the $315 cheque for a few days to make sure the $1500 is in your account.

I'm also sending your bank statement. I couldn't help but notice how much money you're spending at the gay bar. You may want to change some of your habits because $1500 minus $315 = $1185, and according to your statement you spent a bit more than this in one month. You have enough to budget about $200 per month for the rest of the year, less interest payment. I am writing this because I care very much for you and you need to really think and respond appropriately to some of the decisions you're making.

I am willing to help you out but there is a limit to my kind-heartedness. You must respect my wishes for you to be responsible for your choices and accept consequences for your actions. (I have no more money.)

Just a reminder to phone and let the Wellesley Hospital know your Health Care number.

Both Shelley and Nicole asked for your address so that they could send a birthday card to you. They asked me how you were doing so I gave them the number of Trinity College so they could maybe talk to you.

A Gift of Grace

Edward, from our last telephone conversation I am thinking that maybe you're in the wrong program. May I give you some advice? As you know, Nicole kind of bombed out during her first year of university but that was when she realized that she also had taken some courses which weren't suited to her. So, she got a letter of probation. But, the following year she enrolled in courses she knew she would excel in. She was able to do much better because she enjoys math. If you talk to her maybe she could share some of her experiences with you. She would be able to help you make decisions about your courses. By the way, she must care for you a lot because she gets extremely annoyed with some of the anti-gay remarks which she hears from some of her students. I guess she feels protective of your interests.

I'm pleased that you have found someone to care for – Tom that is. He sounds like a great person. I hope he becomes a true friend also.

I'm home right now and it's 1:30 p.m. I have a doctor's appointment this afternoon at 3:15. Then I have to attend a staff meeting which will probably be too long. This year is going very well for me. Diane and I are sharing our expertise and enjoying many projects with our students.

I really would like to see you at Christmas and if you would come home I'd buy a ticket for you with my savings. Just let me know so I can book your flight.

Work hard, Ed and remember – I'll always be proud of you.

Love,

Mom
Watch for a birthday parcel in your mailbox.

A Gift of Grace

November 17, 1995

Edward, age 19, 1st year UofT

We received a disturbing letter from Trinity College at the University of Toronto. It reads:

> "I am writing with regard to your final mark in FSL 100F (Introductory French). Based on this mark, I am somewhat concerned that there may be extenuating circumstances of which this office is unaware, which may have affected your performance in this course.

> "Please make an appointment to speak with someone in this Office as soon as possible regarding whatever options may be open to you. Many students are unaware of the procedures of petitioning or late withdrawal, which could significantly improve their cumulative record. There are deadlines for making adjustments to final marks so the sooner you are able to discuss your situation with us, the better your chances are of correcting your transcript." (Trinity College)

This was followed by a copy of a letter to The Committee on Standing, Faculty of Arts and Science, c/o The Registrar, Trinity College from the University Chaplain. It reads:

> "I write to support the petition of Edward Weatherly for the late withdrawal, without academic penalty, from the course MGT 120F (Financial Accounting).

> "Edward has shown signs of depression and confusion since his arrival at Trinity, and has spoken with me intermittently since early September. It has been quite clear to me all along that he did not fit in his present programme, despite his original hopes. He has now come to this conclusion for himself.

> "I think his intention to withdraw from accounting to pursue a more vocational interest in music is a healthy

A Gift of Grace

one, and hope he can do this without penalty."
(University Chaplain)

*Edward, what is happening to you so far away from me
that I cannot even ask you that question? I knew it was
foolish to take these courses in the first place on the
advice of a so-called Prince, a cast off of society! For some
reason a hideous man who knew you for a week or two
seemed wiser than your family who knows you best.*

December 5, 1995

Edward, age 19, 1st year UofT

Dear Ed,

*I hope you like all these socks and shorts. You may want to wash
the shorts before you wear them but you don't have to.*

Please look after yourself and don't be careless with your health.

I am looking forward to hearing from you.

Take care,
Love

Mom

*P.S. I mailed $150.00 to your account in Wainwright. I couldn't do
it yesterday because it stormed and I couldn't even make it in to
school. This money is for laundry and necessities only.*

I love you, Ed.

Mom

A Gift of Grace

December 7, 1995

Edward, age 19, 1st year UofT

Edward phoned me to tell me he went to the funeral of Robinson Davies, a Canadian writer who died on December 2nd. Edward sounded high at the time he phoned me. He described himself parading the streets wearing a tall, stuffed hat with balloons attached. He also said he had an interview with some TV reporters, telling them some blarney about being very close to Davies.

> *What in the world is Edward doing? Why is he acting so strange? It must be the drugs. I wish I knew a way to get him to stop! I am so far away. I am trying to persuade him to come home for Christmas so I can talk some sense into him. As if that has worked before!*

December 9, 1995

To Whom It May Concern:

I am writing to inform your office that I have decided that my experience as a "Commerce-bound" student at Trinity College did not suit me or my academic or career intentions. My first three months demonstrated that I needed to withdraw from my original courses and pursue piano performance at the Faculty of Music. I am also writing you to petition to remain in residence at Trinity so that I can audit courses from the Faculty of Music as well as study with their piano teacher Rita Spencer. I was previously tormented as a student in Commerce that was brought on by my initial experience in residence and my ostracization dealt by the Episcopon brotherhood. The enclosed letter from Reverend Allan will perhaps document my situation and decision. I have since become stronger and wish to survive these walls as I pursue my art. This hope now depends on your office's decision to enable my National Scholarship first-year residency funding to allow me to stay in residence for the remainder of the year but allow the other half of my unspent tuition to be attached to next year. I, most assuredly, will enter the Faculty of Music next winter session as a newly arrived first year Piano Performance student. I have already withdrawn from my courses before the deadline and I anticipate your reaction to my request.

Yours sincerely,

Edward Weatherly

A Gift of Grace

December 13, 1995

Edward, age 19, 1st year UofT

Ostracized! Tormented! Survive these walls! What is happening to my son so far away? Why does it take a letter from him to a stranger for me to learn of these latest troubles?

Although he wanted to pursue music and registered that way, the Prince of Cathay convinced Edward to enrol in Commerce. Now the walls are closing in on him. Instead of protecting, they seem to me from his letter to be the walls of a prison!

I hide his letter and my journal as well as notes and letters all around the house in places Frank would never look. I can't deal with his response on top of what I am dealing with myself.

So today after I read the copy of Edward latest letter and went to hide it, I found a note I had written on a piece of lined paper tucked there in the hiding place. I read it and I cried without tears at first and then the tears fell on the paper blurring the words, staining the memories captured here:

A Gift of Grace

This is a song from my heart... I have something to share –
I can't keep it any longer. Son –you're my son.
Video --- dress, play house, drama, singing, piano.
Go see what Daddy's doing in the garage,
leave for college, send cookies, I lovingly made lefse,
wrapped them in a tea towel and sent them Express Post.
Respect yourself, others,
You struggle with your identity
Media --- movies, magazines, issues, violence, bigotry, sex, crimes
Queer, faggot, gay
Son --- I love the sound of your voice, you're my sun
MLAs --- laws to keep citizens safe; equal
I can find a cue in any conversation with people just to fit you in
"You eat like that and no girl will want to date you."
Made friends easily
Put downs
Live, learn, know why you're here
Make life easier for others
Material things aren't as important as your own well being
High school
Geek --- didn't play hockey
Figure skating
Shared openly-friendly-but kept the real self hidden
You're far away
I'm proud of you
I hope you find happiness
Respect yourself --- you're beautiful; you're a gift to this world
Me...I cry, I miss you...you left home so soon
Please look after yourself
I send you parcels
Your every hurt is my burden
Your every joy is my triumph
Your every success is mine, too
Sometimes I call just to hear your voice on your voice mail
When you call I save your message
keeping at least one to save and resave
My example should teach you to be loving and tolerant of
others, forgiving of yourself when you do wrong
I want to shelter you from all harm –
but you're not a boy any more
I knew you were different –
exuberant, impulsive, musical,
obsessed with life and every thing in it.
I let go and give you wings to fly wherever you are destined...

December 13, 1995

A Gift of Grace

> *Like the butterflies we raised in school, may you alight on my shoulder to show me you understand I nurtured you through your pupal stage and waited lovingly while you broke through your cocoon to transform into a beautiful butterfly. I hope you return often and that I remain in your heart always as you remain in mine.*

1996

January 4, 1996

Edward, age 19, UofT

Edward took me up on my invitation and prepaid ticket to come home for Christmas. I had hoped he could stay the week, but he went back after a couple of days to Toronto to spend time with Galen and Jean Rogers at their home in the country. I was heartbroken because I would have appreciated playing a few more board games of Monopoly and Trivial Pursuit.

Edward phoned and described their property as very picturesque – snow covered evergreens, beautiful gardens and a gently winding stream with a blanket of snow hanging over the edges. Even swans swam in the cold waters. He described gardens and flower beds, which Galen and Jean had him weed and prune in the fall. They want him to work the soil in the spring, as soon as it thaws.

When he is with them, he sleeps in the guest house beside their outdoor swimming pool. He described several paintings that he was impressed with, some of which Galen's relative painted as one of the Group of Seven. Edward is so impressed with these surroundings and I am apprehensive of the whole scene.

> *But, couldn't it be possible that these people were genuinely interested in our son? After all, Jean made turkey pot pie for supper. What harm could come from a mom who made homemade meat pies?*
>
> *I don't understand the significance of the underlying concerns my spirit is sensing. It's like my "spidey senses" are signalling trouble.*

A Gift of Grace

Edward went to Niagara Falls with Galen.

> *Isn't that a symbolic place for lovers to go? Edward sent me a photo that was taken at Niagara – his eyes in this photo give me the eerie feeling that they are searching for something more than what he is experiencing.*

Edward informed me that Galen has given him and some of his friends many, many tickets to the Toronto Ballet.

> *He is so excited they are exposing him to the best of Toronto's culture.*

January 24, 1996

Edward, age 19, UofT

Angie, a friend of Edward's from UofT, was concerned about this long rambling and very strange email Edward sent to her. She found out my email address and forwarded it to me. I have kept it, cursing and spelling errors intact. What mind was he in when he wrote this?

It seems filled with sheer babble and nonsense!

A Gift of Grace

Date: Tue, 16 Jan 1996 16: 04: 13 EDT
Subject: a very very very very pathetic and "about time" hello

Salute!!! How are you? You are the first person I have got in contact with from UWC besides Matthew since I left last year!! First of all I have to say thank you very much for your stream of letters the past year... I know I am as pathetic as a mole in winter trying to pull off a torrent of polar icing attempts. But, I finally have got my e-mail address and I am now believing in the educational system enough here in Canada to translate my being into a transformed and enlightened state of strong-willed eclectic non-compromisation. Essentially, I miss you and everyone else. My year has been even more of a time of the bizarre and insane. My life in general seems to border on the crazy and incongruous. How was Europe? I will be going for sure this summer for approximately one and a half months. I am dying to go... for I had planned to originally attend to my geneticism this past summer and meet you all but unfortunately my father was on his death bed in Edmonton. Somewhat of a turn around. I am truly sorry that I had teased you sorts when I stated that I would be going over. I passed my IB. Thank God...doing better than I had thought all along; all I really cared about was getting a 7 on my Music, even though I had hitch-hiked to Santa Fe with the sister of one of my first years that night before and got back to Montezuma just in time to write the exam. Graduation was very hard for me. I spent the last 3 weeks of my time there hanging out and smoking endless streams of cigarettes and pot on the patios or with the locals at the Hot Springs. I simply cannot get enough of myself knowing that I am finally writing you. Maybe I am merely because of the convenience and the rapidity of this late-20th century technique of communication.

How are your courses and time at Bryn Mawr? Anyone special trying to carouse with your ingenious methods of table tennis? I hope that all of the quasi-lesbianism that I have heard that run Bryn Mawr hasn't attempted to squash your humour! What did you do for Xmas and New Year's? I spent 9 days of the holidays with my parents and then returned to Toronto to spend New Year's Eve. It was flawless. I was weak. I had supper that evening at a photographer friend's warehouse space. We smoked pot and we listened to his late 1960's underground cartoon solos with this twisted group of artists who were laying low from the scene in New York City. We then went on a bar-spree and bamboozled the fabulous likes of several "it" trend-setting dance clubs through-

January 24, 1996 **127**

A Gift of Grace

out the city. I didn't have time to go home and change so I simply looked around me and created a symphony of random and wore it out on my head => a ten foot snowboarding jester's hat stuffed with packaging bubbles with an extension tied on top with 76 blue and red helium balloons. Even though I wasn't able to get off to Rio for this New Year's festivities I was able to create an international party ambience with my hat. No shirt, pants I made out of glow in the dark fibre optic fabric. This was a fun mixture of late French impressionism that unknowingly met me on such an ill-fated time and space continuum. Regardless, please let me in on your life... I do, even though I haven't showed it, miss you tremendously.

I have tried to cut myself off from the pain of being separated from our mutual group of the most creative, accepting, brilliant and insatiable group of people I think we may ever meet in such a concentrated setting. For me it was an enigmatic time of wearing glasses made of pressure-cooked plastic that enabled me to be a part but not entirely enabling me to see clearly what I was a part of. If that makes sense. I don't currently have access to anyone else's e-mail account. So, if you hear from anyone, please if you could give me a few... I am finally realizing that I am dying bit by bombastic bit every day without contact with you. I got your e-mail from Matthew. He is a terrific guy and even more endearing person in my life since I've been here in Toronto. We are at different colleges. I am at Trinity College and he is at Victoria, as you probably already know. I came here to U of T thinking that my full scholarship and spending money would be a proper beginning to a prosperous time of understanding at an institution of higher learning. I am just coming to an "about time" view of how behind some people are.

I feel much older than my scorpion cells traditionally should feel. I turned 19 high on more drugs than I can count or weigh with, seemingly finding myself but in the end trashing a relationship I had with a model from Ford and lying to him about it. He had arranged a weekend up in the mountains at his cottage – complete with balloons and candlelight. I had been in a slump that week while he was in Buffalo with this hustler who was trying to get information through me about my father by pretending to be Matthew's brother. Very twisted situation. Instead I thought my birthday was a day before it happened, consequently meeting Luke (from Buffalo) later that weekend where he was confused and very upset that I lied to him. I ended up giving him crabs and now know that my time and space needs to have a time of solitude before I can take a jab at the world. The world out here is one of force and is full of secrets. Partly these secrets intrigue me, but on the other hand they are dripping with death. Perhaps my own secrets need to be undone by my own hands before my own secrets orchestrate my demise.

I have so much to tell you. I hope you aren't too busy and can't read my letter. But please oblige me, for I think you might laugh at some of the things that have happened to me over the past seven months.

I ran away from home again this past summer while my father was in the hospital. A tiny bit of stress on my family I might add. I went to Edmonton not knowing where I would stay or who I would stay with or with what means I would survive. I took the bus there and spent the first half of the first day walking the streets of downtown. I met a non-resident student who goes to Trinity here. He and I must have been the only two Trinity students in Alberta at that time, but of course I saw him waiting for a bus and I asked him if I could bum a cigarette. We started talking and we found out about each other. His Dad runs part of the film industry here in Canada, after coming out of his Harvard MBA program. Very neat guy, his name is Gordon... cute but straight. We might go into a "business" together sometime at the end of the month. I am thinking of renting a castle from the city of Toronto and having a bash for next Halloween. It is the perfect location for an ecstasy party for all types... women and men strippers, mirrors, holograms wall paper for advertisement... to name some of the ideas. Anyhow, after seeing Gordon off on the bus, (after taking him to the gay bar to buy him a pitcher of superb Canadian ale) I decided I would walk over to the one gay café... I sat there having my quiet café mocha as if by fate this boy Nolan flew in. He was wearing all Dolce & Gabbanna and sporting a white trash smile to boot. I had met him the previous summer. He invited me over to this place where he was tricking a place for the summer. Unknowingly, he had made a mistake, for I, in the end, would take over his spot and replace his presence with flair and subtle keys for his Cathay Vampire Prince.

I consequently found myself in the living room of the mansion of an exiled Prince of Cathay. His name was Lee X. Choy. He had been studying at the University of London taking Art History as he was jet-setting around with the international group of dukes,

A Gift of Grace

barons and gay elites between London and Milan. But his time in Edmonton had twisted him. He was an old soul and possessed old eyes that could not take the light of day. He lived a twisted existence in the only place that was attending to his life. No one over the seven years that he spent there knew who he really was... until I opened a venue for him. He had been eating the gay boys of Edmonton... over 26 of them after he had created a death environment for them. He would buy this 20 year old hustler with HIV to infect young flawless flesh as he seemingly would be sleeping impotently upstairs in his lair. He had video-taped their infection over the years. 26 should and I am sure more, were trapped in this mansion. I was intrigued by the Picassos, the Rembrandts and the Japanese tapestries and the endless series of masks that dotted the walls and ceiling of his home. The energy was as negative as a bat's underarm. He had taken out all the lights in the building. Nolan, without saying, was thrown out of his life after I arrived uncontrived into his fate that had not been random since his exile. I provided the supposed strength he had been searching for. Once he ate the energy of one boy who was not his ideal, he would kill them and then pay someone to dig up their bones and give them to him which he stored in his basement. It was a fucked 12 days. In the course of time I was proposed to with a stone of jade set in gold which had been taken out of the chest of the Empress Dowager in 1935. I gave it back to him even though it was worth (I had observed in the 1994 Sotheby's journal) over $800,000. We lived at night and we rode around as he told me his story. He wanted me to go home with him to prove to his parents that he was worthy of stature to return and take over the bank and allow his brother to portray his father's political empire. He was exiled so as not to embarrass the family. He wanted me to run his bank. I then, once I left him, changed my plans from music to commerce... a mistake that took me a while to realize... only after almost overdosing on cocaine and ecstasy here in Toronto. To finish this quick... He gave me about 150,000 dollars worth of clothes and artefacts as I gave him back his ring. But also in exchange for my time, he gave me a watercolour painting by Delacroix. Pretty good I thought for 12 days "work." It took me, like I said, a good part of last semester to realize how he fucked me up. We spent thousands of dollars a night and he saturated me like I was his therapist, not his com-panion, with his life story. I have a memory that intrigued him, I would recognize and remember nuances of his home and his numerous dissertations that no one else had. He thought it was the fact that it was fate and that he had gone out to seek me out

A Gift of Grace

like all the others. He was a drug addict though... I never slept with him once, and I have since been infected with the interest of secrets while keeping adequate distance from HIV --- my analysis being that it is intrinsically a societal disease of over consumption. We parted each other as I was going home to repair my family as he was going to the Betty Ford Clinic, before going home to Cathay and repairing his own family. I haven't heard from him since. But, I am still haunted by the memory of the screams and movements of spirits that would wander through the house at night and the barking of his dog that had been, just a month before, kicked to death by Lee's just-previous ex lover who found out he had AIDS at 17 and went psycho before Lee could contain him and cut him up and store his bones in his underground and observable graveyard for the negative energy of society that he thought should be studied and painted. Anyhow, I've gotten over this... but I thought you might be interested in the story. Oh, yeah, paintings would fall off the walls as he would be teaching me about various things at 5 in the morning that I am sure were pushed off by ghosts; the white hair from his dead dog would, even after a nightly ritual of sweeping it up and picking the tufts of hair out of the rugs, return after we had slept. There is more and more to tell about that, but obviously it would probably take a book to catalogue it all.

Anyhow, so I have been spending my time here in this Anglican gothic playground. I have seen Matthew intermittently over our time here at University of Toronto. Angelina had to go home. I never even got to see her here. There is a secret underground, 150 year old brotherhood here in this all-male residence called the Episcopons. Fairly twisted in their own right. This place breeds secreted and covered eccentricity... homoeroticism evident all over. From our wearing academic gowns to dinner in our fabulous dining hall made from oak and gowned itself with precious paintings and a tapestry from eastern Post-WWII Europe. They rip off your clothes in a Pooring Out if you, especially if you are a first year, and your gown, are not up to conventional par as you hold on the dinner table trying to maintain your presence in the hall for one minute. But usually that doesn't happen. So, last semester, after the horrendous British on acid frosh initiations where I was hospitalized with blood poisoning after being dosed with swale in the infamous cake fight to being satirically (DeadPoet-Societyesque) jousted and torn apart for my entrances and exits as a frosh in the quadrangle.

A Gift of Grace

I've seen a lot and been through a lot since I have left UWC. I miss the congeniality, the talks, the laughter, the "being at home with everyone and that's ok if you're different" feeling, the setting, the faculty and most of all the friends. I think you are a part of me whether you want that or not. I have thought of you, Angie, everyday for many, many months. Hard to believe since I am a bastard and don't write very often... but that is partly due to my over-extension and compulsive desire to attempt at revealing all to you in one conversation... or the universe of Angie in one conversation joined in matrimony... fairly hard to do when letters are the medium or e-mail. But I would like for us to talk more... I promise to be good now... after I have come to the realization that there is not one like us and what we have experienced together on this planet. Fairly depressing isn't it? But, I tragically have been searching for others like UWCers... trying not to be the pathetic old women at reunions still caught in the spokes of their old 16 to 19 year old wheels spitting out fragments of a past that they cannot get over. I don't want to get over us or our time together either, but I think I have made more that an effort to find new experiences... even more after Lee X... there is Galen Rogers (a bank CEO)... Bob... Rex... Brad... stories and stories and stories... I think I am quite content to stay in this computer forever and retrieve you, Angie. I hope you forgive me in my insanity and my lack of respect for your time and consideration in writing to me when I seemingly didn't have the time of day for you. I am currently practicing piano 7 hours a day... finally realizing where I have to put some degree of focus... my friend Galen Rogers wants to pay for me to go to Oxford... where he went as he is the head of the Canadian Committee for the Rhodes Scholarship. I want to get into the progressive music scene and compose futuristic worship music of beauty and death... connecting all of our lives together with an intangible communication of time and space and essence of not knowing. I suppose I should do something productive... I've chewed my ashes long enough... time to connect my dreams of my ancestors and my physical conscience world with this membrane of humanity that can, I propose, can adequately be the slip that separates black and white, life and death, good and evil. Perhaps music can define this purpose late into the 20th century where I want to fuck all my souls together (all humanity) and produce a black hole where all answers are found and a Requiem of Life for atoms and bonds (ultimately our bodies as prisms refracting the knowledge and experience and non-experience of the universe) can be created by collecting and reinvolving everything that musically and spiritually

A Gift of Grace

has ever existed and shall ever come into being. But, I just wanted to say Hi....... And I have wrote as if I might never talk to you again, but I suppose you might grant me time enough to write me back... I desperately hope you might do so... thank you Angie for being in my life... You are still in my memory; you are unattainably a grasping branch of the tree that possesses the deep entrenched framework of my mind and action. I love you; thank you again for being in my life. Write and tell me about you since we last talked... I am truly interested. Good luck on you and your classes and your new friends and your journey until we meet (most undoubtedly via the fingers of technology) again.

I am off... la la la la la la la la la la la la la la la la (drifting off)
Kay ser rah ser rah
What ever will be will be...
I love you Angie
And I failed my French IB
OH YES OH YES
Ser rah ser rah...
What ever will be will be
I love you Angie
And again we shall see...

A Gift of Grace

August 19, 1996

Edward, age 19, UofT

Edward came home for about a week during this summer holiday. Most of that time he spent in his room, sitting cross-legged on his bed, reading from a large, thick book of Andy Warhol, and making copious notes in his scrapbook. He insisted that his room light not be turned on and that only his bed side lamp is on. Edward doesn't like the dark, but he also doesn't like bright lights.

"Come out of your room for God's sake!" Frank would say.

This caused a myriad of arguments. For some unknown reason Edward was bent on staying in his room and not socializing with the rest of us.

He left to stay with Galen and Jean Rogers for the rest of the summer and Galen financed a trip for him to Europe. He bought sandals, a backpack and money belt for Edward. Edward considered Galen to be a good friend, and was drawn to his intelligence and prestige. When we visited him in Toronto, he showed me a portrait of this man in the hall of a building in the University of Toronto.

Okay, if this man has a huge portrait in the University of Toronto this must mean that he is a reputable character.

Galen bought a camera for Edward with which Edward had taken pictures of his trip. He smoked a lot in Amsterdam. He phoned home and let me know that he had spent all his money and had none for food.

"But don't worry, Mom, I'll be okay. Lots of people tour Europe with very little but their backpack. I still have my Euro-Rail ticket and I don't have to pay for accommodation because I plan to sleep on the train."

A Gift of Grace

Okay, having this information just alleviated any traces of worry I might have had. Yeah, right!!!

Is this the kid I helped raise and has he no idea how this kind of information affects me? Shit! Now I get to think about him sleeping on the train, have my imagination kick in and visualize all sorts of things happening to my precious son.

August 20, 1996

Edward, age 19, UofT

After Edward got back from Europe, I flew to Toronto and stayed at the same residence as he was in. He smoked marijuana and was so casual about it. I took it upon myself to snoop around and I found a vial of oil in his drawer and a huge box of wine bottles he tells me later he received from Galen.

Edward rationalizes his smoking of marijuana as no more harmful than smoking cigarettes or drinking alcohol; actually he figures it is not as unhealthy.

I remind him, "It is illegal."

I take his casual manner personally.

Fuck!

He shows blatant display of disrespect for me and my attempt to instil a set of values I have upheld all through his upbringing.

I see a plastic bag of weed on his desk, wantonly thrown on top of his textbooks.

A Gift of Grace

How do I get through to this kid of mine?

I tell him it is unhealthy and that he should be taking care of his body, not destroying it.

He grew up disliking pop. That was great at the time because Edward had so much energy he didn't seem to need any added sugar. Now the theory of relativity takes on a new meaning for me and I wish his biggest addiction was caffeinated soft drink.

On the one hand he says he doesn't take many pills when he has a cold, then on the other hand he is willing to invite hundreds of chemicals to infest his lungs and brain.

I went to a few dances with him. One in particular comes to mind. We walked into the dance club and Edward went straight to the bar. I'm left standing around waiting for him. Some guys walked up and asked me, "Are you Ed's Mom?"

"Yes, I am."

"Can I get you a drink?"

"May I get you a drink?"

"Hey, you both can!"
I swear that they were determined to get Ed's Mom drunk, as they made sure I had a drink in my hand all evening. I learned to lick the salt, suck the lemon and chase it down with Tequila. But! I made sure I danced all the effects of the liquor away. There was no way they were going to witness me drunk!

Edward loves to dance and every muscle of his body gets a work-out.

He exclaimed that he would not like to take money from Galen and preferred to do things on his own. He didn't want to ask Dad and me for money and he wasn't about to come home.

God! I wish I knew what to do.

A Gift of Grace

"A person does what he has to do."

Exactly what is he trying to tell me?

We dined at the top of the Toronto tower and spent two hundred dollars, much more than I could afford. But, what the hey, this was my son with whom I was dining and I wouldn't be seeing him until Christmas again; that rationalized the spending.

After our wonderful meal he had the audacity of wishing he had a smoke.

We went to a movie *Trainspotting*. What a show! I did not like seeing it at all, as it caused me more images of darkness. Edward chose the movie we would watch and he changed his mind at least ten times. We went back to the cashier twice to make the changes on our tickets.

We ate out a lot. I bought a U of T sweatshirt and a desk calendar for him. I thought that the calendar would enable him to schedule his studies and help him focus. I went with him to the office at Trinity to register in courses for the fall. The minister wrote a note explaining some special circumstances in Edward's life that may have contributed to his lack of focus last year; otherwise I'm not sure that he would have been able to register.

I have not bothered to ask him about his grades. I have hinted that I am interested, but I just can't bring myself to put too much pressure on him because you never know what might happen.

"We" took out a second student line of credit of five thousand dollars at the bank.

It sounds ludicrous for a student who has full scholarship to have to take out a student loan. I attribute it to his manipulation and my stupidity.

When I got home I wrote him a letter, suggesting that he take a good look at where his lifestyle was leading him.

A Gift of Grace

September 20, 1996

Edward, age 19 years old, 2nd year UofT

Edward phoned and told me he was at a cabin on Lake Champlain… at boys' club or something like that. It didn't sound like any nightclub I knew…

> *What kind of boy's club? God! I hope he is somewhere safe, he is my son and now I have literally no control over the direction his life is taking.*

He is back at university and has a different room at the residence in Trinity College. Edward thinks this is a good thing and that he'll do better this year.

November 22, 1996

Edward, age 20, UofT2

Dear Edward,

Please humour me with my writing.

I have to let you know, Edward, that I don't agree with your relationship with Galen. I don't want to label it, because I don't know him or his motives. I only know you and my role as mother. I appreciate his friendship with you and certainly his financial help. But, if he truly cared for you, would he become intimate with a young man who is just on the brink of his life, when he is as old as he is? I know that you have told me that "It's okay," "I'm not doing anything I don't want to," "We aren't intimate very often," but it still is upsetting for me.

I kept asking you about his motives last year. You said he just liked your company and possibly he liked to photograph you. Fine! Then he financed a trip to Europe. I'm wondering if you were first intimate on your trip to Georgian Bay this last summer. I think you may have felt as if you owed him something. I suppose you do – but not in bed. He may be charming, intelligent, wise in years and sincere in his desire for your welfare. But, I think of Dave. You said he had to have surgery* like you did. He got AIDS and you told me Galen told you that he (Dave) put his watch on the railway track. Why? Was he angry at himself? At Galen? How did he get AIDS? Did he have other partners? Do you have more than one partner? These are questions that I ponder and I know I can't expect answers – I may not want answers. I have thought of the worst scenarios and the best scenarios. I like to think that Galen cares for you and wouldn't do anything to harm you. But, harm isn't always just physical, it can be psychological too.

Is he using his power, money and intelligence to charm his way into your life? He promises to help you with your education, possibly helping you get into Oxford... then, I wonder, what about Jean?

I guess I'm just being a mother and want you to fulfill your dreams. I want you to respect yourself and others, and feel proud of your endeavours in life. I love you unconditionally and trust in you to make the best choices for yourself. You have the personal resources to do the best with your life.

I want to play a big part in your life and want you to share it with me – and Dad, Shelley and Nicole. I don't want you to think I'm being possessive. I just want to be a part of your life. (You said that sometimes you and he do "crazy things." I don't have any idea what that means but I hope it is not unsafe or stupid.)

I don't like the fact that I don't have money to give you. I would get a loan to help you feel more independent. Remember, last summer you said, "I wish I could pay Galen back all the money he has given me so that I didn't owe him. I could be on my own." You said something like that. Maybe you had an idea of what was to develop between the two of you. I pray that it isn't abuse.

A Gift of Grace

New topic: I know that you say you don't smoke anymore. I believe you. I don't think you are smoking cigarettes anymore. But, have you stopped smoking marijuana? I listened to a program on TV about it and people of authority report that smoking "it" damages the brain, heart, lungs and the immune system. It also affects a person's ambition. Scary! I hope you realize, now that you're no longer a teenager (as if age really has some magical influence) that alcohol, drugs and smoking are harmful to an otherwise healthy body and soul.

Well, Edward, I think I needed to write this letter as much for my benefit as for yours!!

Search out what it is you want your life to be like and then set one goal at a time. Then, all you have to do is enjoy living it!

I hope you are doing fine. Attend all your classes, work carefully on your assignments – hand them in on time and study for your tests. I know you know all this but I just threw it in!

Enjoy your cookies and Dinosaurs. I hope the shorts fit.

Love,

Mom

P.S. Please rip this letter into iddy-biddy pieces and garbage it in some remote garbage can...

Our photos are very nice. I'll send one of all of us, one of Dad and me, and one of you and Shelley and Nicole.

> *Edward has an STD from his exploits. At least this one is not fatal. (God, I hope he gets nothing worse!) How he got it is anyone's guess, as I have no idea how many partners this kid has! I dare not ask and I try not to get into a frenzy — but it is difficult. I consider myself an excellent mother and I looked after my children's health during their childhood. Now I have no control and very little influence.

A Gift of Grace

God! I'm ill. Also he has no resistance to anything because he doesn't eat properly. I guess the chart didn't work after all. I thought I had taught him better than that! I guess I didn't teach him to think of others; not even me. I hoped he would remember the things we taught him when he was at home. I am learning I must let go or it will drive me crazy, but I can't do it!

November 30, 1996

Edward, age 20, UofT2

Dear Eddie,

I hope these cookies arrive while they're fairly fresh. I just baked them today and I'm mailing them tomorrow. Buy some milk and have cookies and milk with your friends.

See you at Christmas.

Love,

Mom

1997

January 13, 1997

Edward, age 20, UofT2

Dear Edward,

I'm writing this note during the time my students are writing a quiz in Health. I hope this gets to you before the cookies get stale!

Dad is picking me up at 3:30 so I can mail your parcel and Shelley's before 4:00 – then they will be on time for the truck.

I'm glad you got a comfy chair to work in. I hope your surgery went okay – I'm expecting a call from you tonight.

It was nice having Auntie Mar, Blaine and Helen at our place for the weekend. I'm thinking of maybe applying for a job near Calgary. Then we could visit with Auntie Mar more often. I'm hoping that Nicole and Shelley get a job around Calgary. Then we could drive to the mountains to get away on a weekend. Just dreaming...

I hope you like your parcel.

Love,

Mom

A Gift of Grace

Trinity College
6 Hoskin Avenue
Toronto, Ontario
Canada M5S 1H8

February 7, 1997
To: Sophie Meyer
         Ed Weatherly
From: Bursar
Re: World Debating Championships - South Africa

I am pleased to enclose a cheque for each of you for $1,056.74, determined as follows:

Proceeds of Simpson	
Gift of stock	$1,213.48
Provost's Grant	500.00
Dean of Arts Grant	400.00
Total	$2,113.48
Each	$1,056.74

This is in addition to the $950.00 ($475.00 each) you received before Christmas. This amount was composed of a donation of $250.00 plus the Kingston Prize in Debating of $700.00.

I understand Sophie has written a note of thanks to Mrs. Simpson for her contribution.

Could one of you also write Mr. John Kingston whose gift of $5,000 in 1990 established the endowed fund in memory of his father, Robert Arnold Kingston. Mr. John Kingston's address is 37 Rochester Avenue, Toronto, M4N 1N7. Thanks.

Your enterprise has evidently found support throughout the College. Well done!

Provost,
Dean of Arts

A Gift of Grace

University of Toronto
Statement of Results
Faculty of Arts and Science
Trinity College

May 13, 1997

Mr. Edward Kenneth Weatherly
Trinity College, 6 Hoskin Avenue
Toronto, Ontario
Canada M5S 1H8

Sessional   GPA = 0.07
Cumulative   GPA = 0.07
Status = ON ACADEMIC PROBATION

Course	MRK	GRD	CRS SIZE	CRS AVG
ECO100Y INTRO ECONOMICS	038	E	1433	C+
FSL100F INTROD FRENCH I	021	F	180	B-
HIS311Y CAN INTERNAT RELATNS	003	F	85	C+
POL208Y INRO INTERNAT POL	013	F	301	B-
SCI199Y YR I SEM: SCIENCES	000	F	332	B

Notes:
FOR THE FULL IMPLICATIONS OF YOUR PROBATIONARY STATUS
CONSULT THE CALENDAR AND YOUR COLLEGE REGISTRAR. IN
PARTICULAR, PLEASE NOTE THAT IF YOUR NEXT SESSIONAL GPA
(SUMMER OR WINTER) IS LESS THAN 1.70 AND YOUR CUMULA-
TIVE GPA REMAINS LESS THAN 1.50, YOU WILL BE SUSPENDED.

ASSISTANT DEAN
AND FACULTY REGISTRAR
OFFICE OF THE REGISTRAR AND DEAN OF MEN

A Gift of Grace

May 25, 1997

Edward, age 20, UofT2

Edward went on his World Debating Championships in South Africa. See what opportunities open to him when he is functioning at a high level. Why can't he do this all the time?

Galen bought Edward a computer and synthesizer with the necessary peripherals for him to compose and mix some electronic music.

I wish he was playing the piano; otherwise he is wasting his talent.

He moved into an apartment at the end of April. Galen promised to pay the rent for a year. He also furnished it with a futon and cookware.

Edward went to the Chiapas in Mexico with five other people. Anvil and Edward went to Cancun, rented a jeep and drove into the jungle. Anvil did the filming and Edward was the "boom operator."

They were on a mission to interview Subcommandante Marcos of the Zapatistas Liberation Army, who was hiding from the Mexican government in the jungle outside of La Realidade. The government was exploiting the indigenous in the name of capitalism.

I pray this trip is safe and productive.

A Gift of Grace

Trinity College
6 Hoskin Avenue
Toronto, Ontario
Canada M5S 1H8

June 3, 1997

Mr. Edward Weatherly
Trinity College

Dear Ed,

As you are aware from your 1996 Winter Session Statement of Results, you have been placed, or remain "on academic probation." I would like to draw your attention to some of the implications of this status:

- You may not take more than 2.0 courses in the 1997 Summer Session or 5.0 courses in the 1997-1998 Winter Session i.e. no more than a full course load for your next registration.
- If at the end of the session your cumulative GPA is 1.50 or higher, your status will be "in good standing." If your cumulative GPA is less than 1.50 but your sessional GPA is 1.70 or greater, you will continue "on probation."
- If your cumulative GPA is less than 1.50 and your sessional GPA is less than 1.70, you will be suspended for **one** calendar year. If you have previously been suspended for one year, you will be suspended for three years. If you have previously been suspended for three years, you will be refused further registration in the Faculty of Arts and Science.

If you have any questions, or there are any extenuating circumstances which may affect your academic performance, please feel free to contact this Office and make an appointment with myself or Rodney Branch. Please consult page 487 of the 1997-1998 Arts and Science Calendar for a complete explanation of your status.

Yours sincerely,

Name Withheld
Academic Counsellor

A Gift of Grace

Finally I receive this letter showing his studies at University of Toronto. Starting at UWC and especially over the last two years at UofT, there is a rapid rate of decline in his academic work. This is the opposite of what we had expected from Edward after his high school when he consistently showed excellent performance and raving teacher comments in earlier years.

A Gift of Grace

University of Toronto
Admissions and Awards

Admissions Liaison and Scholarships: Financial Aid:
315 Bloor Street W.   214 College Street
Toronto, Ontario   Toronto, Ontario
Canada M5S 1A3   Canada M5T 2Z9

July 17, 1997

Edward Weatherly
General Delivery
Provost, Alberta

Dear Edward,

I am writing concerning your University of Toronto National Scholarship. We had expected to assess your academic results from the Faculty of Music for purposes of renewing your National Scholarship and were surprised not only by your re-registration in Arts and Science courses, but by your performance in those courses.

It is particularly your performance, of course, which suggests that something went seriously wrong this past year. While I must inform you that we are not prepared again to consider extenuating circumstances to make exceptions to our renewal process, I would very much like to know of your current goals and plans. Are you still considering an Arts and Science program? Whatever your plans, I wish you well and, in the short term, I hope your summer is a good one. I look forward to hearing from you.

Sincerely,

Manager of Enquiry Services and Special Programs

Provost, Alberta
July 28, 1997

Dear Edward,

I am writing this letter in my classroom. I came by to check on my catfish and to pick up the Program of Studies because I want to do some schoolwork at home.

I just got the mail and a letter arrived from Income Security Programs. I plan to phone you and see if you'd like me to open it. In any case I will send if to you.

I picked up an address book "just for you," and I plan to write some important entries – addresses, phone numbers, birthdays – in it for you. I think your Grandmas would really like to hear from you. I can't remember the last time that one of them even saw you! Please either give them a phone call or write them a letter – it doesn't have to be long.

This afternoon I am going along with Shelley to Mossleigh. She is attending an In-service and I will buy some newspapers and try to help her find a place to rent this fall. It has been very difficult to find a reasonably priced place that is available.

I am sending your mail – directory questionnaire, letter from Admissions and Awards, address book and this letter.

Also, I am sending the letter concerning the Canada Pension Disability application. I'll talk to you about this. I copied your birth certificate and had it certified. You should phone and write them a letter to acknowledge receipt of this correspondence.

Bye for now...

Love,

Mom

A Gift of Grace

August 13, 1997

Edward, age 20, Summer

I attended a week long Computer Institute at Lethbridge University and learned how technology can facilitate my teaching and the learning of my students.

I wasn't going to visit Edward this summer because it just becomes so upsetting. But, as the weeks flew by I panicked thinking that I wasn't going to be able to check up on him and obtain peace of mind, if I didn't hurry up and book a flight. I phoned Sun Life Insurance and arranged to cash in some of my RRSPs.

> *Yes, that's what I do. A big percentage was deducted for taxes and I used the remainder to pay for a ticket. Financial intelligence isn't one of my priorities when it comes to my son.*

I phoned Edward when I got in and he sounded relieved when I suggested that I take the shuttle bus to his apartment.

When I arrived he wanted to sleep. He said he was tired because he had been out all night.

> *In fact he had been out until morning consuming mushrooms. Yes, really considerate. Make your mother proud! Get stoned the night before she arrives from the West. But, what does that really matter? "She is only my mom and she accepts anything I do as tolerable... even wonderful!"*

While he slept on the futon, I looked around his bachelor suite. First of all, I notice a very fat journal of phone numbers, addresses and messages. Dishes were stacked up on the counter and the colander was shrouded in an installation of spaghetti.

150 August 13, 1997

A Gift of Grace

Reeking garbage was overflowing its basket and the front closet bulged, packed two thirds of the way up with laundry.

I commented on his habit of scratching and he said it was probably because he hadn't been eating very well lately. Okay, maybe that could be true, but I think he needs to see the doctor and get something to fix it.

He made the appointment and she gave him a copy of Canada's Food Guide. She spoke to him about eating healthy foods. I knew he was getting the exercise, part of a healthy lifestyle, as his mode of transportation was walking.

He has a boyfriend, Max, who works as a waiter at a local restaurant where Edward and I dined one evening. Afterwards we gave Max a ride home. He encouraged Edward to write a resume and hand it out at some places where he would like to work.

In the anticipation of Edward getting employment, I promptly took him shopping, buying half a dozen white shirts, three black dress pants, an expensive black belt and one pair of well made shoes.

This was my way of supporting his launch into the work-force.

August 16, 1997

Edward, age 20, Summer

Each evening I am in Toronto I wait for him to return from his boyfriend Max's apartment. One evening after turning the key in the door, he exclaimed that someone was yelling at him as he crossed the street.

"Hey! Faggot! You mother fucker! Get off the street!"

A Gift of Grace

> *God! I die a little bit more hearing him say that. I am grateful that he can run. Maybe some day he will take a stand but for today, he can run.*

"Are you sure that's what they said?"

"Yes, Mom!"

> *I spoke with Edward about the noise of traffic and just maybe he was being scolded for jaywalking; not his queerness.*

After two nights, I am now sleeping in Edward's apartment and Edward is sleeping at Max's place.

> *Mmm... what have I done to deserve this... or, maybe what have I not done...*

August 17, 1997

Edward, age 20, Summer

Yesterday evening as we walked from one bar to the next, Edward and a friend had a conversation about dancing for a living. They were agreeing that it is now that they must dance 'cause they need to do it when they are young and have the stamina.

The kind of dancing I see in this place concerns me and what else goes on after or between the dances. I thought now was a good time to speak with Edward about going to university.

"Edward, have you registered for university yet?"

"I'm going to take a break from university this year."

"What about some courses from the Royal Conservatory of Music?"

A Gift of Grace

"Yeah, that sounds good. At least the registration will be a good front."

Did he just say "a front" or did the noise of the traffic blur his actual words? I don't want to ask him in case I did hear correctly. Does this mean he won't take it seriously? If so, why am I going along with the stint? Sheer stupidity... Maybe denial...

So yesterday he agreed to go with me to the Royal Conservatory of Music where I plunked down my MasterCard for two courses: one for Midi and the other for the History of Canadian Music. I also agreed to pay for piano lessons. He would look after the arrangement of renting practice rooms in the building.

I am excited. He will be playing the piano again! I can almost hear it in my head as he runs his fingers over the ivories and caresses the ebonies.

I feel like Edward is back on track... once again. His words exactly!

"I'm happy that you came to see me because I feel like I'm back on track."

So I heard wrong last night and am now satisfied about his decision to take a break from university for the year and concentrate on Royal Conservatory studies.

Galen has invited Edward and me to attend his annual Ballet Picnic tomorrow at his place outside Toronto. I was curious to meet this man and his wife, along with their picturesque property that Edward had described to me so often.

Back at his apartment, Edward became engrossed in a conversation with Max and asked me to sit out on the balcony so that I couldn't hear. I complied and ended up there for more than an hour. The balcony had a small round table, small plates with candles and a makeshift chair. I got vertigo as I glanced over the edge to view the city.

August 17, 1997 153

A Gift of Grace

August 18, 1997

Edward, age 20, Summer

In order to get to Galen's home we needed a vehicle, so I rented a convertible and picked up three of Edward's friends. One was Max. His mom is a teacher and he is still hiding the fact from her that he is gay. I really like this young man and hope that he is "the one" for Edward.

> *Max and Edward talk about driving out to Alberta some-time, maybe the end of this summer. I wonder about Frank's reaction.*

We drove to Galen's picnic.

It was all Edward had described. Many vehicles were parked along the property. Tables were set up under a large tent stationed beside the outdoor pool. A huge vegetable garden, flowers and shrubs had been planted to create a beautiful landscape. Front and centre was a statue of a conductor sculpted from intertwining vines. Edward said he would show me the Rogers' name in a book that recognizes special gardens in the Toronto area.

Some guests were swimming and others were playing volleyball down the hill by the stream.

Galen welcomed us and introduced me to his wife, Jean. Some of their families were present, including a pregnant daughter.
Edward had the pre-arranged job of frying the hamburgers. After we ate, Galen took us for a tour, through the main floor of the house which had a neat sunroom used to prepare bedding plants for their gardens.

The guest house has a large fireplace with windows looking out onto the pool area. There are at least two bathrooms and a sitting room with a piano.

A Gift of Grace

This would be the piano that Edward played before they dined.

I'm getting sick.

Galen stopped the tour and went back to the pool area where they were serving drinks. Edward's friends and I followed Edward across a meadow and up a hill to find a small cabin in the woods. There were crystals hanging above the table forming a unique resemblance of a crystal chandelier. It had a second floor. This was their cabin in the woods where the Rogers' family would spend time at Christmas. It sent shivers up my spine as I imagined what may have happened here in the privacy of the woods.

We ran back down the hill and walked past the volleyball players to rejoin Galen and his other guests. I noticed that Galen was enjoying his drinks and was probably feeling little pain. He had few words to say to me, "If he doesn't make it this year, he'll get a one way ticket home."

Whatever that means... his words anger me...

The time came for us to leave and Jean cut sweet peas for me. After saying thank you and good bye, we headed for Toronto.

Edward was planning to go to Eileen's party, so we stopped by her place which was in an established part of town. Her house was built of bricks and its location looked like it could be next door to Hansel and Gretel's. Max had asked Edward earlier while we were still in Toronto if he could join him at this party and had been refused. Max confided in me that Edward made him sad... probably because he didn't think of Max's feelings; only his own. Edward asked me for money as well as the bouquet of flowers that Jean had just given me. He jumped out of the car and went into the house. Max was visibly sad and I think if I were him I would be totally pissed off. So with Edward at the party, Max and I continued the ride to drop him off.

I drove down the road a bit and then Max realized that Edward had his apartment keys. I turned around, but when we got to the

August 18, 1997 **155**

A Gift of Grace

house, Max found out that Edward had left with Eileen and Peggy. I used their washroom. Their house appeared quaint and I got a glimpse of the table set for the birthday party.

We couldn't stay waiting for them to return, so Max asked if I could drive him to his Mom's. On the way there Max confided that both Galen and he love Edward, but that Edward is a pain in the neck.

Yes, I can relate to that!

November 12, 1997

Edward, age 20, Toronto

Back home in Alberta and back into the swing of teaching, life goes on in many separate layers. There is school and when it is done, I think of Edward. I mechanically make dinner and small talk, all the while I am thinking of Edward.

Yesterday on the way home from school and thinking of Edward, I had to pull over onto an approach and write a letter to him. I explained my concerns about the way I had observed him living his life and how he interacted in his relationships.

In a phone call he told me he received two dozen yellow roses for his birthday. I asked him who they were from.

"I don't really know," was his answer, but later in the conversation he admitted they were from Galen.

It makes me sick to my stomach that he is an old man's boyfriend. Then I think of a few couples who are in a relationship and have many years between the spouses. Perhaps this would be OK, but what about Jean? I don't think Galen plans to leave his marriage. I just pray Edward is living his life in happiness.

A Gift of Grace

Edward wears a ring to symbolize their relationship and condones it because it resembles those from Ancient Greece. Edward is still the innate scholar that loves history, yet he is also attracted to power and prestige that this man offers him.

November 18, 1997

Edward, age 21, Toronto

Edward didn't practice the piano, making excuses that he couldn't play on the one at Trinity. No kidding! He lost the key there at least two times that I knew about and he didn't have the money to rent a practice room.

Great! Just great!

Edward asked me to phone and see if I could get a refund. Why couldn't he? I had phoned home during the summer when I was in Toronto asking Frank if he would let me put the $1500 for the cost of the teacher on his Master Card and he had reluctantly agreed. So, now I was in a predicament.

Edward failed to notify his teacher about not being able to show up and of course he had been charged as though he had showed. Sounds reasonable to me and, so, guess what? Mom and Dad get stung again. Frank got only about three hundred dollars as a refund on his credit card.

Ouch! Not good!

Then a few weeks later we get a phone call from the bank in Toronto, advising us that Edward had not paid the interest owing on his student loan. They had called at least two other times and notified us of money owing for overdue payments. Frank took

A Gift of Grace

out $10,000 from his RRSP funds to make full payment on Edward's loan. To my knowledge, Edward did not thank his dad.

I wrote a letter to Edward but I didn't send it. It was upsetting for me to compose it, however, therapeutic at the same time. I guess it would have been upsetting for Edward to receive it. It had to do with his squandering of two $5000 loans and an added 4,000 in taxes and fees his Dad had to pay on the ten grand. There were also $4500 in his Dad's disability funds and approximately $1500 I paid to the Royal Conservatory of Music.

I fear the Royal Conservatory will now have reservations about having anything to do with any request he might have with them in the future. This may be my negative thinking, but it seems realistic, that he may have burned a bridge. And, he may have a hard time registering in courses in the future should he change his mind and want to work toward a teaching certificate.

Lost in my mind of fears and insecurities, I draft a new letter to Edward, scribbled onto a note pad displaying the heading: *Public Education Works... when we all work together.*

Public Education Works... when we all work together

Dear Edward,

Something has happened to you. At one time your aspirations were high and you had energy for achieving great things. You looked forward to challenges and loved learning. Your values have changed. At one time formal education was important and you wanted to become successful. You say marijuana is harmless and I can't help but mention the disrespect I felt when you took mushrooms the night before I came to visit you in Toronto. You show many symptoms of partaking in abusive substances. You don't write letters any more.
Today you say that education is not important and you aren't worried about money. I guess if you don't earn your own way, you will never know the value of money.

I saw you treat Max very unfairly. You went with Eileen and you must have been aware of the fact that you were breaking his heart. That is not the way to treat people. The way you described John made me think he was special. You must have suffered there. Now you are with Evan, a sculptor with no job. Max and John had jobs. I can't help but wonder where all this will lead. You can't continue on this path, Edward!

Scary! Two guys with no visible means of support. You must get a job before you resort to something illegal and get yourself into trouble. This would absolutely break my heart!

Do you need psychological help?

Do you associate with friends at Trinity?

What a shame! I never would have predicted this! You are wasting your talents. Learn from your mistakes and begin a fresh start. You are only twenty-one years old. I wish you luck with reconstructing your way of life.

I long for the Edward I once knew: loved learning; energetic and appreciative of his mother.

A Gift of Grace

I have fleeting thoughts of phoning Galen and asking him some pertinent questions – information I can deal with.

You'd better make some very basic changes in your life. Get a job. Start paying back your loan. Recognize the value of a dollar and respect my signature on your loan. When you deliberately neglect to communicate with the bank, you are affecting not only your credit rating but mine as well! Doesn't this matter to you?

Your actions disappoint me. I think you are feeling guilty about numerous things in your life and for some masochistic reason think that you need to inflict punishment and pain upon yourself. Smarten up and take charge of your life, Ed. You have no one to blame but yourself.

You need to get a job and keep it long enough to establish a credit rating. Because you have no diploma or certificate to show your employer, you must work at a restaurant or maybe work as a clerk in a store. To establish credit rating you need to work and pay bills for six to twelve months. Then you can probably rent an apartment in your name. Until then you will have to share rent with someone and prove yourself a reliable tenant.

Over the last three, four years, you have squandered a lot of money, having nothing to show for it.

All this boils down to the fact that you'll have to get a real job and work for a living. I have always given you the benefit of any doubt, but, Edward, sometimes I think you deliberately lie to me so that you can ignore bigger issues. Somehow you must get in tune with reality. I've lost you somewhere... please think about what you're doing with your life and reconsider the choices you are making...

Love,

Mom

1998

January 18, 1998

Edward, age 21, Toronto

Last month I took a personal day off from school, picked Edward up from the International airport and attended Victoria's wedding in Edmonton before driving home. Victoria was a classmate of Edward's from Provost.

Edward's conversations are becoming more and more disturbing. He says Madonna is his mother. He calls himself Binary Boy and Christian X and uses huge words to describe his grandiose ideas. I can follow his line of thinking up to a point and then I get lost with what really was his point of conversation.

When we got home from the wedding, Frank and I convinced him to phone and make an appointment with a psychiatrist in Wainwright. We are willing to expend an intense amount of energy to get Edward the help he seems so desperately to need. Whatever it takes!

We drove him to Wainwright for his appointment with the psychiatrist. He went in while we waited in the car. We thought it would be an hour at the most, so we just sat and talked. After the first hour, he still wasn't out and we couldn't go off anywhere because we had no idea how much longer it would take. Finally after three hours he came out and said, "Well, I sure wowed her!"

Edward is ever the quintessential actor and was on stage for three hours. Who knows what bizarre stuff he told her.

Shelley and Nicole told me that Edward took some drug or something just before Christmas and had a very bad experience. He only hinted at this information with me.

A Gift of Grace

Sometimes I wish I wasn't so good at reading between the lines. Then I could live in denial and wear rose coloured glasses, thinking I was living my life... I promise myself that some day I will really live my self's life.

At Christmas Edward, Nicole, Darren (Nicole's boyfriend) and I made perogies. We had fun making them and enjoying a feast!

I am teaching grade five in Provost and, ever since I moved there, I have been baking for the staff. I bake biscuits, bran muffins and cinnamon buns. I usually bring cinnamon buns the week that teachers are wildly collecting assignment marks and writing thirty different ways of saying "your child is wonderful, however, he just needs to develop consistent work habits." The staff inhaled any food that was set on the table and I loved making their day.

I understand now that I was baking cinnamon buns for the staff when I didn't get appreciation from personal areas of my life.

My class enjoyed a homemade chocolate cake every time someone had a birthday. I wasn't "saving the world" by baking, I was unconsciously feeding my own soul.

Teaching and baking are my retreats!

When Edward returned to Toronto, he moved out of his bachelor suite and into an apartment with Chanel, a girl he befriended at university. In a bar, Edward met Jim, who became his boyfriend. Jim was from Buffalo. Edward would take the bus to visit him. One night, that is... in the middle of the night, he phoned and was crying. He had another "health concern" and now Jim wouldn't have him for a boyfriend anymore.

It is 2:30 a.m. I now have this information in my head, stewing over something for which I have no control, but have a vested interest in because he is my son. I can't sleep... I lie awake careful not to toss and turn too much so I won't wake Frank and have yet another confrontation. In a few more hours I will be teaching and I'll be okay.

January 29, 1998

Edward, age 21, Toronto

Edward phoned me collect, as usual, to tell me he made friends with a hairdresser (who incidentally is straight) who did drugs. He spoke about her as though he was impressed by the way people were attracted to her when she walked into an establishment. She didn't even bat an eye when he confided in her that he had another "health concern." Heck! She'd had them a number of times and what's the big deal?

He also tells me that he doesn't have the apartment with Chanel anymore and will live on the streets of Philadelphia – I mean Toronto! Then I could only keep in touch with him if and when he will call me. He is staying with various people he meets. I think he will stay with them, use them until he loses his welcome and then will get kicked out.

I continue to keep at least two of Edward's messages saved on my phone. Just in case.

A Gift of Grace

June 21, 1998

Edward, age 21, Toronto

This evening I received a call from a fellow named Jim (Edward has had many Jims in his life, so I am not sure if this is the one who refused to be a friend, a new one or one of the many old ones). He sounded very upset and was at a loss for what to do to with his friend.

"I'm not strong enough to help him and he really needs help or something is going to happen to him. I'm sorry to be telling you this but I just have to. I found this phone number beside the name Mom in his wallet and had to call you. He is sleeping right now. He's caused arguments among the guys staying here and I'm afraid something is going to happen to him. Please help me help him. I can't do it on my own. I'm not strong enough!"

"Do you know where he could go for help? Would you mind walking with him to one of his other friend's places? He has a friend called Chanel. Maybe she would let him stay there for a while until I can think of a way to get him home to Alberta."

Edward lost the apartment with Chanel for whatever reason. He didn't tell me why, but I'm sure it was his crazy lifestyle. Anyway that doesn't matter. What matters is Jim is concerned and took the time to call me and I am taking a stab in the dark about who else can help.

Thank you, thank you, Jim, for phoning me. Thank you, Edward, for keeping my phone number in your wallet.

I asked Nicole to write a letter to Edward.

June 22, 1998
Calgary, Alberta

Dear Edward,

Sorry it has been so long since we have talked. Everyone missed you at Blaine's wedding. We had one chair empty at the kid's table and Harold stated that that should have been you there. The wedding ceremony was the shortest one I have ever been to. Blaine got emotional, which made me get a little emotional. t's hard to believe that he is married. It makes me feel OLD. Oh well.

Helen's dress was very nice. Shelley and I were asked to welcome Helen into our family. Shelley was really nervous but she managed just fine.

Auntie Melody came to the wedding and met up with us at Mom and Dad's hotel afterwards. She asked about you and said to say hi. Christy and Harold are happily single. Christy is in engineering, too. I can't even remember if you know that I am back at school for my chemical engineering degree. It is a lot of hard work but I love it!

I was asked to be the guest speaker at Hughenden Public Schools' Graduation this year. So, public speaking is more like fun to me. My topic focused on how life is full of successes and failures and how you can deal with them. Also, I talked about how it's okay to change your mind about what you want to do with your life. I started out by saying that even as a young child I knew exactly what I wanted to be when I grew up – Dolly Parton. I told them that it was not for the obvious reasons, but because I admired her singing talent and her role as a secretary in the movie, *Nine to Five*. And, I wanted to be just like her! For some reason, they thought that this was funny.

Wherever I go people are always asking me how you are doing. Aside from what Mom tells me I have no idea what you are up to or how you are doing. I am sure it is the same for you. So, I thought I would write a letter to let you know what I have been up to and to find out how things are going for you.

A Gift of Grace

So, Ed, I would really appreciate it if you would give me a call or write me a letter. Mom told me that you are moving out at the end of the month so I thought I had better send this quickly so that you receive it before you left.

Mom said your phone was cut off on Monday afternoon. She left a message on your phone for you on Monday morning and she was wondering if you got it. She would really, really like to hear from you. She misses you.

Shelley had decided to go to Japan to teach English. She leaves in mid August for one year. She would love to see you before she left.

I have been doing a lot of Math tutoring in the evenings, now I need to find something to do during the day. I may work through this temporary agency where they place you in secretarial positions. I am trying to sell my Jeep, because I can't afford it since I am back in university. Dad said I could use the New Yorker to get around in. It still smells of mothballs.

Mom and Dad turn 50 this year! Can you believe it?!

Well, I hope to hear from you soon. I know they have flight specials throughout the year. Maybe I could come visit you this summer.

Take care, Edward. Even though we do not always agree on everything and we do not keep in touch often enough, I think about you often and I love you. wish we had a closer relationship.

Love,

Nicole

P.S. Here is my home address, email address and phone number...

July 9, 1998

Edward, age 21, Toronto

Edward phoned me collect. At least I heard from him, but the conversation did not go well. He told me that he felt I was rejecting his sexuality when I refused to allow him to stay overnight with the boy way back in his school years. How did I know this at the time? Well I suspected it, but it was not out in the open. And, besides... I really don't think it would have had any influence on my decision, but it certainly would have been easier for us to communicate about it.

Didn't he realize that I wouldn't have allowed his sisters to sleep over at a boy's place? Did he also feel I was rejecting his choice of boyfriends? He seemed to imply this.

"Anyway Mom, I messed around with him."

Like, I really needed to find out about that!

August 6, 1998

Edward, age 21, Toronto

I'm not visiting Edward this summer.

I hate my life...

I registered for a Writers' Retreat at Strawberry Creek Lodge held from July tenth to the nineteenth. I wrote and wrote.

A Gift of Grace

I'm getting a life of my own... writing... Edward, I asked you before and you said I could write about your life, but I wonder what the ramifications are? What would be the consequences of publishing it? Would it be considered fiction or non-fiction?

Edward, write to me... share your life...

The lodge is owned by a couple, the lady cooked for the writers and we were free to write, discuss, walk and partake of her very delicious meals. I had a room at the top of the stairs with a single bed and a table for my laptop. I revelled in the serene atmosphere.

In the evening, one of the women would play her flute in the woods outside my window. I would be drawn to walk through the woods and allow myself to be transported to *A Midsummer Night's Dream.*

A writer in residence critiqued one of my articles and agreed I had a story to tell. I just needed to decide what form it should take.

While at the lodge, I corresponded with Shelley on the Internet. She is in Japan, teaching conversational English to business men. She was hired by the Chair of the Board of a large business to teach the Board members. I am impressed by my daughter and so happy she is doing so well, even though I miss her because she is so far away.

This summer I also registered in a one day Women's Conference in Edmonton, a one day Readers' Theatre workshop in Edmonton and a week long stint in Red Deer on Elementary Art Education. Then I spent one week in Lethbridge at the Computer Institute.

I am doing some things I want to do! Yippee!

When I got home from my workshops, there were none of Edward's messages saved on the voicemail. I felt an urgency to get in touch with him, but he had no fixed address. As far as I knew he was living on the streets in Toronto.

A Gift of Grace

Finally, one evening Edward phoned and told me he was in Boston, Massachusetts with a fellow named Anthony, who sold gadgets and traveled around the country booking himself into Trade Fairs. Edward proceeded to inform me that Anthony beat him up in the hotel in which they were staying. He slammed him up against the wall and hit him.

"Edward, get yourself back to Toronto!"

"I can't, Mom! I'm afraid to leave him because I don't have any money to get home."

Two whole weeks went by before he phoned from his cousin's place in Boston, letting me know he was at least safe and he would soon be home in Toronto.

I hate my life...

October 3, 1998

Edward, age 21, Toronto

When Edward finally got back to Toronto, he was really talking up his idea of going on the circuit parties of *Black and Blue* playing the part of "Binary Boy" and "Christian X." He talked obsessively about this until I became ill with the thoughts of what he was going to do with these ideas of his!

I am very concerned about his state of mind. Is it some mental illness or just the drugs talking? I had to figure this out so I searched the Internet for a checklist of signs and symptoms for mental illness. I found one on schizophrenia. I read it and it seemed to me that he is a classic case. He thinks of himself as a messenger, a special prophet destined to spread a secret message to the world. He just has to figure out the code.

"I don't know what it is, Mom, but it is BIG!"

A Gift of Grace

> *I cry, because he genuinely believes what he is saying. I*
> *don't refute what he is telling me because it is his reality,*
> *not mine... I'm trying to keep control of my voice...*

"When I listen to my music, I hear, you are a super star, you are a super star..."

Before when he had grandiose ideas, I could rationalize them as pop culture and his being a bit different.

Somehow I convinced him to come home to spend some time with us before Nicole and Darren's wedding. He went to Chanel's apartment and boxed up all his possessions which he had been keeping in her storage space and shipped them all to Calgary on the Greyhound, COD (Cash on Delivery).

Darren and Nicole got him an apartment on 17th Avenue. I wonder if having his own apartment is a good idea. It never seemed to work out well in Toronto, but he has to have some place to live. It is even a worse idea for Nicole and Darren to have to put him up when they are about to be married.

Nicole is really worried about the impression he will make on her in-laws.

"Mom, what if he comes out at my wedding? I am scared about what Darren's family will think."

> *There is only one solution to that. Don't have him come*
> *to the wedding.*

ility
October 17, 1998

Edward, age 21, Calgary

It was a very moving ceremony. Frank walked his daughter down the aisle. She was breathtakingly beautiful in her white dress. Her blonde hair and blue eyes made her look like an angel.

Nicole expressed fear of Edward announcing his "coming out" on her wedding day, but I don't think Edward said anything about being gay. At least not that I have heard about so far.

Actually, he didn't announce that he was gay but did sit beside the groom's aunt and weave a fictitious plan of his to propagate future generations with digital flesh of non-gender beings.

1999

July 15, 1999

Edward, age 22, Calgary

I am in Calgary to be with Edward and to see what help he needs. On July 9-10 we partied for Frank and my 30th wedding anniversary and a family reunion of sorts at our acreage. Then July 11 was clean-up day, but my heart was not in anything.

Frank could see my pain and anxiety. He urged me to go to Calgary because it was obvious I was not enjoying life much. Shelley was just back from Japan and will soon be heading off to tutor students in Cambridge Bay way up north. She gave Edward a ride to Calgary after the reunion and she phoned me as soon as they arrived in Calgary saying Edward had told her some wild stories on the ride back. She says his thinking is very bizarre.

"Something is definitely wrong, Mom. He has very strange beliefs and thoughts. Mom, he told me about digital flesh that morphs into machine type aliens with digital flesh and then he told me what would occur in the future because of the evolvement of these aliens."

"Did he seem serious?"

"At first I thought it was a joke, but he seemed as if he believed this. I think it is weird for him to come up with this elaborate theory and he did seem to be serious."

"I'm sure he was just making up a story to entertain you. You know he has always been very imaginative."

"OK, Mom."

She changed the topic of conversation.

What is this digital flesh? I have never heard him talk about this before! I did make a mental note of what she said though.

Had I not already been convinced I was needed in Calgary, this sealed it. So I drove down right away and I asked Shelley to jot down notes to document Edward's thinking. Her notes, as follows, will be helpful in getting him some psychiatric health care:

CONCERNS:

While driving to Calgary, Edward talked about AIDS being a conspiracy against gays. When I questioned it, he said no one can prove there is a virus and people die from the drugs – not AIDS. He said the drugs were developed to eliminate gays. When I said straight people get it too and he should be careful – he said not to worry – he is careful. I am concerned that his belief that it is a conspiracy will lead to an illusion of invincibility and, finally, with him contracting AIDS (HIV).

On several occasions he has discussed "religious" ideas with me – usually vague references, but sometimes more than that.

He believes:

* *We will evolve into "beings of light" – literal, not figurative*

* *He is a son of god – Christian? Alien? not defined*

* *He believes that "god" / "gods" are communicating with him through signs e.g. L, 0,10,X – when watching a movie, road signs, he sees 1, 0, or L, O and says, "1,0,0,1,X, ten…" through-out a drive / movie. Casually and consistently. I asked why, he said they are signs for him and he doesn't know if they are communicating with others (he asked me – I said no) but he knows he is meant to communicate these to the world.*

* *Ed is good at talking to convince you he is rational and "normal." He can be very persuasive. BUT he has trouble differentiating reality from delusions.*

* *He can be antisocial – in his room at parent's home all day drawing, writing or sleeping.*

July 15, 1999 **173**

A Gift of Grace

- *Has talked about depression in the past.*
- *Says he needs to prepare himself and become "tougher" (build muscle) for his new phase.*
- *I wish I could remember more but usually it is so different from what I think that I can't understand it, so I don't remember it.*
- *Sometimes he seems to do / say things with no conscience / remorse.*
- *He believes he and Madonna have a special relationship and she has talked to him through her music (I think this is what he meant). He believes he will use her music / his DJ work to send a message to the world.*

August 8, 1999

Edward, age 22, Calgary

Marlene and Nicole had agreed to meet with Edward and suggest that he visit a doctor concerning his bizarre "thoughts" and weird behaviour. He can't go straight to a psychiatrist. He needs a referral.

He agreed to go a doctor, so Darren and Nicole phoned various places and set up an appointment with Dr. Simpson at a Medical Clinic for Psychotherapy and Counselling for Monday, August 9th and with another doctor, Dr. Lodestone, who is in the same field, for Tuesday, August 10. Nicole and I both wrote notes concerning the behaviour that worried us.

Then today we decided to help Edward set up his place properly. So I took him to his apartment on 17th Ave. With a big smile on his face, he pulled a huge stack of magazines out from under his bed.

"Sit. I want to show you my artwork."

He started turning the pages of his magazines and watched for my response. The pages were covered with black marker with interesting parts showcased in unusual ways. This must have taken hours upon hours to complete.

"I like it, Edward."

I take a few magazines and turn the pages slowly, all the while contemplating what he might have been thinking as he deliberately made each stroke of his very black marker. Carefully and respectfully, I place the magazines in a neat pile on his table.

"Thanks for sharing your artwork, Edward. I think you should bring it to show your doctor!"

Marlene and Grandma Kristina came over. Edward was quick to ask them if they'd like to see his artwork. Of course they said, "Yes!" And of course, they said they liked it, but I'm sure we will talk about it later. Is his art weird or is it just that we don't understand it? What did Picasso's mother, aunt and grandmother think of his art when he first showed it to them?

I told them the reason for the gathering today is to help Edward clean his apartment, but most importantly to show him how to do it himself. Mar brought some muffins for Edward and also brought her vacuum cleaner to give the floors "a clean sweep." I helped Edward wash the dishes, Grandma Kristina helped him fold some clothes and we moved his furniture around to better suit his needs. I gave him money to take his dirty clothes to the Laundromat. While Edward was busy with the others, I started cleaning his fridge where I found a vial of a foreign substance.

Mar and Mom left. Then Edward and I finished folding clothes and we draped some of his garments on his bike to help them dry. We went to the nearby Safeway to buy groceries to stock his fridge and cupboards. I paid the $237. I hope it means he will eat properly for a couple of weeks or more. It is obvious he has not been doing that. He is so thin and pale.

When we were back at Edward's apartment he phoned Darren and Nicole to tell them when to expect us for supper. After we put the groceries away we went to Darren and Nicole's place. The four of us left after supper to go to the movie *The Blair Witch Project*. Edward found the movie disturbing and the rest of us were not really impressed either.

A Gift of Grace

After the movie, we were driving to Darren and Nicole's so that Edward would sleep at their place tonight and tomorrow night and we could go to his appointment straight from there. We were almost at Darren and Nicole's when Edward balked at staying over.

"We're almost there," I said.

"I don't care! I want to sleep in my own apartment."

"You can do that the night after the appointment."

"No, let me out of the car, now!"

What could we do but stop, since it looked like he was going to open the door and get out while the car was moving anyway. Darren quickly stopped the car.

Edward got out and turned to say, "Thanks for everything you all did today. I really appreciate everything – the help with my apartment, the groceries, supper, the movie, everything. I do not want you to think I am ungrateful. I know I am being a jerk, but I just want to go home. I will walk there. It's not far."

"It's too far for you to walk at this time of night Ed," Darren said, "Get back in and I will drive you home."

"Promise?"

"Promise."

As we drove off, Edward said, "Besides I am meeting friends who are going to give me a ticket to the Cher Concert."

As we were approaching his apartment, he saw the friends and opened the car door in the middle of the street while the car was still moving! Darren hit the brakes so the car would be stopped before Edward got out. Which he then did, right there in the middle of the street!"

As we pulled away, I looked back and started to sob uncontrollably. So did Nicole. Even Darren looked extremely upset.

Why does he do this to us! Doesn't he know we only care that he is safe and makes it to the appointment on time?

August 9, 1999

Edward, age 22, Calgary

Still anxious to make sure Edward gets some sleep and makes it to the appointment on time; we decided to coax him to stay at Darren and Nicole's until Monday morning. So Saturday night or rather early Sunday morning at 4:00 a.m. we drove over to pick him up from the Toxin Night Club where he said he worked. He said he would be finished work by then, but the place was closed with no one in sight. We drove around to see if he was already riding to his place or was already there. No luck. Then outside his apartment we waited anxiously for him to ride up on his bike. We waited and waited but no show from Edward. Where could he be? Finally Darren and Nicole wanted to go back to their place and wait.

We knew we wouldn't sleep until we had picked him up, so we sat waiting. At 6:00 a.m. just as we decided to go back searching and were about to leave the house, he phoned and said he would be another two hours before he would ride his bike over to his place.

I didn't like the sound of that so I lied, "Darren just left the house!"

He said, "Then go tell him!"

I replied, "I'm in my housecoat! You had better be there for him to pick you up!"

We managed to locate his whereabouts and put his bike in the trunk of my car, first taking the front wheel off so it would fit. Then we went to Darren and Nicole's to finally get some sleep.

A Gift of Grace

Edward slept in the basement. He never even asked me why if Darren had already left and I had been in my housecoat, how was it I was there in the car with Darren and Nicole. I bet he never thought his mother would lie!

August 10, 1999

Edward, age 22, Calgary

I was relieved to find Edward got up and showered, so was ready for his appointment. Thank goodness! So Nicole, Edward and I went to meet with Dr. Olaf Simpson, M.D. at 11:00 a.m. Nicole went into his office first and I waited with Edward in the waiting room reading magazines. With our encouragement Edward brought his artwork and writing along. Edward and Nicole went into the office together, after Nicole had spoken with the doctor separately. Dr. Simpson suggested to Edward that he see a psychiatrist and suggested treatment with medication. The doctor gave Edward forms to fill out and asked that he return them at his next visit at 3:00 p.m. on Wednesday.

Edward agreed with the doctor to take his medicine, but announced on the way to the car that he wouldn't be taking any drugs, "They alter your mind. I'm not ill."

Quite ironic when he is taking street drugs!

Surprisingly Edward agreed to stay with us overnight at Darren and Nicole's. Another night safe... Safe for now!

August 12, 1999

Edward, age 22, Calgary

Since Edward doesn't have a phone at his apartment, we phoned from Nicole's on Monday after the appointment with Dr. Lodestone because Edward seemed to connect with Dr. Simpson. After all, Dr. Simpson knew "Glenn Gould!"

Edward spent Tuesday night at his own apartment. Nicole and I drove over at 2:00 p.m. to pick him up for his second appointment with Dr. Simpson. Again he was ready and waiting. Nicole phoned ahead to tell Fiona, the receptionist, that she and I would like to talk to the doctor alone first. However, when we arrived we discovered that there must have been some miscommunication, because the doctor invited us all in.

He began by asking, "Well, tell me what's with Ed?"

One of the reasons Nicole had phoned yesterday was to let Fiona know we wanted to show Dr. Simpson the substance I found in Edward's fridge. We didn't want to discuss this in front of Edward, which is why we didn't mention it on Monday. So Nicole said, "Ed needs to finish filling out his form."

Dr. Simpson seemed to twig onto what was needed and he escorted Edward to another room to finish the form. While he was in the other room busy writing, the doctor, Nicole and I discussed our concerns. We showed Dr. Simpson our notes of what concerned us most. I also handed him the vial with the foreign substance. He didn't seem too concerned.

Edward has not asked me whether I found it or not. Does he not notice that it is gone? Or does he notice and doesn't want to ask because it is an illegal drug? If so, I have been carrying an illegal substance in my purse for the last three days!

A Gift of Grace

I showed the doctor some of Edward's autobiography assignment that includes some graphic writing. One is the story about Antoinette who is having a dilemma about her sexuality.

Dr. Simpson gave us a prescription for some anti-psychotic drugs and we told him that Edward said he was not going to take any medication. Dr. Simpson said we could mix them in a drink to ensure he would take it.

After the appointment Nicole and I decided we would not fill the prescription because we didn't feel it was right or wise to put drugs in Edward's drink. Besides what is the possible effect of the drug on his chemistry? Especially when we don't know what street drugs are still in his system?

The doctor also gave us a letter for a psychiatrist. His letter compiled our notes and the information Edward gave him on the first visit and also on the form. Parts of Dr. Simpson's notes are incorrect, but we can deal with that when we meet with the psychiatrist. We are pleased that Dr. Simpson provided us with so much detailed information.

As we were leaving, Edward told Dr. Simpson he is going to the Cher Concert tomorrow night. His friends are giving him a free ticket. He stated it so matter-of-factly, like a *fait accompli*, yet we don't know if his friends are that reliable or if his getting concert tickets are a fantasy.

August 13, 1999

Edward age 22, Calgary

Early yesterday evening, Edward phoned me and asked if I would like to go with him to the concert. He said he could get another ticket. I told him no because I was going with Darren and Nicole to Banff today and I wanted to have a good sleep first.

"Do you want to come with us?"

A Gift of Grace

"No."

"OK, I will come over to see you when we get back early tomorrow afternoon."

At 7:00 a.m. we left for Banff. We enjoyed the hot springs, had burritos and nachos at The Magpie & Stump and bought a can of maple syrup for Shelley. We were home by 1:00 p.m. The trip had helped us get a refreshing change of scenery!

When I went over to Edward's at 2:00 p.m., he was still sleeping so I walked down 17th Avenue. I enjoyed The Bear Claw Gallery and I bought a sunflower plant for his apartment.

When I got back he was up and then phoned TELUS to set up a telephone for himself. I let him use my MasterCard for the $100 deposit. I pointed out that he needed $80 and $425 in his bank account at the end of August: one for his phone and the other for his rent. Next month his telephone should be $20 cheaper. I hope he will learn some money management, not keep drawing on my money and not end up homeless like he was in Toronto.

August 14, 1999

Edward, age 22, Calgary

I went to Edward's and knocked three times with no response. I reached to turn the doorknob and the door swung open! The door hadn't been locked and it hadn't even been closed properly! I wasn't impressed and this just gave me another cause for worry. He had been lying down on his bed but got up and I strongly emphasized that he should be sure the door is closed and locked before he goes to bed.

He promises and we boiled some coffee in a saucepan. To continue teaching him life skills, which we have been doing over the past week, I gave him instructions on how to make chilli. He would scrape the thawed hamburger off the frozen beef and then go

A Gift of Grace

into the living room and lift weights for a while. I was patient because I wanted to be sure he did all the work. I enjoyed seeing him cook for us. I wrote the recipe on the back cover of the recipe book I had bought him, *Main Courses* by Jean Pare. He let the chilli simmer while he rinsed some lettuce for a salad. Supper tasted great!

When it was time for me to go because he had to go to work, Edward said I didn't have to drive him because he would take his bike. We said our goodbyes. I backed out of the parking lot and suddenly thought, "There was no bike in his apartment!" I went back and knocked on his door. When I asked him where his bike was he responded, "Oh, my god, oh, my god..."

He couldn't remember when he had it last and that it must still be at work. Since it was raining and it was getting late (7:25 p.m.) I drove him to work. The place was locked.

"That's OK Mom; I can wait in the doorway where it is protected from the rain."

He promised to phone me later that evening to tell me if he found his bike at work. He phoned while Nicole and I were out. Darren answered. Edward told him that someone must have broken into his apartment and taken it. It was a believable deduction since the door was ajar when I had arrived in the morning.

I had fleeting thoughts since he does "make up" stories from time to time. Did he sell his bike to pay for the ticket to the concert? Did he even have a ticket and go to the concert. He hasn't mentioned anything about it and the concert was on Thursday night.

He said he knew he had the bike last week because one morning he got back to his apartment at 8:00 a.m. from work. He remembers this because, while he was still at work, he and some others were in the basement and heard a loud crash. Thinking it was an intruder, someone called the police. Upon investigation, they found two chairs tipped over in different locations. Edward stated that his bike was still standing and he rode it home that day. So he had it then.

A Gift of Grace

It is typical of Edward to lose or misplace his possessions. He mislaid his driver's license at least four times, misplaced his wallet numerous times and lost his watch many times. I remember a gold Mickey Mouse watch I bought for him and he wore it only once. That was when he played at a teacher's wedding held outside in the yard of their home in the country. He must have taken it off before playing the piano and then forgot about it. He phoned the next day, but there was no watch anywhere to be found. They couldn't search their entire acreage, so who knows what became of it. I won't buy him any more watches.

Edward phoned back to say he finally remembered that his bike just might be at Mac's. He couldn't recall which day he might have left it there. I drove to the Mac's and asked the manager if he had noticed a bike outside his store. He did and said it was there for a couple of days, but that it hasn't been there anymore since this morning. He took Edward's name and phone number in case the bike shows up. He also phoned his wife to see if she knew anything about the bike. She didn't. After that I went over to Edward's and told him what I had learned at Mac's.

Then he realized what had probably transpired. He rode his bike home from work, stopped at Mac's to buy some ice cream and left his bicycle leaning against the store. When he came out of the store, he thinks he just walked right past it without noticing because he was eating his ice cream. He mustn't have closed his door properly and just went to bed. So when he noticed his bike was gone and I had found the door open, he assumed someone had been in his apartment and stole his bike. He had seemed very paranoid that someone was in his apartment while he was sleeping. That's why I thought it was important to let him know what the fellow at Mac's said, although I also stressed again he must always check his door before he goes to sleep each night.

Exhausted and distressed, Darren, Nicole and I rented a video to help us unwind. I think we fell asleep before it was over.

August 14, 1999

A Gift of Grace

August 15, 1999

Edward, age 22, Calgary

This afternoon when I went to Edward's, the outside door of the apartment building was locked. I knocked on his window and he came and opened the door. His keys were in the lock on the outside of his apartment door. I remarked about this NOT being a good thing to have happen!

"Open the door with the key, then take out the keys and take them inside with you!!! Make it a habit, please!"

How can he be doing this?

Today I was happy to watch as Edward made dinner without much input from me. He fried steak and onions with two teaspoons of dried onion soup mix, mushroom soup and one half can of water. He washed potatoes and carrots, and I told him it would be okay to boil them in the same pot. Supper was delicious.

I drove Edward to work, dropping him off at a place just off 17th Avenue where he said he would meet Harold, a friend of his who also works at Toxin, and they would walk to work together.

Edward said he would like to go hiking with us tomorrow. I said we'd pick him up at 8:00 a.m. I knew he wouldn't get much sleep working late at Toxin, but he didn't seem to think it would be a problem.

Darren went to Safeway and bought some yeast for making bread in the bread machine. We put everything in the machine and went to bed. At 3:00 a.m. I suddenly awoke worried sick about how Edward was getting back from work without his bike. The smell of freshly baked bread was wafting through the house, so I quietly removed it from the machine and decided to write in my journal.

A Gift of Grace

I will phone him in the morning to let him know when we are picking him up for the hike. That way it won't seem like I am just checking up on him. Meanwhile I don't think I will get much more sleep.

August 16, 1999

Edward, age 22, Calgary

We got up, made sandwiches, packed Nicole and Darren's backpacks and dressed. We phoned Edward to tell him we are on the way over, but he didn't answer. We left a message. Now my fears from last night or rather early morning are causing knots in my stomach. I can usually contain my tears, but my stomach always gets upset.

This is the same anxiety I had when camping in BC. Frank and I went to play cards with relatives camping near us. We left the kids playing board games in the camper, but when we returned around midnight, the kids were gone. I panicked, took the walkie talkie and started wandering around in the pitch black darkness of the Rocky Mountain campground. One of our relatives found me searching and calling in vain. She told me that my kids had gone to Terrace with some other kids. It turned out to be true and I finally heard them return in the early morning after I had a sleepless night. I think it was the first time they had seen the appearance of "angry Mom" as they called it. They didn't understand the frightening experience it was for me and how my upset stomach meant I couldn't eat for hours afterward.

We drove over to pick Edward up and I knocked on the door. Thankfully it was locked with no key on the outside and thank God he answered. He hadn't showered yet, but he got ready without a fuss. He wondered if he could have some cereal, but we

A Gift of Grace

said we'd better get going. No problem. Darren bought Egg McMuffins and hash browns at McDonald's for Edward, him and me. Nicole went off to find something healthier and once she returned we were filling the tank up at the service station next door. I paid for the fuel since Darren and Nicole had paid for everything else so far and we were on our way about 9:30 a.m.

We had a wonderful day hiking up a mountain and enjoying our picnic lunch with the view from the top. Edward seemed to really enjoy the day and spent time asking questions and discussing rock formations with Darren.

During the road trip home, a song came on the radio and he announced, "I don't like this song and they play it over and over at Toxin."

> *I thought to myself, "Good, maybe you'll be receptive to letting us suggest that you find a daytime job." It isn't really safe working and getting home the hours he is keeping.*

We stopped in Banff to walk around before heading home. We ordered a coke in a cafe but Edward refused to order. So when the waitress brought our cokes, she brought Edward some water. He just has to be difficult and yet we all cater to his needs.

Edward brought a book and his markers along, but he chose to sleep most of the drive. At one point along the way, Darren took out his water bottle and offered me a drink, then he took a drink and Edward asked if he could also have a drink. Nicole offered him a drink from the bottle in her bag. I wasn't thinking very fast because I could have offered to get the bottle out of Edward's pack for him. Anyway, Darren gave him a drink from his, letting Edward know that he is usually very strict on who he shares his food and drink with. I think that's a wise practice.

> *Edward seems to see no boundaries in what others would see as a common courtesy. For instance, he'll ask to borrow any garment. With his previous health concerns and any we don't know about, who knows what can happen.*

A Gift of Grace

August 18, 1999

Edward, age 22, Calgary

We received a copy of the letter from Dr. Simpson to the psychiatrist to whom he has referred Edward, along with the notes he had made the day we were in his office:

Dear Dr. Belmont,

Thanks so much for seeing Edward so quickly. I have enclosed his history for your interest.

Sincerely,

Olaf Simpson, MD

The enclosed history:

> The Medical Clinic for Counselling and Psychotherapy
> The Bow River Professional Centre
> Calgary AB
>
> Re: Edward Weatherly
>
> This man came to the clinic today with his sister and mother who are becoming more and more concerned with his increasingly bizarre behaviour. They estimate that his behaviour has been quite unusual for the past five years and was remarked on by teachers in New Mexico, where Edward had gone on scholarship several years ago. They wrote he had lack of focus. His sister, Nicole, told him that he should come with her to the clinic to "get better."
>
> Edward was born in Provost, Alberta and attended different schools in Czar, Hughenden and finally in Provost where

A Gift of Grace

he took grade eleven. Then he won a scholarship to the International Baccalaureate program in New Mexico. As a boy of eight years, he accused some bikers of sexual abuse but later retracted his story. During high school in Alberta he achieved grade ten in the Royal Conservatory of music program. After his studies in New Mexico, he won a scholarship to the University of Toronto where he attended for about two years in general studies and commerce, before failing and meeting a much older man who took Edward as a lover. He then moved to Mexico in 1998 for a few months to work on a film about the revolutionary movement currently involving Marcos in Chiapas.

In 1998 when he had taken his 69 year old lover, who bought him gifts, he also began stripping in nightclubs in Montreal, Toronto and Washington, this ending about three months ago. He says during this time, he used heroin (perhaps), crack and marijuana. He says that he's never used injectible drugs. He was tested for HIV about 18 months ago and was found to be negative.

Currently, he says that he wants to use his musical training to put together a multimedia project. He says that he often receives frequencies from outer space and from God that are telling him how to write music and make it into multimedia. He said something during the interview about the "Bronfman Branch," and something to do with Glenn Gould's production, "The Idea of North" which he was going to put into "contrapuntal multimedia" and appreciate its "innerness, ecstasy and narcissistic aptitude." Somehow connecting to this was the rock star Madonna, Andy Warhol and other famous figures from American pop culture, he said, who are going to broadcast his message to the world.

Edward often used his hands and fingers to make X and O signs and finds the letters O and I ubiquitously, symbolizing false prophets, among other things.

Before he came into the room, his sister, a schoolteacher aged 25, spoke for about 15 minutes and gave me a précis of what the family in general has noted bizarre in his behaviour:

A Gift of Grace

– Edward believes that AIDS is not a disease but a conspiracy against homosexuals –– the drugs used to treat homosexuals are really what are killing them

– he believes that billboards and television sets are speaking to him alone and have tasks and messages intended for him alone.

– he is often defensive and angry

– he is often very paranoid

– he's often antisocial, withdrawing into his room where he does drawing and painting for hours on end or works at his writing

– he believes that he has a special audience with American rock star Madonna who will help to broadcast his ideas to the world at-large

– he tends to prevaricate at times with his family, i.e., he is now telling his sister that he is a bouncer in a local club, but when she checked, the club had been closed for a long time.

– he has taken to using a black felt pen in outlining figures in fashion magazines and proclaiming that he is another Picasso

– he has broadcasted that he will be rich and famous some day

– he appears to lack a conscience lately, i.e., he will make a promise to go out with one person and then at the last minute leave that person for someone else

– he is obsessed with the idea of dark and light. When he was living in Toronto he was going through a "dark period"; now he is going through a "light period" in Calgary.

– believes that someday, because all men are made of binary combinations, they will only be "digital flesh."

– believes that he is a prophet

– reads coincidence into everything such as messages in fortune cookies

– states that things occur in the sixth dimension, which only very bright people, such as him, are able to understand

August 18, 1999

A Gift of Grace

– believes the CIA is wiretapping his apartment

– he wishes to make a video so that he, by masturbating on the moving image, as the Christ Child???, will regenerate the Earth's population as we now know will become obsolete. He believes that the gods are communicating with him through signs; when watching a movie, road signs and such, he sees a combination of ones and zeroes and believes that it is his task to communicate the meaning of the signs, which only he understands, to the world.

– through digital music he has choreographed a dance with Xs and Os.

– he calls himself "binary boy" and believes that all humans will some day evolve into digital flesh

–he believes that one day all his artwork will be in New York galleries

– he refers to himself as a prodigy and messenger

– he is in awe of power and money

Initial Impression:
This young man has symptoms of the following:
    - schizophrenia, paranoid type
    - homosexuality, ego, syntonic
    - narcissistic personality traits

He will be referred to a specialist immediately.

Olaf Simpson, M.D.

August 19, 1999

Edward, age 22, Calgary

Nicole is very good at getting Edward up, making phone calls to ensure he is OK, picking him up and getting him to appointments on time. Tomorrow Edward will be seeing a psychiatrist referred

A Gift of Grace

by Dr. Simpson. However, Nicole phoned the psychiatrist a few days earlier to ask if she and I can accompany Edward. We thought it was imperative we are aware of the treatment they planned for him. With this knowledge, we would be in a better position to monitor his behaviour, such as ensure he takes his medication and keeps doctor appointments.

Nicole reported the psychiatrist, Dr. Anne Belmont was rude and uncompassionate during the phone call. When asked if Edward should bring his artwork and writing along, Anne responded, "Why would I need to see that? I'll take your word that it is the way it is."

She also said, "I have never had anyone come into my office accompanying a patient. Edward is 22 years old and the meeting is confidential."

Nicole retorted, "Ed does not have a problem with Mom and me coming in with him, why would you?"

Actually, from reading the pamphlets from Special Services, family involvement is crucial to successful treatment and rehabilitation of patients. We understand that Edward can sign a statement consenting for his doctor to release pertinent information to us. We will request this to be done.

Nicole and Anne did not get off on the right foot over the phone. Then today to our astonishment we found out that she is a psychologist, coordinator for the psychiatric services of the clinic where she works and not a psychiatrist, as Dr. Simpson led us to believe. The Dr. Belmont who is a psychiatrist is not Dr. Anne Belmont, but her husband Terry. If Dr. Simpson thought he was referring us to a psychiatrist named Dr. Anne Belmont and, if psychological services were all that was to be provided, we could have stayed with Dr. Simpson. Why did we need an appointment with a psychologist to refer us to her husband, the psychiatrist, when Dr. Simpson had already referred us to what he believed was the psychiatrist? We were not impressed.

We were also worried Edward would get antsy about telling his life story to so many different people. And psychologists cannot prescribe the medicine Edward so desperately needs.

August 19, 1999 191

A Gift of Grace

Nicole phoned Dr. Simpson and told Fiona, his receptionist, that Dr. Anne Belmont is not a psychiatrist. Fiona was dumbfounded because that is how Anne is listed in their directory. Nicole left a message for Dr. Simpson to call us. Nicole also phoned Dad in Provost and Shelley up North to express her complaint about Anne's lack of ethics and compassion for her brother.

This evening Dr. Simpson returned Nicole's call. Since I was there, Nicole handed the phone to me and I told him about our concerns. Dr. Simpson agreed Edward should see Dr. Terry Belmont, the psychiatrist, not Dr. Anne Belmont, but I was trying to explain that she insists, before we get in to see her husband, we have to go through her first.

Nicole took the phone and asked Dr. Simpson if Edward could see him instead of Dr. Terry Belmont. He replied, "I prefer to have Edward see Terry before he comes back to me."

So there is nothing to be done but go to the appointment and see what happens.

August 20, 1999

Edward, age 22, Calgary

After Anne met with Edward, she asked us to come into her office. She asked us what we would like to tell her about him. Nicole expressed her concern about Ed's obsessions with messages he sees in media (TV, billboards, magazines and even in fortune cookies) that hold a special significance for him.

Nicole shared the following information with Anne:

Edward believes he is a "Digital Prophet," regularly decoding algorithms of 1's and 0's, which he says he finds secretly embedded in various pop-culture multimedia. For example, while reading the advertising text on a poster or video billboard, he converts the letter "L" to the number "1" and the letter "O" to the number

"0," putting these digits together to make the number "10," which is the letter "X" in Roman Numerals. Edward believes that these revelations of the letter X contain a top secret message that he is supposed to further decode and then spread to the masses via digital media and DJ culture, as the clubs and circuit parties were places of worship for him.

Edward agreed to see Dr. Terry Belmont at Special Services in the Foothills Hospital just next door to the Cancer Clinic where Grandpa Ted had his cancer treatments. It brought up sad memories and we hope it will not be too upsetting for Edward.

On the way out to the car, Edward was visibly upset because Anne commented that he was "psychotic." It wasn't the right word to use with him! We did our best not to get too negative about her even though it required a lot of restraint. We don't want him to refuse any more visits to psychologists or psychiatrists. When we were back at her place Nicole phoned Dr. Simpson and expressed concern about the misconception of Dr. Anne's credentials as well as her manner in dealing with our family's needs.

Then Nicole took us to Spolumbos for meatball sandwiches for lunch. We dropped Edward off at his apartment and agreed to pick him up at 2:00 p.m. tomorrow for the appointment with Dr. Terry Belmont. We took Edward back to his apartment.

I came inside while Nicole waited for me in the car. I noticed a receipt from a sauna dated 99/08/17 for twenty dollars. I was disappointed because a few days ago he had showed me his feet, which appeared to have signs of athlete's foot. I told him he could pick that up from shared bathrooms or other areas where people go barefoot, such as a sauna.

Hint, hint...

After I was inside, he begged us not to tell Auntie Mar about what's with him and the results of today's meeting.

"I'm not crazy!"

I was finding it difficult to get up and leave him alone in his apartment, but at the same time I realize and respect his request

A Gift of Grace

to have some time to himself. He also insists he will not take any prescription drugs.

"I've had experience with mind-altering drugs and I know what they do to you."

I did not want to argue at this point, ask him what street drugs he still takes or try to convince him that he must take medicine. All Nicole and I asked him to promise was that he keeps the appointment tomorrow and remain open minded.

We had his very best interests in our minds!

He agrees to the appointment but he still insists he will **not** be taking the drugs.

Edward started to cry when I got up to leave. "I'm sorry for what I have done in the past. I know I have disappointed you."

I sat down not knowing how to respond.

He sat, shoulders hunched and crying... "You didn't come for me!"

What in the world does he mean? Come for him? When? Where? I spent so much time going to see him and trying to help him both in Calgary and Toronto. I didn't know if I should ask him what he means or just let him cry.

His tears burst through and he truly had a "good cry." I was surprised. Crying wasn't something I saw him do much.

More guilt... I hug him, but his body is limp and unresponsive...

I sat down again and agreed there were times we had been disappointed in his behaviour, but it didn't mean we loved him any less. I also told him that he has always been very determined, so I know he is going to do just exactly what he wants to do and I have no control over his final choices. All I can ever do is listen to him and offer unsolicited advice.

"I have always been there for you! All you have ever had to do is call and I come running!"

"I feel broken… I wish someone would just lock me up!"

> *Oh, my God! Here I thought he is feeling so much better since coming to Calgary. What more can we do? We are doing everything possible to ensure he regains control of his life.*

"I love you Edward and **nothing** can ever take that away!"

We sat without talking. I cried. He cried. We look into one another's eyes and we weep openly.

"I'll call you later tonight."

With that I walked out to the car where Nicole was waiting and we drove to her place. Mar was there visiting with Darren. We fill them in on the appointment with Anne. Days ago when Mar and Nicole spoke with Edward, Mar thought that maybe he had ADD (Attention Deficit Disorder). Now she realizes it's much more serious.

> *With medicine and psychotherapy, I am certain he'll recover. I'm sounding like this is going to be a piece of cake and very much straightforward – treatment and recovery. What else can I believe? "I am broken" are words that will haunt me forever, I'm sure.*

I followed Mar out to her house in Chestermere. She made a delicious chef's salad and we watched a video. It was late when Nicole phoned to tell me Dr. Simpson wants Edward to see the psychiatrist right away. Since there was nothing I could do now, I told her I would come back to her place in the morning.

A Gift of Grace

Before I go to bed I plan to read some of the book, *Is There No Place on Earth for Me?* The book is written by Susan Sheehan about a woman with schizophrenia.

I wonder why Dr. Simpson is so concerned that he would phone so late in the day to ask us to have Edward go in to see the psychiatrist immediately. This, as well as Edward's words, weighs heavily on my mind. I am not sure I can concentrate on the pages in front of me or even sleep.

August 21, 1999

Edward, age 22, Calgary

I managed to read some of the book before I went to sleep but there was not much sleep. So I got up at 7:30 a.m., showered and read more of the book until Mar got up. I had breakfast with her.

> *I love drinking my coffee this morning, from my thin lipped cup with the fluted top surrounded by flowers; the iris stands boldly... my sister gave it to me... she is my bestest friend in the whole wide world...*

Nicole phoned and said because of Dr. Simpson's phone call we were able to make an appointment to see Dr. Terry Belmont at 3:00 p.m. today. We agree it is extremely important for Edward to experience a positive meeting with the psychiatrist and also important that he agrees to take medication. I have a good feeling that he will agree, but I still experience the emotional apprehension of what will transpire at the 3:00 p.m. appointment.

I phoned Edward and told him I watched a movie and stayed overnight with Auntie Mar. I told him about the appointment and that Nicole and I will pick him up at 2:00 p.m. I said Auntie Mar sends her "positive vibes" – she says that often, so it would not alert Edward that I had told her anything.

A Gift of Grace

Since Nicole and Darren have really opened their home to me while I am in Calgary, I stopped on the way to buy some lilies and a vase for them. It's not just their hospitality that I appreciate. They are doing so much else for Edward and offering me moral support.

When I got to Nicole's, she phoned Edward and told him she had to wait until her clothes were dry. He had phoned earlier to check if we were on our way.

When we got to his place, he asked if we would stop by the bank. It was 2:40 p.m. already but Nicole stopped at the bank anyway. He told the teller that when he deposited his money in the bank machine, he had pressed the "cheque" button instead of the "cash" button. She told him it would make no difference, but Edward wanted to check for sure. The teller got his account file, but because the deposit was last night, it still hadn't shown up. The teller assured him it will probably have the right amount in his account tomorrow.

We arrived at Special Services, Foothills Hospital at 3:05 p.m. Nicole and I agreed earlier that we would not discuss any aspects of his upcoming appointment since there had been some negative feelings about Anne's competency. I had some apprehension, but Edward was seeing a psychiatrist today and I choose to believe this man will be professional and do his best job for my son.

After Edward had been in with Dr. Belmont for about an hour, the receptionist told Nicole and me we could go into the therapy room if we wished. We did and Dr. T. Belmont informed us that Edward had agreed to take medication to relieve his symptoms of psychosis. There were three pills in a vial beside Edward.

"Is that okay with you, Edward?" I asked

"Sure, if it will help my music."

I have secretly hoped that Edward would some day play the piano again and sing. He has been caught up with the idea of mixing different artists' music to create new pieces, but I regard that as a waste of his inherent talent.

Dr. Belmont asked the receptionist to check his schedule for next week to set up another appointment. One is made for 3:00 p.m. on Tuesday, August 24.

A Gift of Grace

Darren and Nicole had made an appointment today with a realtor to look at a house and then had been invited to a BBQ supper that evening. Edward's appointment went longer than expected and ended at 4:30 p.m. Nicole had to drop off Edward and me at Edward's before she could head home. On the way, Edward asked if Nicole would stop at a music store. Edward went in while Nicole and I stayed in her car to wait for him.

"Nicole, don't you have an appointment and BBQ tonight?"

"Yes, but Darren changed the appointment with the realtor from 4:00 to 5:00, so we'll still have time to make it to the BBQ at 6:00."

"Oh, I didn't realize these times were so soon! Now you'll be late. Why didn't you just tell Edward you didn't have time to stop?"

"Mom, I didn't want to refuse Edward because I didn't want to tick him off."

Focus seemed always to be on what will help Edward stay on track, meet his needs, keep him from running away... not tick him off... our mental health is at risk here, too. Why should we have to tiptoe around him?

August 24, 1999

Edward, age 22, Calgary

I phoned Edward this morning and reminded him we would be picking him up in the afternoon for his appointment with Dr. Belmont. He thought his appointment was on Wednesday, but he agreed to be ready by 2:30 p.m.

I had typed a *Letter of Consent* for him to sign yesterday giving a release of information regarding his treatment at the Foothills Medical Centre to his father, his sisters and me. Nicole and I debated about when would be the best time to have him read

A Gift of Grace

and sign it. Yesterday he had said he wasn't going to take his pill (and ended up taking it) and so we thought we shouldn't chance making him unduly agitated just before going in to see the doctor.

As it turned out, I gave it to him yesterday when he was sitting at the kitchen table and he signed it. I handed it to the receptionist before Edward when in to see Dr. Terry Belmont. When Edward came out, he showed me a bottle containing some Olanzapine (Zyprexa). I noticed it was labelled 5 mg and seemed as though it had seven pills in it.

Then Dr. Belmont called Nicole and me into his office. A doctor of psychiatry from Budapest, Hungry had been present in Edward's therapy session and stayed in while we were there. Dr. Belmont confirmed Edward has schizophrenia.

> *I'm not crazy. My son has schizophrenia. Surprisingly it's not any easier having it confirmed.*

Dr. Belmont also wanted to see us to form a plan with our list of needs and wants for Edward as well as for our family. He asked who would be the family contact for the treatment team. Since I'm four to five hours away, Nicole was willing to be responsible. I'm hoping Edward will be able to accept responsibility for taking his medication and transporting himself to his sessions. We were handed a duplicate of the pamphlets and sheets that were given to Edward.

When we were done, Edward asked about going for a drink or some food (that's what we have usually done), but Nicole said we'd go home. She asked him what he'd like and he said he'd like some hamburgers. He mixed the ground beef and grilled three burgers on the BBQ for us.

Edward and I went to Chinook Centre and shopped for a pair of running shoes and an entertainment centre for his apartment.

When we got back to Nicole and Darren's, we cleaned up and went to the Tuesday night movie, *Sixth Sense*, with Bruce Willis. This show was about a psychiatrist who treats a young boy who he believes has schizophrenia because the boy says he can see and talk to dead people. Even though it is a horror film, I see parallels.

August 24, 1999 **199**

A Gift of Grace

I drove Edward home and we carried the shelves for the entertainment centre into his apartment. We talked about his medicine and I told him how it made me happy that he was cooperating and taking the meds. I told him Dad asks about him every day and loves him very much. I also told Edward his Dad and I want him to lead a healthy life, earn his own living and find happiness. And, we are very pleased he is taking his medicine.

I asked him if Dr. Belmont is helping him and he responded, "Yes."

He seems to be remorseful for some past activities... but, on the other hand, reminds me that he has wonderful memories of interesting people and beautiful music.

Edward described a bit about what he feels is his calling in life. He has known many gay people in Toronto who were unloved and cast out by their families. He wants to change that.

"Everyone deserves to be loved by everyone else and their God."

I told him to phone Toxin and tell them he won't be coming in any more. I also told him not to go to the shady nightclubs or the sauna anymore.

It was my opinion there are most likely unsavoury characters there. Hey, my son is one of them. I just want him not to associate with the others. There must be other places to meet young gay men. I guess you need a sort of radar since they won't be walking around with a sticker on their forehead. I must admit that I have a certain radar sense on behalf of my students. I make sure I empower them with a voice as they will need it to work through some of the cruelties they are destined to experience.

I got back to Nicole's at 1:15 a.m. and cried all the way there... I empathize with my son and the rest of my family...

I'm going to look at the upside! I have a great deal of faith that Edward will take his medication and we'll see improvement in his thinking as it relates to others, as well *as the riddance of his "positive" symptoms of schizophrenia. Positive symptoms are behaviours that are **added** to the person's personality. I take exception to the use of the word "positive" symptoms of schizophrenia because they are not 'positive' in the conventional sense of the word. Edward has delusions and most likely hallucinations, **added** to his personality. (These are definitely not something a person would want added to their personality!)*

On the other hand, he has also shown some "negative symptoms." These include his new habit of staying in his room and not coming out to socialize. Edward was always known as the most friendly, outgoing person around!

(N.B. Positive symptoms are, for example, hallucinations and delusions. Negative symptoms are, for example, flat affect, apathy and poverty of speech.)

August 25, 1999

Edward, age 22, Calgary

I phoned Edward in the morning and asked if he'd taken his pills at the right time. He said he had.

Today we went shopping and decided to look for books on schizophrenia. Darren brought along the books he already had on the topic. Then he, Nicole and I searched through shelves at Chapters and in second-hand bookstores. I'm interested in reading psychology medical journals at the University of Calgary. I want to learn about the latest developments in brain research to understand how the brain functions normally, as well as its dysfunctions.

While we were doing this, Edward was in the music store and purchased three CDs. I couldn't help but notice that he wanted to return the first set.

> *Edward demonstrates an impulsive personality... He probably gets it from me!*

He asked me, "Do you think it was silly of me to spend eighty dollars on CDs?"

"Probably, just know that you'll need to pay your rent of four hundred twenty-five dollars plus your phone bill which will be approximately eighty dollars for the first one."

"I'll have enough."

August 26, 1999

Edward, age 22, Calgary

I phoned Edward in the morning and asked if he'd taken his pills at the right time.

"Yes, I have, Mom!" he sounded agitated.

Darren, Nicole and I went to the *Calgary Schizophrenia Society* and asked about getting a daytime job for Edward so it would be easier to plan a schedule for taking his pills. We were greeted by a friendly woman named Wendy. We told her about Edward's interest in music and, specifically, CD mixers. Also surprising to us, he actually expressed an interest in construction work. Wendy said she would phone us on Monday after she checked with a couple of agencies.

I shared with her that Edward seems to have a poor self image. When he walks down the sidewalk, he comments, "People walking down the street are saying, 'Look at that poor fucking bastard!' "

Wendy says the job he gets may be half time. She expresses the importance of Edward experiencing success at his jobs so he isn't

A Gift of Grace

fired and then ends up feeling like a failure. She tells us that a job may be supplemented by money available from AISH (Assured Income for the Severely Handicapped). Schizophrenia is considered a severe handicap.

She stressed the importance of Edward being on medication long enough so that symptoms of psychosis do not appear while he is working at a job. He is presently working from 8:00 p.m. to 2:00 p.m. at a gay night club called Toxin. Wendy seemed as vehement as we are about getting him out of this scene. Her best scenario for us was that Edward would have recovery in six months. Then she threw out doom and gloom at us…

She said she hated to inform us, but she'd be blunt… "He could very well end up in jail!"

Wendy told us to take advantage of any "in" he gave us to get him out of working at Toxin.

This is what I have been trying to do – plant a seed in his brain to desire a daytime job.

"You really do need to advocate for Edward so that his needs are met and he recovers as soon as possible. Schizophrenia cannot be cured but can be treated with medication and psychotherapy."

I am aware of the possible need for psychotherapy treatment for Edward to come to grips with any guilt and resentment emerging from his reflections upon past experiences. Wendy listened with interest while we described our confusion over Anne's title as doctor, the psychiatrist, rather than doctor, the psychologist. She was surprised because her office's experience is that patients have a more positive relationship with Anne rather than with Terry.

We left just in time to pick up the application form at AISH. We had planned to stop by City Hall today to see if they had any jobs for Edward, but it was too late. Wendy had given us information about a Drop-in Centre for members of the Schizophrenia Society. So we stopped in there and listened to a young fellow play his violin. After he finished, he came over to us and introduced himself as Quinn. He told us he has schizophrenia. It hasn't prevented him from being a volunteer at the Society in Calgary.

August 26, 1999 203

A Gift of Grace

This is comforting news.

Then it was time to go back to Edward's for a quick bite and to get him to Toxin on time. Back at Darren and Nicole's, I phoned both Frank at home in Provost and Shelley up north to give them the update.

August 27, 1999

Edward, age 22, Calgary

I woke with a start at 6:00 a.m. My stomach was instantly upset. This has been happening a great deal over my anxiety about Edward. I took a Tums from the bottle that Nicole had given me yesterday to reduce the physical effects. I got up, left a note for Nicole and tried a couple of times to phone Edward. There was no answer.

I drove to Edward's apartment. I knocked two times on his door and then noticed him in the front passenger's seat of a car that was driving into the parking lot. When he got out, I greeted him and he asked me how long I'd been there. I answered that I'd just arrived. I told him that I was thinking of him and couldn't sleep, so I thought I'd bring over some milk for him and Drano for the clogged sink.

I was concerned that he had been up all night and hadn't taken his pills. I poured the Drano into the kitchen sink and while washing my hands in the bathroom, I counted four pills in his medicine vial. It seems the right number, but he will need some more.

"How did work go?"

"Okay, I am quite sedated and very tired now. I have to get a day-time job, nine to five with weekends off; a normal job. But I have to work at Toxin until the end of the month so I can pay my rent. I'll give them a week's notice. My manager, Brandon, said he would need a week's notice."

204 August 27, 1999

A Gift of Grace

"You could give your notice now; work Saturday and Sunday nights and that would be okay. I have some contacts for you for getting a job."

I told him he can apply for AISH and I'll help him pay this month's rent. I asked him when he takes his pill.

He answered, "I take them at 3:00."

I hope he means a.m. when he gets home from work and before he goes to sleep because I wondered if he would be able to function if he took them just before work.

"Is that a.m. or p.m.?"

"p.m."

"Should I phone the nurse to see if that's an okay time to be taking your pill? Aren't you supposed to take them just before you go to bed?"

He said, "I don't care. You can phone the nurse. What time is it?"

"7:00 a.m."

He checked his telephone messages. I said that he'd find a few calls that were from me but I had left no messages.

"You've been worrying about me."

"You'll have to put up with me and my worrying."

Edward responded, "That's okay, it isn't as if you haven't put up with me for a long time!"

When Edward was 16 and I would worry about him, he told me, "Mom, if I die tomorrow, it's OK because I have lived an amazing life."

"Goodnight. I know you want to sleep. I love you, Edward."

"I love you more!"

A Gift of Grace

I noticed that he appeared patient with me and didn't use his usual agitated tone to dismiss me.

I drove to Nicole's and went with her and a friend to Eaton's. They're going into receivership so have good sales. Edward asked me to buy him some cargo pants. I bought a pair as well as a belt. After lunch I went to his place. When I got there, I used his washroom and noticed he had three pills left. We decided to walk down 17th Avenue to find a good restaurant for supper.

Before we left the apartment, Edward shared, "Mom, there's talking on the street about me, some good and some bad. I know that is a form of psychosis, right?"

I agreed, but told him the pills will help. We had supper at the Chameleon; half orders of linguine and clam sauce and chicken. I felt bummed out. Fatigue, worry, finances all were weighing me down.

Edward announced, "I need a daytime job."

"Well, Edward, give notice to quit right away. Dad and I will help pay your rent if need be. There are agencies that will help you."

After I got back to Nicole's, Darren had gone out to meet up with some of his friends. So Nicole and I watched a small part of the video, *Picasso*, which we had rented to understand his state of mind because he died in an asylum and was believed to have had schizophrenia. The video was pretty pathetic and not at all what we expected.

I phoned and spoke with Shelley in Cambridge Bay. She's going to a dance tomorrow night. She seems to be pretty happy where she is.

August 28, 1999

Edward, age 22, Calgary

I slept in until 10:45 a.m. I phoned Edward and left a message for him to call me when he woke. Later I called and the phone rang once on his end and then there was silence.

Darren and Nicole were getting ready to go to Johnson Canyon. I would have loved to go but thought I'd better check on Edward. I drove to his place, but he still wanted to sleep. His dishes still aren't done from when I unplugged the sink, so I soaked them and went out to pick up a few things for him. When I returned at 3:30 p.m., he was still sleepy and asked if I'd fix him some scrambled eggs and bacon. I did and then ate with him.

I vowed not to mention his pill but eventually I couldn't help it because it was getting late. He showed it to me and popped it into his mouth. I said, "Shouldn't you drink a glass of water with that?"

"No, I can swallow it without."

I asked to read the sheets of information he received from the psychiatrist.

"You got the same ones," he said, handing the one describing Zyprexa to me. "I asked for my own copies because I want to know the ingredients. These sheets are useless. There are no ingredients listed. I can see through the wording on the page. It is written ever so carefully so patients aren't alarmed and will take the pills. I'm not fooled by this at all! I'll take the rest of these and then that's it!"

My stomach always reacts to his non-compliance with instant feelings of diarrhea coming on.

A Gift of Grace

"Do you think the medication is helping you?" I had read it is possible there could be some positive results in just a few days.

"It makes me sleepy."

Then he abruptly changed the topic.

"What's four times seven?'

"Twenty-eight."

"I need a better job, one with forty hours."

"Yes, Edward, you do."

"Maybe I'll look on Monday and Tuesday."

He wanted to sleep so I left.

Back at Darren and Nicole's I decided to make a list of things to discuss with the nurse at the *Early Psychosis Program* at the Foothills Hospital.

BRING
– Edward's autobiography
– AISH Record Contact form
– letter of consent for the release of information

PSYCHOTHERAPY
– personality
– conscience
– memory
– behaviour: demanding, abusive, manipulative, inconsiderate, lack of common courtesies
– vocational therapy: help plan ahead for education, set short and long term goals so that he can be self-supportive. He is presently unable to pay for rent, groceries, telephone, public transport, laundry

SAIT (Southern Alberta Institute of Technology)
– are there co-op programs involving courses and work experience to help ensure job placement?

A Gift of Grace

ALBERTA COLLEGE OF ART AND DESIGN
– take a course

VOCATIONAL / OCCUPATIONAL THERAPIST
– need a job
– skills, interests
– AISH form
– Wendy is helping
– family funds have diminished
– budgeting money

ALBERTA HEALTH CARE
– is there any way that Edward's premium could be paid because of his disability, at least until he is more self-sufficient?

DRUG COVERAGE
– will his medication continue to be paid through his treatment plan?
– how will any other prescription drugs he may require, be paid for?

BLUE CROSS (Alberta health care insurance plan)
– do we need to apply for this?

MORALITY
– risky behaviours in the past
– would psychotherapy help eliminate these behaviours?
– Edward thinks there is a conspiracy against gay people. He says it is the medicine that kills them.

SOCIAL LIFE / WELL BEING
– says he's bored and depressed at times
– very important aspect because Edward has always been friendly and outgoing
– he needs to have the opportunity to meet people who can relate to him, especially people who are gay, who are intelligent, maybe have schizophrenia, and for sure have other interests, other than the bar and nightclub scene
– met Darrel from the Schizophrenia Society; maybe Edward could participate at some time in the future
– introduce to clubs such as art, painting, music, drama, fitness, swimming, piano, singing, CD mixing

August 28, 1999

A Gift of Grace

MEDICAL
– thorough
– blood tests
– HIV test
– Hepatitis B immunization
– routine
– STDs

> *Being healthy is very important; Edward has expressed his dissatisfaction with being "skinny" and he is not satisfied with his body build.*

MEDICATION
– would medication injection better suit Ed's needs?
– do you administer small doses until the doctor determines what kind of drug and what dose is most effective?

SYMPTOMS
– what does the doctor think caused his symptoms?

FAMILY THERAPY
– anger and resentment
– moods swings mirroring whether Edward is doing well or not
– need for re-energizing; we are burnt out
– tense relationships – frequent arguments, strong feelings of anger and resentment among family members

BOOKS
– when should I share with Edward the books I have bought on the topic of schizophrenia?

INDEPENDENCE
– eventually (after he has taken medication for a while) to have Edward be more independent by getting to sessions on his own, using the Public Transport – i.e. phone and get the route, purchase a bus pass...

Edward phoned about 11:00 p.m. He had slept most of the day. As he described it, "I missed the day!"

210 August 28, 1999

A Gift of Grace

He was supposed to work at 8:00 p.m. at Toxin but said he had a sore eye. He tried phoning to say he wouldn't be able to go in. However, Toxin didn't answer.

A plausible story? I don't think so. Really?

"How do you feel?"

"I feel depressed. I wanted to give the manager a week's notice, but now I probably don't have a job! I won't be able to get a good reference either!"

"Do you want to come over here and stay overnight?"

"Yes, but ask Darren and Nicole, first."

I asked him to stay over because I would worry about him staying by himself tonight feeling as he does.

I went over to pick him up. He packed his toothbrush, toothpaste, shorts for hiking and put his pills in his backpack. Then he shaved without putting the light on in the bathroom. He doesn't want me to put the light on in his living room either. He uses colourful mini Christmas lights strung on the floor, alongside the bed, to act as his night light.

Before I left, we had started watching a rented video starring Randy Quaid playing the role of a criminal. After an electrocution, he survives because lightning strikes the transformer. A psychiatrist analyzes him; he escapes and proves he has become a new personality.

Is there an underlying message in support of electro shock therapy?

Anyway, Nicole didn't think it was a video to watch with Edward. So they finished watching it while I was picking up Edward. When I came back with Edward, we all watched *Austin Powers* hoping it would brighten his mood.

August 28, 1999 **211**

A Gift of Grace

August 30, 1999

Edward, age 22, Calgary

Nicole and I met with Mabel Nelback, Clinical Nurse Specialist, of the Early Psychosis Program at the Foothills Hospital in Calgary, Alberta. She gave us forms to fill out about how we are feeling (that is, our well-being) in relation to fulfilling the caregiver role for Edward. She answered our questions about getting financial assistance. Apparently it takes about three months to get set up for receiving AISH and the amount will be $800. On the other hand, Welfare Assistance would be $400.

Mabel suggested that he apply for Blue Cross. His medication is provided to him through the clinic right now, but it will become more expensive with an increase in dosage. Then we'll probably have to pay for prescriptions.

We asked about jobs. Mabel said they don't push patients to get jobs until they are on full medication. Nicole and I told her he needs to work to help pay rent and maintain some self-esteem. Last month when Frank and I were down, we took him to the bank to deposit the cash he got from Toxin. He was $10 to $15 short for his rent. I gave him $40.

He had then commented, "I feel proud of myself in a twisted sort of way."

I was also concerned about how he would spend his daytime hours. Mabel said there is a program to help patients fill their day, but it is most unlikely that it would be suitable for Edward. We noticed a poetry club and art group posted on the bulletin board in the hospital. Maybe Edward could join one of those.

We agreed that a half-time job and a course at Viscount Bennett would probably appeal to Edward's intelligence and sense of purpose.

We asked about hospitalization to help monitor his medication but Mabel didn't recommend it. She says it's for chronic patients

A Gift of Grace

and would be depressing for him. She spoke very highly of the clinic at Special Services, Foothills Hospital.

We informed her of the Letter of Consent Edward signed for the release of medical information and the treatment plan to his family. I asked about the results of psychotherapy and effects of the medication. Apparently, some personality traits we don't like may disappear or at least become less annoying.

Psychotherapy and meds will improve Edward's ability to make better decisions concerning his life style. Yippee!

We asked about a medical and Dr. Belmont said he would arrange to have one for Edward. We think it's important that he have a thorough check-up so we can all know his health status. This would include an HIV test.

He has expressed apprehension about whether or not he has contracted HIV. It is something I worry about as well. Mental illness is enough of a life sentence without the added dangers of HIV.

Mabel gave us sheets of information and a video (20 minutes) to view and return. I purchased a book, *Living and Working with Schizophrenia* by J.J. Jeffries.

Mabel commented positively about his recovery to a functional state, "After all," she said, "his psychoses, positive and negative, have only shown up in the last five years or so."

I wonder though if the episode with the biker sexual assault was not a lie but a delusion. I also wonder about his lack of interest in playing the piano. We had never had to encourage him to play, but I recall the year he was in grade ten and performing at the Musical Festival in Lloydminster. He was not being his usual enthusiastic self about playing.

That year he was smoking some marijuana with a friend who had just moved to Czar. Frank was working in Slave Lake and I was commuting to Provost to teach. I was concerned about his safety that whole school year. Now I am beginning to believe it probably was more than just pot and adolescence.

August 30, 1999 **213**

August 31, 1999

Edward, age 22, Calgary

Edward and I agreed that I would phone him at 9:00 a.m. and then I'd go over about 10:00 a.m. Nicole woke me at 8:00 a.m. and I showered and carried my things out to the car because I would be going home today after supper. I drove over to Edward's and bought a coffee at Mac's near his place. I spoke to the wife of the owner about Edward's bike and she told the same story as her husband.

I knocked on Edward's door and he let me in. He still had his mini Christmas lights on strung along the floor beside this bed. I thought he uses them as a night light, although it seems he has them on every time I'm over whether it's dark out or the middle of the day. He shaved in the dark on Sunday night at 11:30 p.m.

I ask him about it. He says he is opposed to having the room lights on because there is too much going on when the lights are on. He claims he can focus better with the lights off.

We met Mar for lunch at Moxie's. We talked a lot. Edward expressed an interest in playing the piano again and taking the seven courses he would have left to complete his ARCT (Alberta Royal Conservatory Teaching Certificate). Mar said he could possibly practice on the piano in her school. This sounded great!

I do know he needs a part-time job to help him feel as if he is contributing to his rent and other expenses. Nicole is taking him tomorrow to a place where he can copy resumes free – fifteen per day! There is career counselling at that place and two hundred jobs listed on the bulletin board. The program has been set up for youth from fifteen to twenty-four years of age. Generous Auntie Mar lent her Walkman to Edward.

After lunch, Edward and I took a bus downtown so I didn't have to look for parking. I bought some cologne and a watch for him, then some perfume for me.

Oh, oh! I bought another watch for him!

Then we decided to walk to the Safeway on Eighth Street. After that we took a taxi to his apartment.

While riding in the taxi, Edward asked me, "Do you think I should be taking anti-depressants?"

This took me off guard and I guess because of the look on my face, he asked, "Why are you scowling?"

"Oh, you just took me by surprise! "

God! I don't mean to be scowling. Is he depressed now? Will he need to take both anti-psychotic meds and anti-depressants?

Somehow, I got out of that one without causing him to become defensive and irritated. Maybe the pills he's been taking are actually starting to kick in. He's becoming reflective and more aware of his moods.

We drove over to get some groceries. When we got back, I put them away and I fried some stuffed tenderloin while Edward did his laundry. Together we prepared stir-fry with sauce, all in the same electric fry pan. It was delicious. When we were eating, he said that since he has started taking his medication, his thoughts are more logical.

I nearly flipped! This is what we have wanted to hear for such a long time!!!

He said he was sorry for telling me so much stuff that was going on in his life. I forgave him and told him it was okay, because he needed to tell someone and it may as well be me.

He announced, "I fucked up!"

A Gift of Grace

"Yup!" I said, "You did! But... by taking your medicine, you will be able to make more realistic and healthier choices."

"I feel sorry for you. Auntie Mar has Blaine and he's doing well."

"Don't get hung up with guilty feelings of the past. Dad and I understand that you are trying your best to live a healthier lifestyle."

I think Frank needs to come and stay at his sister Nora's and visit Edward once in a while. They need to break the communication barrier that cements their inability to talk. I'm confident that they will find it easier to converse once Edward is on the proper dosage for his illness.

After supper he went to Mac's and bought a black comb. I cut his hair with the scissors and trimmed his neck with the razor. I always cut his hair when he was at home. He wore it longer in winter but as soon as summer came I put the small attachment on the clipper and shaved his head. I am happy to be cutting his hair for him again.

When Nicole came over to say goodbye, she exclaimed, "Mom, you should feel really good about what we've done for Edward this summer!"

Nicole makes me so happy!

"I appreciate your willingness to be so involved and so persistent in getting the best care for Edward."

December 2, 1999

Edward, age 23, Calgary

After I left Calgary in the summer, Edward went into the three-year Early Psychosis Program for the treatment of patients with a mental illness at Foothills Hospital. I went back to teaching in Provost in September. Nicole is his primary liaison on behalf of his parents.

With the long days in the hospital, he was wondering what he was going to do with all his time. Nicole brought him some large poster paper and Mr. Sketch markers. He loved this. He drew and posted his artwork all over his room, as well as in the hallway.

Edward was released on November 30. I hope it was a long enough time, but I doubt it. We will just have to wait and see.

2000

May 6, 2000

Edward, age 23, Calgary

On February 28 this year, Shari, my sister died at age 58. We called her "Big Shari-Lee" because she was the oldest and like a second mom to my brothers, my younger sister and me. She died in the same month as Dad, ten years apart.

Her death was unexpected, but it was hard to take time to grieve. We still had matters of concern with Edward. After three months Edward was released from the inpatient Early Psychosis Program at the end of last November. This was unsettling because we knew that he hadn't been hospitalized long enough for him to be stable and responsible for taking his meds and not the street drugs.

When we asked the social worker regarding the possibility of psychotherapy for Edward, she said, "We do not do psychotherapy with people who have schizophrenia."

We were quite surprised.

He was supposed go to Foothills on a regular basis as an out-patient to monitor his progress, but he didn't always show up. Where was he? He seemed to disappear from Calgary for awhile. We found out later he had gone to a gay event called "White Party" in Palm Springs, California during Spring Break.

May 30, 2000

Edward, age 23, Calgary

When he returned, Nicole phoned to report that Edward is not doing well.

She didn't go into detail but she said, "Mom, he is acting so crazy and I'm afraid of what he will do next. We need to get him into the hospital!"

"I know, but how can we do that when he refuses to go voluntarily?"

"I found out I can apply to a judge to get a warrant for his arrest, but you need to write a letter telling all his issues and reasons for wanting him hospitalized."

Nicole says, "This letter must be hand delivered to the judge, before we can have Edward committed to the hospital. It has to state he is at risk of injuring himself or others, before it will be considered for involuntary admittance."

It wasn't something we wanted to do, but we felt it was necessary in order to help Edward.

"OK, Dad and I will do that."

"OK, Mom, but do it quickly."

We wrote the letter and Nicole hand-delivered it to the judge.

A Gift of Grace

June 19, 2000

Edward, age 23, Calgary

Based on our letter, Edward was admitted to hospital on May 24, 2000 and a Notification of Certification (Edward certified insane) was issued with an expiry date of June 24, 2000.

One month, then what?

This past year, Nicole had chosen a university course, because of her interest in understanding her brother's brain disease. She had this interview as part of her assignment. While he was in hospital, Nicole asked questions and wrote down the answers her brother gave to the following questions:

1. What were your feelings when Mom and Dad suggested that you phone and make an appointment with the Mental Health Centre?
   I wasn't and am not afraid to talk about my experience. I had no problem going to the Mental Health Centre.

2. At what point did you realize that the medicine was helping you?
   The medicine's effects were fairly immediate. At first I was tired and groggy, but gradually "tuned" in my awareness to everyday tasks.

3. List all the symptoms of schizophrenia that you think you have.
   Classic symptoms would include hallucinations (even though I know they exist) both auditory and visual.

4. Since schizophrenia does not have a cure, are you convinced that it is important to take your medicine every day?
   If there is no cure... how would you know that this particular medicine is what has made me make progress with my life? I agree to take the medicine only because if it doesn't affect

me it doesn't hurt to try I guess. Neuroleptic straight-jackets come to mind but aren't necessarily the case. I don't like to analyze my mind anymore, since people seem to think that there is something wrong with what I think.

5. Did you at any time wonder if there was something "wrong" with your thoughts?
No, but recognizing that other people might find them so. Bright minds find opposition from mediocre spirits (whatever).

6. Do you accept the fact that you have a mental illness?
Not really.

7. Do you feel loved by your family? (Because you are…)
More now than in the past.

8. Who do you care about today?
Everyone.

9. Describe your thoughts while you were in Toronto.
Which thoughts in particular? I could write a book.

10. Describe your thoughts now.
I could write another book.

11. If you were to describe your mind/brain metaphorically, what analogy would you use? Explain.
A star.

12. What are some of the major stresses in your life?
Money, money, money.

13. Have you accepted the diagnosis that you have schizophrenia?
Sure.

14. When you were off your medicine for that month a while ago, did you recognize a return of any thoughts of delusion, voices, messages, aliens, God and other such things?
Even taking the medicine my beliefs haven't changed. If anything they've gotten stronger. My faith had grown that's all. The medication if anything has slowed me down to function perhaps even on a placebo level so that I can do the things most people have to do to live.

A Gift of Grace

15. People with schizophrenia may experience the following: (Please describe these as they relate to you.)
    a. auditory hallucinations (voices that seem to be warning you, tempting to control you, or giving you messages)
        Too complex to describe.
    b. olfactory hallucinations (the ability to smell non-existent smells)
        No.
    c. visual hallucinations (see apparitions such as God, the devil, messages and such)
        All the time.
    d. persecutory delusions (convince you that you are the victim of organized plots by powerful adversaries)
        No.
    e. delusions of being controlled (generating unwelcome but uncontrollable thoughts)
        Not particularly.

16. Some day do you think you would volunteer to help other people deal with this treatable brain disorder?
    Treatable, but no cure… sounds like a human guinea pig to me. But apart from my thoughts on a global alien conspiracy concerning the production of pharmaceuticals for the purpose of cloning thoughts and behaviours in the masses… sure, the typical schizophrenic needs help. Usually these individuals are gifted and are unrecognized as such.

17. What goals have you set for your future in the
    a. Short term?
        Maintain my workout routine, keep my job, save money.
    b. Long term?
        Go back to school, pursue my art and music, and embrace love and light.

November 16, 2000

Edward, age 24, Claresholm

We were so disappointed over Edward's release from hospital after he had been admitted in May. When he was there he was safe, getting treatment and we all could live a normal life.

We learned about a facility called the Claresholm-Raymond Care Centre and it sounded like a good place for Edward to stay while getting used to taking his medication and living a healthy lifestyle.

We did the necessary phoning and arranged for an appointment to see if Edward would be accepted as a patient. We were actually worried Edward would be able to fool the doctor with "a smoke-screen of brilliance." (This was a phrase Nicole found in a book she read when she took her "brain course" at university and it definitely suited Edward.) So we wanted to be sure we were involved in the interview process.

We drove there one weekend and met for the intake interview involving Edward's medical history. Medical reports from Foothills Early Psychosis Program helped them with their decision to have Edward stay there. He was admitted on November 8 and is sharing a bedroom with someone else and sharing the entire living quarters with about four other people.

Edward is learning some life skills. He has to help plan the menu for meals and shop for the groceries for a week at a time. There are cleaning jobs to do as well. He also walks to a nearby business to help chop wood and stack the logs for small payment.

After he takes his meds for awhile, he starts thinking rationally about his escapades and gets depressed, "I'm twenty-five and I'm being left behind – all my UWC classmates have gone on to universities and fulfilled their dreams."

Edward has said to me several times during the periods when he most struggles with his psychosis and addictions, "Mom, I have to go through the dark before I can reach the light."

A Gift of Grace

"No Edward," I say, "You can live in the light. You don't have to go through all the dark stuff."

> *Maybe you haven't come to realize your life's purpose yet, Edward. You are still processing your past experiences to the level where you can let them go and move on to brighter days.*

December 16, 2000

Edward, age 24, Claresholm

Claresholm is a long way south from where we live. Last Friday, I insisted on seeing Edward and ended up driving through a blizzard on the south side of Brooks. The snow was beaten into the signs and I couldn't see where to turn. I sure didn't want to suddenly stop because I might get rear ended! I finally took a risk and turned off onto what looked like a safe place. I was lucky that it was a side road where I could safely wait out the storm. I stayed there for three hours crying and thinking how stupid I was to go out when a storm was brewing. I had panic attacks until the snow began to slow down and I could see the road. Then I drove the rest of the way and booked into a motel.

When I visited Edward, he didn't say much and I had a difficult time carrying on a conversation with him. I noticed that he didn't participate in many of the activities and wasn't at all interested in playing the piano in the common room.

I drove home wondering why I was crazy enough to go out in a storm and try to visit with someone who doesn't seem to care if I am there or not.

> *Back at the Middleton's, I loved listening to Edward play the piano in the small sewing room. He seemed to need to pound the keys at times and then at other times stroke them gently. With the windows open, his music would permeate the air, caressing the pink hollyhocks along the wall.*

I miss that right this minute and my throat constricts and tears fall. God, I miss him and I don't think he even cares enough to ponder my emotional state...

December 30, 2000

Edward, age 24, Calgary

While Edward was in the Claresholm-Raymond Care Centre, they realized he had a substance abuse problem. So they referred him to the AADAC, Lander Treatment Centre in Claresholm as an out-patient, while he was still an inpatient at the Care Centre.

We were called to a meeting on December 24th. We went and they suggested a guardianship arrangement for Edward because he could not be responsible on his own. We decided not to do that.

They told us he could come home for Christmas, but had to be returned on 29th so he could start the AADAC program on December 30th. So we took him home to Provost.

It was not much of a visit because Frank, Edward and I were all in a depressed state of mind. None of us talked much and we went robotically about our schedule. We returned him on the 29th.

2001

March 30, 2001

Edward, age 24, Claresholm

We received this progress report:

AADAC, LANDER TREATMENT CENTRE – PROGRESS REVIEW

Phase I:	March 10-22, 2001
Completed:	Yes
Name:	WEATHERLY, Ed
Referral:	Claresholm Care Centre

Substance Abuse History: Mr. Weatherly began using alcohol at 14, binging on the weekends. By 18, he felt he had a drinking problem, as he was drinking three to four times a week. Mr. Weatherly began using marijuana at 16, and felt he had a problem with it by 18 as he used it daily for extended periods. At 20, he began using cocaine, his drug of choice. He typically binged on crack cocaine and felt it became problematic within the last year. Mr. Weatherly has not had extended abstinence from any of the above substances, though he had not used any of them since his admission in a psychiatric care facility October 1, 2000. This was his first residential addiction treatment experience.

Motivation: Mr. Weatherly came to treatment to learn how to live without drugs. He also came because he wanted to be clean so he could determine how much of his schizophrenia was related to drug use, stating he felt his schizophrenia might have been drug-induced. He also wanted to find out why he uses drugs and to develop some other activities to do instead of use.

A Gift of Grace

High Risk Situations Identified: Cocaine: unpleasant emotions, urges/temptations, social pressure to use

Participation / Progress: Mr. Weatherly participated in all program aspects. Though his journals were brief, they often reflected a fairly deep understanding of himself and his issues, and in small group he was open and honest in discussing his issues, including his homosexuality. The main issue he addressed in treatment was the lack of acceptance he felt and how he had escaped this with heavy drug use and promiscuity. He stated that he felt abandoned by his father because he had not accepted him when he told him he was homosexual. He stated that his diagnosis of schizophrenia in the summer of 1999 had made him feel even more unaccepted, and that he struggled at times with feeling accepted anywhere outside a major metropolitan centre with a substantial "gay scene" (e.g. Toronto, Vancouver). Through treatment, he realized he could not rely on external sources for a sense of acceptance and that he had to learn to accept himself, as this was an important step in having a successful recovery as well as healthy self-esteem.

Regarding his high-risk situation of unpleasant emotions, he planned to stay with his feelings and analyze them for an understanding of where they were coming from, rather then repress them, or use drugs or sex to cover them. He also planned to express his feelings to someone close to him (e.g. his mother or any of three very close friends).

Regarding his high risk situation of urges/temptations and social pressure to use, he planned to avoid gay bars and the "underground scene" because of the ready availability of drugs there, and to begin developing networks of non-using peers who had mutual interests like art, music, and/or gay culture and politics.

He also planned to remind himself that urges to use, especially when having had used cocaine heavily, were normal, and that he had to "reach out" and talk to someone about them.

In summation, Mr. Weatherly developed some good relapse prevention plans that, if implemented diligently, will increase the likelihood of healthy recovery. To maximize this likelihood, he must continue to explore and work on low self-esteem and lack of acceptance, as well as work through his feelings (abandonment, resentment) around his father refusing to accept his sexuality.

March 30, 2001

A Gift of Grace

In addition, because of his history of poly-drug use, he must be very wary of substituting drugs (including alcohol) besides cocaine as his drug of choice.

Recommendations: The following recommendations were discussed with Mr. Weatherly:
- Continue to participate in the Claresholm Care Centre program until he is discharged. Mr. Weatherly planned to do this.
- Attend N.A. (Narcotics Anonymous) meetings regularly. Mr. Weatherly planned to do this.
- Return to this Centre to attend the Phase III program. Mr. Weatherly planned to do this if he was not working or if his workplace permitted him to take time off for treatment.

Name Withheld
Addictions Counsellor

June 12, 2001

Edward, age 24, Provost

In May I received phone calls from Edward that worried me as he felt things were going very badly for him in Claresholm. I urged him to stay in there another month because he was due to be released in June and then we would help him get his AISH application filled out, so he could get it reinstated.

Edward was released from the Claresholm-Raymond Care Centre as an inpatient on June 6th. They said he would receive injections of his medication as an outpatient and his next injection was to be June 19, but we had to get him back to Calgary for a follow-up appointment with Dr. Belmont at the Foothills on June 18th and then to see an AADAC Counsellor in Calgary during drop-in hours. It seemed pointless to take him back the next day to Claresholm, especially when he can receive his injections in Calgary. Besides he would probably live on the streets in Claresholm, if we left him there.

A Gift of Grace

I picked him up and brought him to Provost to await the visit with Dr. Belmont on June 18th. Just like last Christmas there is little communication. Sometimes to break the silence, I was tempted to ask, "What's on your mind?" I resisted the temptation because he felt I could already read his thoughts.

He would probably think since I already know what he is thinking, that I would be asking just to trip him up and see if he's going to lie to me now!

A Gift of Grace

Provost, Alberta
September 7, 2001

Dear Dr. Belmont,

Since Edward was released in June 2001, nothing much has changed. For a brief period of time, he appeared to be on track and focused on keeping his life in order. This was a façade. All the while he was attending a drug and alcohol rehab program he was using street drugs. We know that these negate the medication he gets for schizophrenia.

Edward is completely out of control again. He has recently quit his job, pawned all his valuables, and is talking of going to Toronto where he thinks he is being called to fulfill his life's work… which amounts to self-destructive activities. Also, even if he wanted to go back to work, his employer would not accept him. His roommates have given up on him. Unless things change, they want him to leave.

Edward is unable or unwilling to help himself, and we as his parents are continually hitting a dead end with The Alberta Health Act and its protectors. This hinders any really effective treatment plan. It is a sad case when the system that is designed to protect the individual aids in the patient's demise.

Please advise us. We are at our wit's end as to what to do next in order to help our son.

Sincerely,

Frank and *Bea Weatherly*

September 8, 2001

Edward, age 24, Calgary

Edward's life is once again spinning out of control. He no longer has an apartment to go to or any money. Through his friends Colleen and Susan (a lesbian couple) he got a job at the Elbow Casino where they work and he rented a basement room in the house where they live. I had really hoped it would work out for all concerned.

From talking to Nicole, we learned the situation is desperate. He quit his job or was fired. He is using street drugs instead of his prescription meds. His roommates could no longer have him there.

Nicole said she needed a letter so she could get a warrant for his arrest and take him to an intervention at Foothills Hospital.

We sent a letter to Nicole for her review. She responded as follows:

Mom and Dad,

The letter you sent for my input sounds good, but I edited it a bit. In my "professional" opinion this is how you play the game.

LETTER

We are Edward Weatherly's parents and support necessary measures to obtain the appropriate medical treatment for him. He is homosexual and has been diagnosed with schizophrenia.

During the last while, Nicole, Edward's sister who lives in Calgary, has observed an alarming change in his behaviour. After he walked out on his job at the Casino and was complaining of side effects, Edward's medication was reduced from 20 mg to 10mg. Also, Nicole received a message from Edward's roommates asking to speak to her privately about their concern for his welfare. They told Nicole that Edward has become delusional again, and

A Gift of Grace

they reported that Edward's behaviours involve obsessions of a sexual nature, involving promiscuity and drugs, as well as posting nude pictures on the Internet. This is disturbing news.

We believe Edward must be hospitalized. In addition to his positive and negative symptoms returning in full force, he has been engaging in self-destructive behaviour the entire time. Not only is he a danger to himself but he may also pose a health threat to others. We fear that he may have AIDS or contract AIDS in the near future through his promiscuity.

His drug abuse (ecstasy, cocaine and pretty much anything he can get his hands on) is complicating matters by interfering with the effects of his medicine and putting him at great risk. We feel he requires immediate attention to focus on regulating his medicine, getting him into a drug rehabilitation program and possibly intense therapy on lifestyle choices. Hospitalizing Edward would separate him from his dangerous lifestyle and outside influences so that we can help him get on the right track.

He has many more health concerns in addition to regulating his medicine for schizophrenia. The medicine alone will not help his other health concerns. Edward will most likely agree to take the increased dosage on Tuesday to avoid hospitalization, but in the meantime he will be involved in the same destructive behaviour as before. It will be a lot more difficult to help him with all of his immediate needs if he is not hospitalized. We fully support Edward being hospitalized, so that he can get the help he so desperately needs. We fear for his safety.

Edward is an intelligent person who has, in his past, done extremely well academically, musically and socially. He was very goal-oriented and achieved high standards in all activities he engaged in. He received many academic scholarships and music awards. Edward received his IB from the Armand Hammer United World College, New Mexico and attended the University of Toronto on a full scholarship. It was here that he became significantly delusional, and, after researching his symptoms on the Internet, we concluded that he had a mental illness and it appeared to be schizophrenia. We convinced him to return home and his family collaboratively worked to make appointments for him with Dr. Simpson and Dr. Belmont.

A Gift of Grace

We are hoping that you can initiate a treatment plan for Edward that would serve his individual needs. Should you require more background knowledge than what you have in his file, Nicole would be an excellent source of information.

His behaviour has a huge impact on his family, because we love him. Edward is seriously in need of your help so that he can have a chance of living a better life. Thank you very much for your professional assistance. Please let us know the status of his treatment plan.

Note: Edward can be extremely convincing to others that he is in control of his life, but he is very much out of control.

Sincerely,

Frank and *Bea Weatherly*

September 13, 2001

Edward, age 24, Calgary

Frank and I are feeling the stress on our relationship and I find it more and more difficult to communicate my opinions on how we should go about helping Edward. Frank decided he and Shelley, who was at home visiting, should drive to Calgary to be involved in an intervention planned with Dr. Belmont.

Edward's two roommates would be at their house and asked him to come over so they could talk. Nicole was to park down the street to see if Edward would come as requested. Edward was there and he was compliant. Nicole had the police come, handcuff him and take him to the Foothills Hospital. I know this was painful for her to see her brother handcuffed and taken away in a police car.

A Gift of Grace

> *I empathize for her feelings about our methods of getting him to the hospital. Would I have been strong enough to do what she did?*

I hadn't insisted on going in the morning. Frank said there were enough people involved and I didn't need to ask for another day off from teaching.

Then in the middle of the morning I had such a severe panic attack, I told my principal I was going to Calgary and he needed to get me a sub right away.

I took the Dodge Ram, picked up Mom at Hillcrest Lodge and started heading toward Calgary. We were on the outskirts of the city when it felt like the truck was having a flat tire. I slowed down and steered to the edge of the road. I got out and examined the wheel. Oh, my God! The wheel was at a forty-five degree angle and was nearly off the axle! I walked to the nearest business and phoned for a taxi to take us to the Foothills Hospital. The Dodge would have to wait until later.

We arrived when the intervention was almost finished and were not greeted with much warmth from my husband. He didn't need me. I was supposed to stay in Provost, but I just couldn't stay there when this meeting was occurring.

The outcome of the intervention is a bit of a blur, but everyone let Edward know the impact his actions had on them... and that he needed to stay clean... no drugs/alcohol... take his meds...

> *We love you Eddie; we want to help you. A round of hugs...*

September 16, 2001

Edward, age 24, Calgary

Edward was admitted to hospital right after the intervention there on the 13th. He was examined by two physicians at the Foothills Hospital:

September 15, 2001
Dr. Montab

Facts observed by physician

- Schizophrenic symptoms
- Paranoid-agitated
- Risk to self
- Form 8 sister (Nicole had submitted Form 8 to have him committed to the hospital again)
- Unwilling to stay as a patient

Facts communicated to physician by others

- Significant thought disorder
- Delusional
- Refusing to take meds

September 15, 2001
Dr. Seastone

Facts observed by physician

- Guarded
- Wants to leave hospital
- I am uncertain how he really views illness

Facts communicated to physician by others

- History of psychotic disorder with risky behaviour

November 1, 2001

Edward, age 24, Calgary

We wrote the following letter to the hospital.

To Whom It May Concern

We are very frustrated with the mental health system. Our son, Edward Weatherly, was hospitalized in May 2000 and again on September 13, 2001. I have been phoning once a day to speak with Ed's nurse and I get told he is a model patient and that he shows only minor delusions, that being Xs, 0s and 1s. Ed is intelligent and he is knowledgeable when it comes to manipulating people and reaching his goal – to get out and go to Toronto. He is capable of bluffing the staff and getting them to think he is well.

We know that he has been taking street drugs and this is greatly interfering with his medication, and consequently, this ability to think clearly about healthy choices. He has reverted back to thinking that he must return to Toronto, where he can dance (nude) for money and be a model for pornography. He is adamant that drugs, promiscuous sex and pornography are acceptable. He tells me that pornography is not illegal. So... does that make it okay? No, it does not.

Earlier, when he was medicated and away from street drugs, he expressed remorse for his past and called it his dark life. He thanked me over and over again for getting him out of Toronto. PLEASE, HELP HIM!!! Help us get him the treatment he so desperately needs. His family loves him dearly and it literally breaks our hearts to see him destroy his life from not getting the proper treatment. This treatment can't be a bandage for a short length of time, but a plan of action that would see Edward past his drug addiction, receiving therapy on a regular basis (instead of 15 minutes once every month or so) and then living in a supervised environment. This would allow him to fulfill some of the dreams he had when he was a youth.

He is presently getting sucked into modeling with a fellow by the name of Afton, a photographer.

Edward does not deny that he has recently smoked marijuana and cocaine. It showed up in his blood tests.

Edward is out of control, and needs assistance to get well. It is our belief that he requires hospitalization long enough to become rational, and get rid of his delusion that he is the Christ Child (Christian). Then, he must receive help to overcome his addiction to drugs. After that, we can help him locate a place to live where he would receive monitoring so that he can live a clean life. We love Edward, and need your help to get him the treatment he requires. When he is taking street drugs he is making some very irresponsible choices.

Sincerely,

Frank and *Bea Weatherly*

November 15, 2001

Edward, age 25, Calgary

Edward was still in the hospital on his birthday. To lift his spirits Nicole took one of his pieces of art and had it framed as his unique birthday present. While doing this act of kindness, she thought of silk-screening his artwork onto T-shirts. She had the concept of doing this as a business for Edward to be self-supporting and came up with the name IDEGO Multimedia.

We have not heard from the hospital and it still looks like they will soon release him back to the streets of Calgary to go god knows where!

2002

January 1, 2002

Edward, age 25, Calgary

Most people write their resolutions on the first day of the New Year. I am going to do the opposite. I am going to make a list of Edward's activities last year. My look back at 2001:

- Lived in Calgary
- Hustling for money for drugs
- Smoking crack, using dirty needle
- Frequenting gay "bathhouses"
- Living the street life
- Using shelters when he can
- Lining up at soup kitchens when he can
- Very depressed
- Having unprotected sex
- Fired from Elbow River Casino because of his addiction to drugs
- Arrested because he was delusional and his roommates, Colleen and Susan, were worried about him
- Pawned computer and DJ equipment to leave Calgary for Toronto,
- Ended up not leaving but buying crack with the money instead
- Very depressed

I hope 2002 will be much better for all of us.

February 21, 2002

Edward, age 25, Calgary

I took the black tux Edward got from the Prince of Cathay to school and my students cut it up to clothe their wire sculptures of Sir John A. MacDonald. A class of twenty-nine sculptures was displayed at the Teachers' Convention in Edmonton on February 15 and 16. It naturally followed the study of the book, *One Sir John Too Many.*

Edward is thankfully still in hospital. I want to bring him home to Provost when he is out, but Frank is adamant that cannot happen. I understand why he says this because of all the heartache Edward has put us all through.

Maybe I'll write an Open Book, sell it and make millions, and he'll feel some of the suffering I'm experiencing now when I recall the outright wasting he has done with my hard-earned money, my generous nature and uncondi-tional love which I have always shown toward him. Frank doesn't know the half of it in terms of money I have given Edward.

I have notes written on scraps of paper while engaging in telephone conversations with Edward and kept in secret... stashed all over the house... under the lining of my lingerie drawer, in folders in my work room, between old books where no one would accidentally come across them --- hiding what I wrote... but subconsciously needing to hang onto them...

This diary too is hidden because I have written things I do not want revealed to Edward's father. Many are secrets I am afraid to share with anyone. Maybe someday I will dare.

June 13, 2002

Edward, age 25, Calgary

On March 3rd, I moved from the acreage and rented a house in Provost. I finally had it. I had travelled by myself to Calgary the previous weekend and vowed not to return to the acreage. I realized I had not been happy for years and had repeated the mantra "I hate my life" over and over, until I was no longer in touch with "who am I?" I had made up my mind and I was determined to carry out my decision without letting outside influences deter me.

Frank can make me so angry at times. For example, I asked him last spring to get some old manure for my flower beds. He grumbled about it, but eventually did get some from our neighbours, who had already offered us some manure. He has made all the decisions about where we are to live and I have adjusted to the moves as best I could. Each time I had to start my garden all over again. Well, I didn't have to, but I do enjoy the feel of digging in the rich earth and planting seeds that later flourish.Then I feel such a sense of peace surrounded by beautiful flowers and such pride when I offer my family fresh vegetables from the garden.

It was difficult to leave because Frank was in poor physical and mental health. Both of us were depressed and hating our lives. Yet I always worked on our marriage. I did everything I could to have enjoyment together because I knew some day there would just be the two of us and I was tired of having separate existences. One day last fall we went to the Big Valley Jamboree in Camrose, Alberta and sat on the bleachers. We talked and enjoyed"elephant ears" and coffee. Why can't we do more things like this? Why do we each have to go our separate ways each day barely talking? Why do I have to be the one to start every conversation? Why do I continue to smile on the outside when inside there is so much pain?

It seemed my life was in compartments. One compartment is for teaching, which I love. Another compartment is for Edward and the drama that surrounds him. Still another one is for the girls.

A Gift of Grace

Then there's the compartment for our marriage. Every day I shut the door as I exit one compartment and open the door to the next. I thought this system was working for me, but I found out one day this spring to my surprise it had never really worked after all!

As Frank always says, "Get real!" My life as a whole wasn't real. I made one last ditch effort. I wrote a list of changes that we could make together to improve our relationship. I suggested counselling as well. He barely glanced at the list before he started yelling.

That was it! The breaking point! The camel... I packed a bag, got in the car and went to a hotel for the night. I went teaching the next day and then looked for rental units in Provost. I handed in my resignation for the end of the year. I have to move away because everyone knows Frank and everyone loves Frank, except perhaps me! To have any kind of a separate life, any new beginning, I have to move away.

I sewed cushions as a farewell gesture for all 31 students in my class. I cut the squares from old denim jeans. Then I cut the top parts from new material that had a print of the solar system. We had just finished a sky science unit. They are my last class in the regional school division and I want to leave them a legacy, a gift that I have made which they can use for star gazing, watching the rodeo, sitting at soccer or baseball games...

I just realized these were the things I had asked Frank to do with me. If you ask me now, who I love the most, I would say my children. My children... the biological ones and the classroom ones...

With Frank having no more say over my life, I brought Edward out to Provost to stay with me. I will be moving to Calgary and bringing him with me there as well. I can do what is best for me and my children now. And no more hiding my diary!

A Gift of Grace

July 16, 2002

Edward, age 25, Calgary

I taught in Provost until the end of June and then moved to Calgary. Nicole and Darren broke up this spring as well. Nicole did everything she could to make it work, but it was not to be. So she is renting the main floor of a house and I moved in with her. Now I have a small bedroom, three comforters as my bed and anxious about getting a job. But, I have a comfy pillow!

Nicole is determined to have Edward's artwork silk-screened onto T-shirts. This means we had to make important decisions about types, colours and sizes. She ordered the shirts and I helped finance the endeavour. We took many photos of the shirts.

Nicole stood on a chair in the driveway in the back yard while I moved the Bristol board until it would be a successful shot, without any glare from the sun. Later Nicole had the photos posted on a website she created for this venture.

Nicole and I take many brisk walks along the pathways of Edworthy Park discussing the impact of divorce and philosophizing about what the universe intends. We participate in support group meetings for families of addicts and learn other families have similar stories of frustration and heartache to share about their loved ones.

My sister, Marlene, helped me with the paperwork for getting me into the *Calgary Board of Education*. And, I had the laborious task of writing a resume, something I had never done before. It ended up being a great exercise for me because it forced me to gather supporting documents and memories which revealed how much I had accomplished with my students and how much I learned from my professional development workshops and conventions.

Marlene offered to take me out for dinner at a seafood restaurant the night before my interview with the representative from CBE Human Resources. We both ordered the pasta with fresh scallops. As a CBE administrator, she was going to give me some coaching on how to have a successful interview... I need employment! I am at risk of not getting hired, since I am at the top of the pay scale grid and I am new to the division. We enjoyed our dinner and I came away with her great coaching tips.

Later that evening I chatted with Nicole and it got late. At about ten to twelve I got sick to my stomach and started heaving!

"Don't worry; I've had it before... it's just food poisoning."

Somehow that wasn't that comforting.

She had an exam the next day, so she went off to bed.

"You'll just have to take your pillow with you into the bathroom and sleep there until you get over it! Good luck on your interview tomorrow..."

The next morning I felt tired and wired. The interview was scheduled for 10:00 a.m. Driving downtown to the office I was grappling with the thoughts of telling what I had experienced last night. I managed to do the appropriate thing and hold back – not sharing the drama!

Yippee! I am successfully screened for subbing with the CBE!

July 21, 2002

Edward, age 25, Calgary

I got into a discussion with Edward about his life. He can't stay with us because our living space is too small and we can't trust him to stay clean and sober.

I convinced him he needed to go with me to check out the services of Renfrew Treatment Centre. We found it is only a two-night, one-day facility for alcoholics to dry out, but they said it will help Edward, so I left him there. I am really running out of ideas for him to get his life on a healthy track.

> *I feel ashamed, angry and hopeless that I can't help him... help himself...*

We paid for a booth at a special event in Calgary called *SnowJam*. The event planners arrange to have a snowmaker come in and create some real snow for special events. Kids show off their unique skills on skateboards on the curved cement, while motocross enthusiasts travel up and down ramps, twisting and turning and thrilling the crowd.

Nicole had taken many of pieces of Edward's art and named them: Happiness, Audience, Control, My Self... She showed her ideas to Edward and he agreed her titles fit. Then she had the art and titles silk-screened onto T-shirts, hoodies and tees, all with the IDEGO logo.

So we take this opportunity to sell art T-shirts.

> *We will make a difference! This project will provide a healthy focus for Edward and a sense of purpose.*

A Gift of Grace

I brought Edward over to Nicole's to help us fold shirts and put tags on the garments. He promised to help us carry the boxes of shirts to the site and set up our booth the next day. I see this as a good thing; he will see that what we are doing is helpful to all of us.

I believe Edward will become more responsible with life choices after he realizes his life has a purpose. He does have a message to spread. It is BIG and IDEGO and Nicole's efforts will make this happen.

When it comes time for him to lend us a hand in the morning, he doesn't show up, so we make many trips carrying out boxes of shirts, getting caught up in the upbeat music blasting through the air. One of my nieces came out to help us sell T-shirts and hoodies. She is the perfect model for the clothes and attracts many people to our booth.

As they stop by, we explain the art that came from Edward's gift of a vision that is huge in spite of or maybe because of his mental illness. Many respond that they too have a loved one with a mental illness. Some confide they too have a mental illness. Other people share that they have been in the Early Psychosis Program at The Foothills Hospital in Calgary, just like Edward.

We explain how IDEGO will spread Edward's message – using time, energy, money and love to turn a negative into a positive... Edward is sad he never received his degree. He may not have his degree from a university, but his life is a degree in survival. Out of all he has been through, he will share his message through IDEGO.

He always said, "I have a message. I don't know what it is, but it is BIG. And someday I will do something. I don't know what it is, but it will be HUGE!"

Eddie, we now know your message and it is huge. It is hope, instead of despair. It is the unique art that you created through your special vision of the world. It is that "I am! I am good and worthwhile and out of my story others will feel they are worthwhile too."

We have a good day on Saturday sharing our story with people who show up at our booth. We love the excitement generated

A Gift of Grace

by kids coming by and enthusiastically checking out our T-shirts, tees and hoodies. We sold a thousand dollars worth of clothing. It starts raining just before it comes time for us to carry the boxes of shirts back to the car for overnight storage. It was made difficult by the rain, but we get the job done. Edward never did show up.

Where is he?

We get back home. We talk and share the progress of our day, but a dark cloud appears when we think about the whereabouts of Edward. I get sick to my stomach worrying about where he is and what he is doing. I have to find him and know he is safe. I implore Nicole to drive up and down 17th Avenue, so she gives in to me and waits in the car, while I go into the coffee shops showing Edward's photo. I get, "Nope! Haven't seen him!"

I can't sleep. Nicole and my niece can't sleep. We stayed up Saturday night talking and went to bed sometime around 2:00 a.m. Then at 3:30 a.m. the phone rang. It was a collect call from Edward.

"Sorry, Mom, I'm in Toronto."

"What!! How'd you get there?"

"I took the Greyhound bus."

He seems to have this recurring desire to go back to Toronto. Maybe supplying him with enough money to keep him off the streets of Calgary was what gave him the resources to buy a ticket. Then he was always receiving gifts from me and others that he would pawn for money for drugs. Not the time to worry about that now.

"Where are you?"

My stomach screams panic, but I remain calm, I am so thankful to hear his voice.

A Gift of Grace

"Standing outside at a phone booth."

I knew it wasn't productive to ask him for all the details of the "why." I just focused on the details of how we were going to get him back home.

"Do you see a hotel nearby?"

"Yes, there's a Holiday Inn."

That's good. He must be in a fairly good part of town.

"Go to the hotel, tell the manager your situation and them ask to use their phone to call me."

"Sorry, Mom. I panicked and had to leave."

Don't lose him...

"Edward, the important thing is that you phoned. Speak with the man at the desk and ask to use the phone... and call me... right away!"

"Hello, Mrs. Weatherly? Your son is here and has asked me to phone your number."

"Yes, thank you... please help me. Edward needs someone to look after him tonight. He is not well. I will give you my credit card information and I would appreciate it if you would use it to pay for a room for him, as well as provide him with something to eat. Also, he will need cash for a taxi ride to the airport tomorrow. Put all this on my card."

"Okay, Mrs. Weatherly. What time is his flight?"

"I haven't arranged that yet, but, if you give me your number, I will phone you as soon as I book it."

I called Travel Cuts and then informed the fellow at the Holiday Inn of the flight number and airline. I couldn't sleep. It took

July 21, 2002 **247**

A Gift of Grace

about two hours to figure everything out with his room, food, and taxi money. My stomach is a mess of nerves... but I am grateful. I think of my Dad as our guardian angel. Edward will be home in eight hours, I will pick him up at the airport and we'll talk. I am happy, things will be okay! I fall asleep on my comfy pillow.

At noon I left to pick him up, wondering what story he was going to tell me this time. We exchange grievances and agree to try to make things work out.

Edward tells me that he didn't want everyone looking at him in the booth and talking about him. He feels they will judge him by his illness. I know he doesn't like the word "psychotic" used by his psychologist. He is also uncomfortable with his new label, "schizophrenic." He definitely feels the stigma.

Why don't the professionals say he has psychosis or he has schizophrenia? Rather than he "is" these labels. I don't know if that would have made him feel better, but it sounds better to me.

I looked through the brochures at the support group office, hoping to find a facility for Edward. I came across a treatment centre for drug addiction and alcoholism called "Fresh Start" located on 68th Street. After checking this out, he agrees to stay and registers for a lengthy time period.

October 21, 2002

Edward, age 25, Calgary

Edward was doing well at Fresh Start. I visited him every day on my way home from teaching in the NW part of the city. But soon he was released with nowhere to go.

Now Nicole, Edward and I all share the same main floor of a house with only two bedrooms. It is cramped and inconvenient.

A Gift of Grace

Edward sleeps on the couch and we go to bed and get up earlier than him. As I walk by I keep asking him if he has taken his pills.

"Yes, Mom, I took my pills!" He shoves the vial a couple of inches from my face, "You think I'm crazy, don't you? Don't you?"

He is agitated.

"Yes, Edward, I think you're crazy. Take the pills," I said with a smile.

The chatterbox is going off in my head. Did I just use the word "crazy" -- how crazy is that? This is what I do in school; I use the word that is labelling to take its power away.

November 27, 2002

Edward, age 26, Calgary

One day before going to school I dropped Edward off at the Foothills Hospital. He was going to admit himself into the hospital, as he was having what he described as "disturbing thoughts." When I returned home after teaching he was in the house.

"I didn't get in. They don't feel I'm at risk enough to get a room in the hospital."

God, I know Edward doesn't "look" like a mentally distraught person but, if you chatted with him long enough, you would come to realize that his conversations are not going anywhere. You follow his line of thinking and then he gets off on another topic very easily and you don't realize you're on another topic until it hits you that he has completed a full circle. He uses these "big" words, some of which are in the dictionary, but others are a combination of words he has blended.

A Gift of Grace

While he was staying with us, often a discussion would turn sour, he would bolt and we wouldn't have any idea where he had gone. It was difficult living with all of us in the same house and he felt I was hovering over him. So he moved in with a friend renting in the basement of the house of an elderly couple. This seemed like it would work, so we moved his belongings over there!

We invited him over for Thanksgiving, but we didn't hear from him. We went over to his apartment and found him sleeping in the entryway. When we asked why he was sleeping there, he admitted he had used drugs and when he came back to get into the apartment, he couldn't find his key in his pocket. When he left earlier, he didn't lock the door, but his roommate must have. He had only had the apartment ten days, but Nicole and I were worried about the elderly couple being put at risk because of his irresponsible behaviour. So we told them a bit about our situation and proceeded with the task of moving him out!

So now Edward was staying with us again, sleeping on the sofa. He had something burning in his mind and wanted to tell me what it was.

"Will you go for a walk with me?"

I walked down the street with him and we hadn't gone a block when he confided that he had some of his photos put on the Internet. He was paranoid about what he had done.

"Yes, Edward, you made a mistake. Leave it in the past. You can't do anything about it now. They're out there. You aren't the only one that has done that! Learn from your mistakes! So, you made a mistake. Don't make the same mistake again! I love you."

One night we had another argument. I was prone to give in to Edward and Nicole was adamant about setting boundaries with him. She tried to get him to think reasonably and change his actions. He went for the door with both of us shouting after him in different ways of telling him what to do!

In the moment I was at my wit's end and shouted, "You can jolly well find somewhere else to sleep tonight!"

He stormed out the door.

*My upset stomach and overactive imagination wreak
havoc with me. I relive the worrying I've done over and
over in the past, about the consequences of his risky
behaviours and final curtain closing with dreaded dark
diseases and death.*

Nicole and I cried and argued. I was seething with anger and my
own feelings of hopelessness... what are we doing?!

Later he phoned and he was at some homeless shelter.

Thank you for phoning...

"He doesn't have a toothbrush or any razors."

It was 10:30 p.m. We were spent. I asked and Nicole agreed to
take the bag of toiletries to him.

Finally I heard her returning. I had been waiting. As she stepped
inside the door, she appeared with a tearstained face. She related
what transpired... she rang the doorbell... a man appeared and
she asked for Edward Weatherly. Edward came to the doorway
with a glassy stare. She couldn't help but notice the yellow blister
on his thumb, probably from cooking crack... I pictured this alley-
way drug transaction in full detail in my mind...

They exchanged greetings and Nicole handed him the bag.

"Thanks, Cole," They hugged.

"I love you, Ed."

"I love you, too." They hugged.

She cried all the way home. Not knowing if she will ever see him
again...

A Gift of Grace

December 10, 2002

Edward, age 26, Location: Not sure

Nicole must have been waiting for me to come home because as soon as I walked in the door, she asked, "Mom, do you want a glass of wine?"

"Sure."

"Do you want to sit in the red chair?"

"Sure."

I sit. She sits.

I sip. She sips.

"Mom..."

"Yes?"

Nicole has this big grin on her face. I have no idea what's up!

"I'm a lesbian."

"Really?"

"Yes, Mom."

"Okay."

We skål and sip, as we converse, and I sense a renewed contentment in this young lady.

This time, I guess, Edward paved the path for his big sister.

2003

March 6, 2003

Edward, age 26, Toronto

Edward is in Toronto again. He hitchhiked to Regina, phoned Galen for the money to take the Greyhound the rest of the way.

So in spite of all we did to help him or get him help, the latest being staying with Nicole and me, Edward ended up on the streets of Calgary and then abruptly left. Even though Galen helped him get to Toronto, Edward is living on the streets there according to his phone calls.

I get phone calls from Edward when he needs money. I send it by Money Mart and I don't ask him what it's for. I don't want to know. I have fleeting thoughts of wondering, but I don't want to know.

> *I put my head in the sand and don't voice my true feelings and opinions even to myself.*

I am teaching at school in NW Calgary. I teach my students to cultivate their "voice" in my Speech Masters lessons. I observe huge improvements in their development of self-esteem and confidence. They are a retreat from my reality with Edward.

July 20, 2003

Edward, age 26, Toronto

Shelley and Joe were married in June in a beautiful wedding ceremony in Calgary. Helping her with wedding plans, complete with chocolate fondue, was a bright light in my life. She has become such a confident young woman and I am so proud of her. She teaches in the school system in Cambridge Bay, Nunavut, where she met her husband. Joe is a pilot and has a passion for flying.

Edward was visibly absent at their wedding.

Nicole has her Chemical Engineering degree and her prized ring. I completed a year's teaching experience with the Calgary Board of Education. We shared a few glasses of wine...

Over the summer Nicole moved to Vancouver and put her engineering career on hold to begin working on a 3D-animated documentary about Edward's life and artwork.

IDEGO signed a contract with an animation company to begin the pre-production of the documentary.

Nicole has a passion for doing what she thinks needs to be done for her brother, as well as for other people and their families.

We empathize with the heartbreaking struggles of people with mental illness along with the multiple complications of alcohol and street drugs. It seems like something positive we can do now, while Edward is out-of-control and doing whatever he is doing in Toronto.

I have an orange bowl, spoon and ticket with the words and date: EDWARD WEATHERLY 14.03.03. I wonder if he needs it when he gets in line for the soup kitchen...

I am alone so I register for dance lessons with Alberta Dance Sport. I am in desperate need of a distraction.

September 23, 2003

Edward, age 26, Toronto

Edward is still in Toronto, lost somewhere in dreadful delusions. He refers to himself as a Digital Prophet. He tells me he has plans to write a Digital Requiem for lost souls. He seems to be obsessed with the "dark and the light." He talks about his name being Christian X and he is Binary Boy when he is creating/mixing music. He explains grandiose plans for the universe and its present take on gender.

He says that while watching TV, reading magazines or travelling in a car and encountering billboards, he sees 0s, Xs and 1s that are translated in his mind to be a code for him to interpret for the masses. I feel it was not a good idea to question him too much on this because that was his perception and reality, not mine. However, it is another sign for his family that he needs medical help.

As I take my head out of the sand, I conger images of Edward in psychosis partaking in activities of an unhealthy nature. I secretly hope he does not get infected... with the ultimate death sentence: HIV/AIDS. But how long can his guardian angel continue to stick with him?

Edward phones from what he says is an apartment complex where he says he lives and works. From his vague job description, I know in my heart of hearts, his "job" is one of self-destruction.

He tells me, "I have to do all the dark until I can get to the light."

I re-emphasize: "No, Edward, you do not! Just learn from your mistakes and begin a new day of doing things right!"

My mom (Grandma Kristina) says, "Everything comes out in the wash." I cry and cry, hoping and praying that he "comes out alive."

A Gift of Grace

He told me he didn't have bedclothes. I sent him the big blue and yellow flower printed comforter that I had when I slept on the futon at Nicole's. I sent the comforter because it once comforted me and I loved it... it had the colours of the flag of Sweden... my maternal grandmother's roots.

Edward has been drawn to Toronto over and over. When I quiz him about this he gives me an explanation that has to do with "feeling like he belongs there and is safe there."

But how can that be? Toronto is where he had bad experiences so I cannot fathom it possible to still feel akin to such a place!

I know he has told me before that there is a gay community there. Isn't there one here? One where he could find one safe, clean person to be with?

September 25, 2003

Edward, age 26, Toronto

I started reading Danielle Steele's book, *His Bright Light: The Story of Nick Traina,* a story she wrote about her son. His smile on the cover compelled me to purchase the book. I know she lost her son due to his mental illness, but can't bring myself to finish the last few chapters.

The shame of mental illness coupled with his manic depressive disorder had him spiralling out of control. At first she had a personal manager for him, but he was left alone for a short time. I don't want to read what happens then. I fear if I read it and something bad happens, I will worry it will happen in my life.

I can relate to her anxieties and fears about Nick, his personality and challenges. One of the factors is the social stigma over psychological disorders. Shame, embarrassment and a code of silence continue to be the norm. I will read the rest of her book when I feel Edward is safe.

October 12, 2003

Edward, age 26, Toronto

Edward tells me he lives in the Boys Apartment in Toronto. The description he gives sickens me. Young men living "free" with cameras on them day and night watching... Selling the images around the world for those into this sort of thing... what else could it be but pornography? Reality TV?

Edward says he has a rash that is getting worse and worse. I ask him if he has seen a doctor. He says not yet but he is going in for another test for HIV at the free clinic.

Now my stomach is queasy. How many times can I go through with the anxiety and stress of waiting for his phone call to tell me whether he has or hasn't contracted HIV? It is taking a toll.

Edward says he met a doctor from Texas and is going with him to the Black and Blue Festival in Montreal from October 8-14. He will call me when he is back in Toronto.

He says, "Mom, you would agree with the idea of the Black and Blue Festival. It celebrates that we are all different, but are all human beings. We can be ourselves no matter what race, religion, politics or sexual orientation."

I might agree with those ideals, but to me it seems like a great big party with any excuse to drink, take drugs, have sex... I have to not think about it.

I am trying to focus on my personal life and finding happiness. I have met someone and so I do not obsess over Edward so much.

October 24, 2003

Edward, age 26, Toronto

Edward called. He says he is back in Toronto. When he got back he was at "The Barn" and his friend Pedro saw the red spots on Edward and said, "Sweetheart, that's a sign of syphilis."

"Don't worry, Mom. I'm going to have it checked out at the same time I do my HIV test."

How many times can Edward "miss the bullet?"

He sent me a note:

HAPPY BIRTHDAY MOM!!!!!

I hope your brunch was fun with your friends this afternoon... you have a great day! I promise you'll get a handwritten letter from me... but the reason I'm writing now is because I love you and everything you have done for me in my life and continue to be a part of me. I have been too sick to really tell you how I truly appreciate you MOM and I'm sending you BIG HUGS and a big kiss from me right now. Happy Birthday and remember always that

I LOVE YOU

Eddie

November 12, 2003

Edward, age 27, Toronto

Edward was supposed to go to the clinic on his birthday to hear the results of his HIV test. He told me that he thinks it will be positive this time. So he didn't want to hear the news on his birthday.

He told me where he could pick up any money I might send him for his birthday. He says he is not feeling well.

"I think I am psychotic, Mom."

Oh if only that were it. The only problem…

"I can't stay in the Boys Apartment anymore. They won't let me stay with the rash."

So back to the streets!

He promised to phone me tonight. I am sick with worry.

November 13, 2003

Edward, age 27, Toronto

Edward phoned.

"Hi, Mom?'

"Yes, what is it?"

"I got a phone call and I'm positive…"

A Gift of Grace

"Of what?" I asked hoping for anything else but the inevitable.

"HIV."

Tears well up and flood my face... it has finally arrived. News that my son has HIV... I knew all along the news would come... I just didn't know when... well, today is that day.

"Do you know what you have to do now?"

"Yes. The people at the Mapleleaf Clinic are telling me what to do. They deal with HIV/AIDS patients all the time. They specialize."

Well at least there is a health team on his case.

Why am I feeling a sense of relief?

"Oh and by the way. The spots are syphilis" pause...

"Don't worry there is a cure for that. And Mom, I really need more money."

November 24, 2003

Edward, age 27, Toronto

Edward phoned. He was excited that he met a "spiritual sage," whose name was Glenn. Edward said he reminded him of Glenn Gould because of the gloves he wore.

Wearing gloves! Well, it is winter after all!

Edward explained Glenn's partner had HIV and so Glenn knew a lot about it. Glenn let Edward stay with him and Edward was

A Gift of Grace

painting artwork on his own leather shirt to wear to the Midnight Club.

Another phone call he tells me Glenn kicked him out.

The next phone call:

"Mom, guess what?"

OK, now what!

"What Edward?"

"I met a new friend. Her name is Beula Davenport."

"That's good, Edward."

"She's helping me get off the streets. I'm staying with her right now, but she is trying to get me into the Fred Victor Centre."

"What's that?"

"It's a place to stay. It's for the homeless to get off the street."

"That's very good."

Yes and we've been there before - homeless, then help, then homeless again. Endless cycle...

"Mom, Beula is a "Harm Reduction Worker. She's helping me get AISH and Ontario Disability. She really understands because she is an ex-junky."

Okay. Edward has schizophrenia, he has lived on the streets. Be thankful he is now with a friend, a Harm Reduction Worker, and he has a place to sleep.

"Oh Mom, can you send more money?"

November 24, 2003 **261**

2004

January 1, 2004

Edward, 27, Toronto

So here is my recap of Edward's activities in 2003:

- Committed to hospital
- Hitchhiked to Regina, phoned Galen for money to take the Greyhound to Toronto
- Tells me he has had visions of Hell
- Missed Shelley and Joe's wedding
- Childhood friend Alex died
- In Toronto with lots of partying
- Dancer at a strip club
- Hung out at shady nightclubs
- Drugs, drugs, drugs
- Sex, sex, sex
- Lived in Boys Apartment under a camera 24/7 to pay for his room; Unprotected sex
- Told in November that he is infected with HIV
- In a study with a health team in Toronto
- Diagnosed with syphilis, had to take penicillin
- Urgent to cure syphilis before deal with HIV
- Hearing loss probably due to syphilis
- Went to Fred Victor Centre
- A junkie who partied with him in underground, now is Harm Reduction Worker, let him room with her, helped him with AISH, to get off streets and got him on Ontario Disability
- Tells me he has nightmares, is overwhelmed and feels out of control
- Waiting for someone to lock him up to protect himself from himself
- Making graffiti in alley ways,
- DJ in underground; psychosis out of control

June 6, 2004

Edward, age 27, Toronto

Edward is phoning me regularly now from Toronto, with requests for money. I send hundreds of dollars at a time through the services of Money Mart in Crowfoot Landing.

This is too easy... I'm thinking it's not the right thing to do, but I am at a loss of what to really do to make any difference...

Edward phones and tells me that he has met someone special "Damon" and he is excited about this news. The two of them helped one another "get off the street" he said and they are sharing an apartment that has a loft. Damon too has HIV.

Damon's dad has helped them with renting a piano and Edward is happily drawing his artwork on huge pieces of canvas.

Edward made arrangements to have his artwork on display in an art gallery called Gallery X in Toronto. He mails me several cards advertising the show on February 23 to March 26, 2004, with the reception on Thursday, March 4th from 6-8 p.m.

Shelley and Joe are in Montreal now. They bought a house there. She says she will be able to check up on Edward from time to time.

Edward and Damon are planning a reunion to bring me, Shelley, and Auntie Mar... to Toronto... or rather we bring ourselves, but all congregate...

A Gift of Grace

Sent: Monday, July 26, 2004 10:11 AM
Edward, age 27, Toronto

Subject: MESSAGE FROM EDDIE

HI MOM!!!!!

It's Monday and I'm using one of the computers at the ACT library (free)...

I told you I'd write you so here I am finally writing you an email... a lot cheaper than collect phone calls I know!!!! Anyhow thank you again for the $ you sent me last week... really helped us out a lot!!!! I have been looking after myself and can't wait till you come and visit me here in Toronto!!!! We're thinking of having a dinner for all of us – You, Auntie Mar, Shelley, Damon and Me at our place... French cuisine maybe...??? some wine... music and maybe hopefully a piano concert for après dinner!!!

I don't know when exactly you are coming to Toronto... the 10th or which day I can't remember, if you said or not, all I know is that it's in the morning I think??? Damon and I went to Long and McQuade (a music store) and checked out pianos to rent or rent to own and they are very nice... Would be awesome to be able to start practicing at home again as it has been too long and I've always wanted to be able to do that????? We possibly can rent a computer as well from the same store as it turned out Damon's friend from university works there now and can get us a discount deal...

Anyhow I can't wait till you come to see me, so much has happened and most importantly I MISS YOU!!!! Maybe you guys can look on the Internet as to what you would like to do or see or whatever when u are here... welcome to stay at our place if you want to we'll just make room for sleeping arrangements if you want... but probably you would get a hotel room but you don't have to... I'll call you this week about what we find out about pianos and stuff... I'm thinking I could maybe take one course at U of T maybe... piano lessons maybe at the Royal Conservatory (since I'd have a piano at home to practice on) and maybe a modern dance class I've always wanted to do that... work on the computer at home... digital recording studio – Damon and I

A Gift of Grace

would work on our art digital and otherwise all at home... see how it goes anyhow...:)))

I'll call you maybe (Monday) or tomorrow ok???? I want to call Shelley but I can't find her number (don't tell her that please) only have her Montreal one... I want to talk to her about you all coming to Toronto!!!!!!

Have a great day Mom!

LOVE YOUR SON,

Eddie

August 20, 2004

Edward, age 27, Toronto

Marlene and I fly to Ottawa and then Shelley drives us to Toronto to visit Edward. We want to see firsthand how he is doing and where he is living.

Then we walk to the part of Toronto, Cabbagetown, where Edward lives. Some people say there were many Polish immigrants in the area at the turn of the century and they were so poor that they could only afford to eat cabbages planted in their yards. The characteristic smell of cabbage cooking is what gave the area its name.

Since Edward didn't have a phone, we had agreed before we left Alberta that he would wait outside his building at approximately the time that we would arrive and we would sit on a bench on the opposite side of the street and watch for him. It worked!!

It was great to see Edward and meet his friend. We walked up the stairs to the second floor. I noticed sparkles on the floor in the hallway. He showed us their apartment and the rented piano. On their mattress they had the comforter that I had mailed them.

August 20, 2004 **265**

A Gift of Grace

(He should have had the other one I had sent him before, but he says he "gave it away to a homeless person!") A trail of sparkles was glistening here and there and pretty much everywhere! Edward has a fascination for gluing sparkles on his artwork.

He showed us some of the posters he has gathered off the streets and is storing them under the stairs. We have a cup of tea and take a walk around the neighbourhood. The next day we went to visit Gallery X and took photos of us in the space where Edward had his show.

I took one minute clips of Edward playing the piano.

Edward took us to meet his health team and we all gathered in the office and were introduced to each member. I got an uneasy feeling when one of them said that Edward doesn't need his medication for schizophrenia because he is able to manage his symptoms. I disagree. But, I am comforted when we are in Dr. Paul Melon's office. He has an excellent manner in which he explains why Edward must take his medication.

He puts his hand on Ed's forearm, looks him in the eye and says emphatically, "Honey, just take the damn pills!"

We went out for lunch and dinner and enjoyed one another's company. Shelley, Mar and I planned to stay for three days and on the last day, we agreed that Edward is doing well.

On the way back to Calgary, I reflected on the activities of our visit. My gut feeling is that we weren't there long enough to truly assess how things were really going for Edward. So, I chatted with Shelley and Mar to see what they thought. They felt he is okay, but I experience anxiety thinking about his welfare, as I know he is smoking marijuana.

*I know as his mother that Edward needs to take his meds for schizophrenia so his mind becomes stable, take his medication for HIV so he doesn't get AIDS, AND **NOT** take any street drugs not even marijuana, if he is going to have a chance of some quality of life...*

A Gift of Grace

August 24, 2004

Edward, age 27, Toronto

I write the following letter to his doctor:

Dear Dr. Paul Melon,

Thank you so much for meeting with me last Wednesday, August 18. Our discussion gave me much confidence in you and your Health Care Team.

At our meeting with you on Thursday at 5:30, you explained to Ed, Damon and me about the importance of taking meds for schizophrenia to contain "stuff" to prevent him from spiralling, making unwise choices and risking the formation of new strains of the virus. You also explained the importance of taking meds for HIV on a regular basis, without recreational street drugs messing with his sensitive brain. Making healthy choices is paramount; in Ed's case it's his music and art.

The pharmacy in your building was closed when we left after the meeting, so the next day we stopped at the pharmacy in the local drugstore. Ed didn't have his card and they didn't have the drug available anyway. So, he went to the pharmacy at your building and they weren't able to dispense any loxapine because they had to get some in from somewhere else.

Some time has passed since our meeting. I am under the impression after talking with Edward on the phone last evening (Tuesday, Aug 23), that he is having some trepidation about taking meds for schizophrenia! At the beginning of the conversation he said he hasn't been able to get the prescription filled and then at the end he said that maybe he wouldn't have to take them, if he felt they were going to give him stress. (Actually, I thought they would act as a stress reliever.) The influence of marijuana is probably a factor. You said during our meeting that you would discuss this at another time with Damon and Ed, together/ separately.

August 24, 2004 **267**

A Gift of Grace

I guess the point of this message is twofold:

- Edward has not started taking his medication for his mental illness and this is holding up his start for taking HIV medication, if the plan is to have him somewhat stabilized on the schizophrenia meds before starting the HIV meds.

- Ed's CD4 count is low and viral count is high... this could get worse... Shouldn't he be starting his meds for HIV sooner rather than later? As you know, I am his mom and want the best chance for him...

Ed told me he has a meeting with Jordan (social worker) today; does he know that Ed has a prescription for loxapine? I ask this because Celine (infectious disease specialist) said during our family meeting, that Ed was managing his schizophrenia symptoms and wouldn't need to take medication.

Edward and Damon do not have a telephone yet and hope to have one by the end of the month... so that means we correspond when Ed phones collect (which happens at a pay phone. He says he doesn't like to discuss the real important issues because he is out on the street where he can be overheard. Or, I'm thinking it is his voices that are troubling him.)

Thank you again for your professional assistance and caring manner. I look forward to your response.

Yours truly,

Bea Weatherly

August 25, 2004

Edward, age 27, Toronto

I decided that I must visit Edward again to see what daily life is really like for him and Damon. Right away I book another flight to Toronto and plan to spend four days. School will be starting soon and I have to ease my mind about how he is living his life.

We agreed to watch for one another and this time I will be staying overnight at their place. So, I drag my teal blue suitcase for blocks. I'm headed for Cabbagetown walking from where I got off the shuttle bus, which transports people by making a loop, dropping them off at different hotels along the way. Then I sat on the bench across from his building. It was a beautiful sunny day. saw an elderly lady standing at the bus stop. Three young men were having a heated discussion and crossed the street after noticing the green light.

I was in the moment and enjoyed watching people. It gave me a sense of what it is like living in Cabbagetown. Then I spotted Edward at the pay phone. Quickly I crossed the street and he gave me one of his big smiles and a hug! He took my luggage and we went to his apartment and immediately made tea.

We spent the day checking out what they need to make things comfortable. We shopped in an "economical store" for a wastebasket, rubber gloves, and cleaning agents for serious scrubbing of bathroom and cupboards!

Making another trip to the store, we bought oranges, two jugs of milk, bread, butter, eggs, peanut butter, cheese, yogurt, Kraft Dinner, onions, perogies, and two packages of bacon.

We shopped for a table that would work in their small space and found the perfect table with two chairs that fit nicely in their apartment.

While Edward and Damon were out, I cleaned. I started with the bathroom. Sparkles clinging everywhere and I couldn't get rid of them!

August 26, 2004

Edward, age 27, Toronto

I get to know Damon better and he seems to be a very caring person. Edward made the futon (which is located at the bottom of the stairs) into a bed for me and I find it quite lumpy but it's okay. I am on a mission to find peace of mind with my son. Each night I write in my journal about the daily activities and my thoughts. Each day's entry gets more and more emotional. I find they both are smoking a lot of pot and drinking tea.

Damon buys and smokes pot under the pretence that the pot helps him deal with his HIV. Edward says he smokes it for the same reason... For a false sense of reality? So that it will kill the brain cells housing the negative thoughts of the past... or present?

Pot does not help Edward in any way; it messes with his brain and it screws up his mother.

But, hey, now his mother has bought into the idea of buying the illegal substance. I recognize that at this moment in time, rationalizing it as my theory of relativity, the young men "need" the pot. I notice they are both very edgy and unsettled.

So, we walked quite a few blocks to make the purchase. Standing outside a building, I gave Damon three twenties and then all three of us entered the building. Damon spoke with a man, but I couldn't hear what is being said. I knew Damon was receiving an earful. I surmised what's happening. So Edward and I left and walked down the street. Damon stormed out fuming! I had exchanged money with Damon outside a huge window with one way visibility.

"We're screwed! We can't buy any now because of you!"

Now they wouldn't sell him any pot because I was along and I might tell the powers that be. So Damon will no longer get to buy from these guys.

I swear!

All three of us walked down the street and turned off into a parking lot.

"Now you've jeopardized my health!"

"It isn't her fault!"

"I won't be able to buy from them and it isn't easy finding another place!"

"Screw you!"

"Fuck you!"

"Fuck you!!"

Damon and Edward continued to shout at one another. I was working hard at keeping my cool 'cause it wouldn't do any good if all three of us went berserk. Damon threw his keys at Edward and gave me back the sixty dollars. After they yelled back and forth, things started cooling down. I gave the money back to Damon, he went back and, some time later, he returned with the goods.

All's good in our reality.

We walked without talking back to the apartment. I put on the tea kettle, the guys rolled their joints. We walked out of the apartment, down the hallway, out onto the rooftop area to smoke, drink tea and reflect on the escapade: a reckless adventure or prank.

Oh! By the way, I have never smoked weed... as long as second-hand doesn't count...

A Gift of Grace

August 27, 2004

Edward, age 27, Toronto

Each night I stayed, it was Edward's habit to get up in the middle of the night and come down the stairs. He drank from the jug of milk in the fridge, stopped and sat on the edge of my bed before making his way up the stairs to his bedroom in the loft.

One night he had an extreme nightmare and asked, "Can I lie down with you, Mom?"

"Edward... not really!"I said. Then I added, "I love you, Edward..."

"I love you, too, Mom..."

We hugged and then he climbed the stairs... I wept and wept and wept...

This scenario brought the memories of numerous times in his childhood when he would experience a nightmare and come to my bedroom door to implore me to climb into bed with his dad and me.

So I would end up going to Edward's room to console him while he fell back to sleep, until Frank would yell at me, "This is ridiculous! Get back to bed!"

His father had boundaries.

But this night was the pivotal moment when I saw that Edward wasn't able to get well if he was smoking pot, taking his meds in a haphazard fashion and having wicked nightmares. I resolved to get him the heck out of Toronto.

One day, Damon spent time with his brother and I took this gift of time to have a talk with Edward. We went to a small café for a $2.99 breakfast where the shutters were open and we could watch passers-by.

A Gift of Grace

"Edward, how do you think you are doing here in Toronto?"

"Good."

"Well, Edward we need you now. Nicole has been working on the film for a while now and we really need to get it completed."

"How would I help?"

"If you went to Vancouver, you could support Nicole and her endeavour to complete the film."

"What would I do?"

"You would help our company a lot! You already play a big part... I think now is the time for you to become a concrete part of what is going on. Nicole needs you!"

"But what about Damon and me? What'll I tell him?"

"You'll know what to say when the time comes. Tell him the truth. Tell him how you really feel and not to hurt him. You are not well, Edward."

He seems relieved by what I am telling him.

"But his dad helped us rent the piano, for us... for me, mostly! What about all my stuff and my art?"

"Edward, you've done this before. Box it up and send it to Nicole's address, COD. I'll pay for it."

I hope to "get" Edward out of Toronto yet again, if I can convince him that he has an opportunity to help Nicole with IDEGO.

I trust that a closer relationship with Nicole will ensue and help them both...

August 27, 2004 **273**

A Gift of Grace

October 26, 2004

Edward, age 27, Toronto

Dear Mom,

Here I am finally writing you a proper letter out of my scrapbook that you bought me from home. I can't wait till Christmas hopefully I can come and see where you are living. It was great to have you here to see me and connect with who my health professionals are. It was so great for you and Shelley and Auntie Mar to meet everyone who has been working with me here in Toronto.

I apologize that this letter didn't get to you for your birthday, but just the same, I wish you a BIG HAPPY BIRTHDAY MOM!!! I really am excited about Christmas Holidays so we have to work out how I can come see you. I'm sending you a big 56th birthday Hug and Kiss from me and I hope you had a great day! It looks like my matters of health are finally allowing me to be "on track" again as I'm thinking clearer and feeling more in control of my life every new day. We (Damon and me) probably won't make it to California the days we thought because of our passports and identification for Damon as he needs ID from the US before we can apply for a passport. But I'm still going to apply for mine as well as another copy of my birth certificate (which I still have but it's probably good to have another one) and transfer my Driver's License from Alberta to Ontario. It's really too bad that Dad can't drive [he's now legally blind], but it sounds like Auntie Samantha [Frank's sister] wants him to move in with them – or at least be in a house they are building on their property so he can be as independent as possible.

I love you so much Mom and I am so happy to know that you have seen where I'm living and who I'm spending, well working on a relationship that is finally meant for me to become reality... I continue to keep my faith that all our times of trials and struggles with everything will allow us to be closer now more than ever before. Thank you for your continuing support of my being healthy as I know I can be and that means I can work with everyone on IDEGO's team and be an active member of our family.

I love you MOM!!!

Love,

Edward

2005

February 20, 2005

Edward, age 28, Vancouver

I just knew Edward couldn't live in Toronto anymore. That's why I convinced him that he needed to go to Vancouver and help Nicole with the film. He seemed relieved to leave Toronto.

Nicole orchestrated things in Vancouver so that Edward had a health team there to assist him in taking control of his health and well being. She knew it wouldn't be wise to have him live with her, since his life is so erratic and he needs to become more responsible for himself. She looked into a place suitable for him and found the age old, The Salvation Army. Edward's shelter is Harbour Light, a place for homeless people earnest about turning their lives around. He now has a place of residence in Vancouver! Also he has just completed a 12 week Addictions Rehabilitation Program at Salvation Army's Harbour Light and also the Harbour Light Defence.

On Family Day weekend I flew to visit Nicole and Edward in Vancouver. Nicole has an apartment overlooking Coal Harbour and Edward is at Harbour Light in East Vancouver. While I'm not allowed to visit him in his room, because of restrictions which help in monitoring the program, I am allowed to sit with him on the rooftop place of serenity... with permission for cigarettes only.

He got kicked out one time but spoke with the manager and got himself back in. While he was out, he slept overnight in a nearby shelter that lets homeless people stay one night at a time. This meant his life included eating his evening meal at Harbour Light and then making sure he was at the shelter in time to get a bed for him to sleep in.

Edward is facing consequences for his actions and advocating for himself. I am so proud of him for starting to take control of his life. We help him just enough, he helps himself and that helps me.... Life is great!

"Do you play the piano?"

He asks for the key from the Chaplain and invites me to sit in the pew in the chapel. He removes his ball cap and sets it on top of the piano, keeps his down filled coat on and sits on the stool. He begins to play Rachmaninoff's *Second Piano Concerto, 1st and 2nd Movement*, enveloping a stretch of time... a breath mint for my soul. Then some of his friends enter the room. One of them plays the guitar while Edward and two other men sing songs.

This is great! I love it!

Edward is ecstatic to inform me that I can help him in the soup kitchen at suppertime. He is the "head soup person" and I have been given the honour of serving the bowls of soup! I notice the focus on cleanliness and having a system of assembly to serve the people. Everyone has a specific job, and I can't help but notice that everyone also jokes around and has fun. Regular volunteers are scheduled to assist with the jobs.

I stand at my post and promptly, at five o'clock, I begin to see the line of men and women approaching the window. I serve each one a bowl of soup, feeling great to be helping and thrilled when they make eye contact and exchange a smile.

Then I left for Calgary and signed up for some dance lessons and a watercolour course at the University of Calgary. I am glad I can have me time again.

November 12, 2005

Edward, age 29, Vancouver

Shelley and Joe now have a beautiful baby girl, Madeleine. She is the delight of my life! I am so happy for them and I'm bursting with pride! I have a granddaughter!

She was born on Edward's birthday, November 10th...

How about that!

Madeleine is a welcome miracle of warm sunshine! She makes me happy when skies are grey...

2006

February 25, 2006

Edward, age 29, Vancouver

Last July, Edward went to the UWC reunion. I paid for his trip in the hopes it would inspire him. It obviously did because he wrote the following article, which was published in the February/March 2006 issue of UNITED WORLD COLLEGES.

The United World Colleges mission statement is "UWC makes education a force to unite people, nations and cultures for peace and a sustainable future".

UWC UTOPIAN DREAMS & UTOPIAN DELUSIONS
by Edward Kenneth Weatherly, UWC-USA Class of 1995

October 22, 2005   7:55 p.m.

Dear UWC Network,

Upon graduating in May 1995 from UWC-USA, in Montezuma, New Mexico, I not only left with my diploma, I left with a deep rooted set of ideals of peace, love and international understanding – and I was ready to do my part to help make the world a better place. Little did I know that my journey would be momentarily derailed by paranoid schizophrenia, a treatable brain disorder that affects 1% of the general population, changing my life forever.

I first began to descend into psychosis while attending Trinity College at the University of Toronto. I started to exhibit symptoms of schizophrenia that became visibly noticeable to my friends, but

A Gift of Grace

my delusions seamlessly entered my reality. I tried to hide the fact that I had started to sense that something was not quite right; however, at the same time, I was so convinced of my delusions that initially I resisted help from my friends and family.

I thought I was a "Digital Prophet" regularly decoding algorithms of 0's and 1's, which I found secretly embedded in various pop-culture multimedia. For example, while reading the advertising text on a poster, or billboard, I would convert the letter 'O' to the number '0' and the letter 'L' to the number '1', putting these digits together to make the number '10', which was the letter 'X' in Roman Numerals. I believed that this revelation of X's contained a top secret message that I was supposed to further decode and then spread to the masses. Although I failed to determine what this message was, I believed it was BIG.

The quest I was on, while in a state of altered reality, bridged me from mainstream society to the dark-side of underground gay subculture, in the heart of Toronto. My delusions and hallucinations got so out of control that I subsequently was unable to complete my studies at the University of Toronto. Instead, I proceeded to set up digital camp with a home recording studio to work on a multimedia project, fuelled by my psychosis. During this period, I was manically trying to fulfill my mission, spreading the message to the masses. Although I was excited about my new-found calling, I felt alone and scared a lot of the time, as my brain tried desperately to make sense of the overload of stimuli that gregariously paraded around me. Aliens continually communicated with me wherever I went, while echoes of my life-changing experience at UWC-USA still resonated within me.

Eventually, through the chaos of my psychosis, came my long sought after road to recovery. In 1999, I received a diagnosis, having paranoid schizophrenia and a chronic drug addiction. It has been a year now that I have been in recovery, living in Vancouver, British Columbia, and now living a healthy lifestyle, physically, mentally, spiritually and emotionally.

However, I am still on a BIG mission, except this time it is based on my new-found reality: I am determined to spread the message about the complexities of mental illness, addiction, homelessness, homosexuality and HIV through a 3D-animated documentary feature film based on my life and artwork.

A Gift of Grace

The documentary is being produced with the huge assistance of my sister, Nicole Weatherly, who has helped to lead the way for me to come back to health and reality. Together, with the help from the rest of our family, we created IDEGO Multimedia, a company whose mission is to promote awareness and understanding of diverse social issues, within the context of art.

This long road, since my time as a student at UWC-USA, has been a turbulent one to say the least. My experience at UWC has had a profoundly positive impact on my life. I am forever grateful for this opportunity, having formed incredible memories and having made life-long friendships. I am finally opening up about my life as a UWC graduate who has struggled with schizophrenia and other challenges, including addiction, homelessness, homosexuality and HIV, with the hope of helping other people who may be living in the pain of silence that too often hides these issues in secrecy and ignorance. There is hope.

I will always love you,

Edward Weatherly

Edward has told me more than once that it was a good thing he went to UWC in New Mexico. He was not sure where he would have ended up if he had not been accepted and had to take grade twelve in Provost. This was a turning point in his life and it certainly was one in my life as I attempted to let go of my son.

He is proud to be a UWC graduate and a part of its huge extended family. He hopes and prays that this message can create dialogue among UWC graduates or anyone whose heart has been affected by the baffling progression of psychosis caused from a mental illness such as his.

February 25, 2006

A Gift of Grace

March 14, 2006

Edward, age 29, Vancouver

I received a brief note from Edward, but not even his cheery tone can help me. Through thick and thin I seemed to carry on and carry loads for others. I survived breast cancer, a failed marriage, and the ups and downs of being there for Edward. Finally in 2003, I met the person I thought would be the love of my life. After two years with him, he suddenly dies. What more can I take!

Nothing it seems! I experienced a severe emotional meltdown. I applied for a sick leave from the Calgary Board of Education. I was granted one that will end after Spring Break.

> *There are times I am not even here for myself, much less for anyone else.*

April 20, 2006

Edward, age 29, Vancouver

I am back teaching. During my leave of absence Shelley came down for a week to help me. Her strength and wisdom buoyed me up when I most needed it.

And Madeleine! She came with her Mom. She is a spirited happy grandchild. A ray of sunshine that beamed right into my heart...

My daughter and granddaughter were here for me when I needed a lot of support. It was a precious week and whenever I'm down I will think of them. Especially Madeleine, the next generation of invincible women in our family...

May 19, 2006

Edward, age 29, Vancouver

I receive the following letter from Edward and I cry a flood of tears because my dream for him to manifest his complete recovery is starting to come true!

Dear Mom,

Well, it is late Monday night and I know it has been too long since I wrote you the letter that I promised. The last letter I wrote you was an amends letter and had a format similar to the letters I wrote to Shelley, Nicole, Dad and Aunty Mar. So, I will try and duplicate the essence of what I wrote to you but since you didn't get it in the mail last time I will try again.

Basically Mom, I am now taking responsibility for the actions of my past and am proactively leading my life in a way that honours me and those around me. I can only imagine the heartache I must have caused you over the years, full of worry and anxiety, and, now that I am having clarity in awareness of how I affect my loved ones, I recognize that I need to let you know just how deeply I love you – always have and always will unconditionally.

I am taking control of my new life by treating myself with respect and integrity and plan for big things in the future. Of course, living daily recovery is a major priority for me and each week as you know I go to at least three meetings for support with regards to my addictive side as well as the schizophrenia side of me.

I have done a lot of work to regain the direction I have in my life and I do not want to backtrack and go back to how I used to live. I want to go to school – maybe even university again at some point and save money and apply for student loans so I could pursue the goal. Forward is the direction I am going and plan to continue on that track and train/frame of mind.

A Gift of Grace

I want you to know Mom that I support you and your new life on your own as well. You have always been there for me and I will do my best to be there for you whenever you need me. I can't imagine the stress of what happened with you but I know you are strong and can make it through.

For all the love you have ever given me so selflessly and freely to me over the years, I will never be able to truly show you what a wonderful gift of life and love you have given me. I will now cherish myself and make choices that are in agreement with my true values and will show you respect and love in the process.

On this Mothers' Day, I want you to have this letter as a testament of my love for you. You are such an important part of my life and I will love you forever.

Love, your son,

Edward

December 28, 2006

Edward, age 30, Vancouver

Edward had been living in a group home with a treatment plan to support him in dealing with his addictions of drugs and alcohol. I visited him in Surrey during the Thanksgiving weekend and found his demeanour very depressed. He would hardly carry on a conversation with me. It was difficult for me to really assess the condition of his health. I knew he was seeing his psychiatrist and filling the prescriptions for Risperdal and taking the meds. His lack of emotion told me that. However, this lack of facial expression and lack of speech also failed to signal how he was truly feeling.

Just as Edward used a black Mr. Sketch to draw throughout magazines about seven years ago, well, he did the same thing this year with a book he purchased for my birthday. He told me that he was going to mail me a special book written by Madonna Ritchie entitled, *Mr. Peabody's Apples*. Then he sent it Express Post.

A Gift of Grace

The story is about a great teacher who dedicates his life to helping others and stressed the value and importance of love for all people. Madonna dedicated the book to teachers everywhere and that is probably one of the reasons why Edward bought it for me. Only, it is impossible to read because it has black marker pretty much over all the words, allowing only a young boy to peek through! Maybe the young boy is Eddie!

I moved and lived in a condo until this month when I purchased a house. I liked the photo in the paper and when I viewed it with the realtor; I walked through the yard first. It is so inviting, even in winter! It seems as though the yard is full of perennials and many of them are roses. The deck is smallish and overlooks a garden of promise. Maybe I've been promised a rose garden! I love my life!

Christmas was coming and Shelley and Madeleine were coming! That gave me reason to prepare for a happy holiday. Nicole is in Calgary and Edward was coming from Surrey. He will need a return ticket and I will pay for it.

Imagine… all three of my kids together at Christmastime! And, my granddaughter… this is too good to be true. I invited some of our extended family to join us.

We enjoyed one another's company, but when it came time for Edward to fly back to Surrey, he became sad.

"I know we agreed that I would fly back to Surrey, but I don't want to."

"You have a good program there, Edward, and you can look forward to moving into the new Phoenix Facility."

"Yeah, I guess. I will have my own room there."

He saw his niece, Madeleine for the first time. The kids and I hadn't spent Christmas together for many years. And, now he was flying back to B.C.

The house felt cold and empty when all the bright lights of my life left.

2007

January 3, 2007

Edward, age 30, Vancouver

Edward and I had agreed that he would fly to Calgary, spend Christmas with us and then fly back to Surrey.

"I may want to just stay and live with you, Mom."

The girls didn't think that was prudent since Edward's track record wasn't good.

"He will screw up and place an emotional burden on you," says Shelley.

"Yes, and then Mom will go crazy again," says Nicole.

After Christmas, Edward flew back to Surrey. I phoned him and we had a "heart to heart."

"What will Nicole and Shelley say?"

"It is between you and me, Edward. Can we live together?"

"Yes, I think we can. I would love to live with you... and I am house trained now!"

I chuckle...

"I'm finding it sometimes difficult living with eight Alpha males and having to be 'on guard'."

I remember him telling me that once a week they take all the food out of the deep freeze, clean it and put the food back

A Gift of Grace

inside. They share bathroom and kitchen duties and everyone does their own laundry.

His meds make him quite drowsy and the guys aren't allowed to sleep during the day, and definitely not on the sofa. If they are found sleeping on the couch, they get a "Pick a Day," which means they have to pick the day that they will do everyone else's chores!

I went to a few of his self-help meetings in Surrey. The walk was not that far but the facility was a room full of what appeared to be straight men and women with varying lengths of sobriety. Their stories helped me further understand where Edward had been and was now beating the odds in his journey toward a clean life. Edward appreciated the counselling he received from the Resident Manager of the treatment facility. However, he wished he could have permission to attend a gay self-help meeting. The manager thought it was contrary to the premise of their organization.

"I need to know that you will find a place to attend support meetings and stay clean or my mental health will suffer and you won't be allowed to live with me... and that would break my heart."

"I promise, Mom."

Edward made all the necessary arrangements to have his health records sent to Calgary and I booked and paid for his one way airline ticket home to me.

A Gift of Grace

September 27, 2007

Edward, age 30, Calgary

Edward moved to Calgary to live with me on January 6, 2007. He has been living with me since then and is doing very well. He has independently looked after all his health needs, appointments with health professionals and all the other things he needs.

After living here for three months, he wrote up a resume and while I was at work teaching, walked to the shopping centre and delivered his resume to a few businesses. A day later he was elated to inform me that he got a job working from 7:00 a.m. to 2:00 p.m., Monday to Friday at a store in the nearby mall.

A month and a half later, however, he announced that he had requested part time, and his manager agreed. So now he will be working Mondays, Wednesdays and Fridays. He shares with me his reason.

"People are talking about me."

"What people?"

"My voices are telling me I am no good."

"Oh Edward, just let all those 'nigglies' go. If you are going to make up stories you may as well make up the good ones."

"Yes, Mom, that is what I am doing. Since I have come to live with you, my voices are quieter. I am not so afraid of everything. I don't always feel like someone is going to hurt me."

"Why are you such an angel, Mom?"

I think my Dad has been around to guide me and guard Edward. He was generous with his time and money and offered a helping hand where needed.

A Gift of Grace

I am reminded of and comforted by the words of Abraham Lincoln, "All that I am or hope to be, I owe to my angel mother..."

We often pick up a "large, double, double" at Tim Horton's and I drop him off at work. I remind him not to listen to the negative voices today. After work he walks home. He now has the freedom to have a snooze before helping the neighbours or meeting with a friend for coffee.

Edward now is thoughtful and remembers the birthdays of family members. He vacuums, does the dishes and his own laundry. He helps two widows with mowing the lawn and shovelling snow, as well as ours. His assistance is greatly appreciated.

Wow!

I have been driving him to most of his meetings on Tuesday, Thursday and Saturday each week. They are held at a church. He says this group of gay and lesbians is about the only group in Calgary where he feels comfortable as a young gay man.

I find this disconcerting that he must struggle to find acceptance in society. His schizophrenia causes him to be paranoid about what other people in public places might be saying about him and society isn't completely in tune with the essence of his being.

The fact that he chooses to live the life he is designed for – that of a gay person – means that it is difficult to socialize freely in Calgary, Alberta. Because he is treasuring his sobriety, it is not an option to hang out at any of the very few gay bars in the city.

I am happy that he chooses to live his truth, not a lie.

I give hugs and Edward asks for hugs. We both are grateful for one another's understanding and support.

September 27, 2007

A Gift of Grace

I was googling on the net for a group of people with whom I would feel comfortable networking. Meetups jumped up and one in particular caught my attention. I had been telling people I was going to write a book some day because I had stories in me that were being "paged." Only, the truth is, I was searching to boost my home business and widen my vision for contacts and leads.

Well, I clicked on *Writing* and found a group called, "Calgary Writers' Meetup." The website seemed like this was the group that was supposed to appear at this time in my life. It offered what I needed – an outlet for sharing my life's experiences and a deadline for writing and publishing a book! And, yes! I will have money to reach my goals. I will travel and help my kids finish producing our documentary.

Today I regard myself as a writer. I never did before. I know I have experiences to share and an inner strength and spirit to become a role model for others. Also, I know I'll get started with paper, pencil and eraser.

At the end of August I attended my first meeting and dared to invest in my writing skills; I believe I have a story.

In the past, Edward would write me letters that would be more than letters. Really they were essays. I encourage him to write now. We agree it's a miracle he has overcome so much adversity and express our gratitude often.

One time when I visited Edward in Toronto he led me down the back alleys and showed me his graffiti. Then he took me out onto the busy street again, grabbed my hand and guided me to an exclusive jewellery store. There were guards outside. Edward asked the lady to unlock the compartments and take out extremely expensive pieces of jewellery to try on.

I was uncomfortable because we had no need to be in a store that expensive. Now I can't wait for the day we can go in and he can buy me fine jewellery.

2008

February 18, 2008

Edward, age 31, Calgary

Today is Family Day. February 18! 18 years ago was the first Family Day. 18 years since my father passed away, but this Family Day is one not to mourn but rejoice! My Dad is looking down on us and celebrating our success.

This year is going to be the greatest!

I have begun to put together my book and it will be published this year. For years I have been asking Edward if it is okay with him if I write this book, realizing it will impact him.

"Mom, just write it!"

So, these words gave me a gift of freedom to express myself out of my harbour of guilt and heartache. Writing has been cathartic as I relive the pain and sorrow of past events. Now I will hand my manuscript over to him to read and hope that he will find some healing in the knowledge that the truth will provide hope for others in despair.

I didn't get a sub job this morning – I was alert at 6:00 a.m. in anticipation for my cell to vibrate an alarm but nothing. The upside… I guess today is the first day I stay home and officially start writing my story!

Now, after I drop Edward off at his meetings I drive to the Second Cup and write. I share my story with different people who seem interested in listening. I share with the clerk at the Seven Eleven, my financial advisor, my dentist, hairdresser, aesthetician, doctor, the lady standing in line at the checkout counter… Their reactions reveal there is merit in releasing my story.

A Gift of Grace

I drove Edward downtown twice this month so he could go to the accountant's office to lift his bankruptcy off his record. He finally received the necessary signature and now begins the process of renewing his credit. The lifting of the bankruptcy lifted Edward's spirits.

"Mom, that has been bothering me for a long time and now I took care of it!"

"I bet that really feels good Edward!"

He filed his Income Tax Return before me this year!

Edward has made new friends and joins them when they offer to give him a ride to do some volunteering at AIDS Calgary.

Edward has started working Thursdays, too, so he now has a four day work week.

Yippee for him!

Nicole has become our social convener. We have a reservation at a fine dining restaurant on Saturday night! We end up sharing appetizers and dancing to a fantastic jazz and blues band. I love music. It soothes my soul...

We have tickets to listen to a show, *Courage to Hope*, by Frank O'Dea, co-founder of Second Cup, and comedian Phil Callaway, at the Jubilee Auditorium. O'Dea was a homeless alcoholic who got himself off the streets and on to success! Proceeds go to benefit the Jack Neufeld Family Charitable Foundation and The Mustard Seed.

Then there is Macbeth at the IMAX theatre...

A Gift of Grace

February 24, 2008

Edward, age 31, Calgary

As I am writing today, Edward is playing Rachmaninoff's, Second Piano Concerto, Second Movement and I am crying with joy. He has just recently started to sit down more frequently at the piano and play...

He gets up... and reads the text on the screen...

"What do you mean, I might go to jail?"

"Well, you were working at a job and you were taking drugs off and on...What was your job at Toxin?"

"I was a bouncer!"

Then he grins and breaks out into a chuckle... I think because he tries to imagine himself throwing some guy out because of rough behaviour! Like he could or even would do that!

His face breaks out into an even bigger grin..."I really was just the doorman!"

Today, Edward, a friend and I listened to Dr. Stephen Post present his message; *It's Good to be Good.* Dr. Post is the first speaker of *The Forever Funds Speaker Series* established by The Calgary Foundation. This special event we attended was funded by The Calgary Foundation and supported by the Calgary Health Region as part of their Exploring Health and Healing Conference.

Edward brings me a cuppa tea and I love my life...

He sits at the piano; playing Rachmaninoff with no lamp... his music sheet is illuminated by the moonlight shining through the front room window.

A Gift of Grace

I love to hear him sit and play so effortlessly...

Many years ago Edward's piano teacher, Martha Hazelton informed him that he would gain the emotional part of playing after he had had some of life's experiences.

Well, Edward you've had life experiences beyond imagination, so play on...

I trust you will uphold the beliefs and values we taught you at home, treat yourself and others with respect and continue to believe in your ability to find happiness.

Lessons I Learned

1. Find a checklist of signs

2. Notice a pattern of behaviour

3. Check on the Internet to identify symptoms
   Symptoms are divided into positive and negative
   - Positive symptoms are, for example, hallucinations and delusions.
   - Negative symptoms are, for example, flat affect, apathy and poverty of speech.

   For more information, see the following website: www.sfnsw.org.au/schizophrenia/symptoms.htm

4. Admit there's a problem

5. Find a support group
   Learn strategies from the professional who facilitates the meetings, such as how to set healthy boundaries with your loved one

6. Seek a coach, mentor or counsellor

7. Persevere –
   - Don't give up; giving up on pursuing health care for Edward was NEVER an option!
   - Expect the revolving door – no obstacle is greater than the spirit within
   - Keep on top of the Health Care System
   - Programs that work: Fresh Start, Renfrew, Early Psychosis Program, Claresholm-Raymond Care Centre, AADAC Lander Treatment Centre in Claresholm, Toronto Healthcare HIV Research Study

8. Seek different perspectives on the person's behaviours from teachers, siblings, relatives, neighbours and friends

A Gift of Grace

9. Give unconditional love

10. Have the courage to advocate for your loved one

11. Seek the expertise of professionals – social workers, psychologists, psychiatrists
    Bring your notes with you so you can provide the necessary anecdotal information for the professionals to make a more accurate diagnosis.

12. Keep an open mind – other issues may cloud the mental illness – be aware of the complexity of the individual

13. Give yourself a distraction
    - Dance
    - Paint
    - Write
    - Go to a movie that gets you laughing and lightens you up
    - Overcome a fear which in turn will boost your confidence e.g. downhill skiing

14. Become knowledgeable about schizophrenia
    - Learn about the illness
    - Find books in Bookstores, Public Library
    - Contact Schizophrenia Society
    - Figure out how to talk to your loved one –"What's on your mind?" may backfire
    - Talk to people, chances are you will make a connection with someone who knows someone with schizophrenia, because one person out of 100 are diagnosed with schizophrenia in the world regardless of culture (World Health Organization says there were 1% or 5 million people worldwide in 2000 who had schizophrenia.)

15. Above all, don't lose your sense of self!
    - Find affirmations and quotes that resonate with you
    - Promote positive thinking by attending seminars, reading self-help books
    - Pamper yourself
    - Go on a retreat to write

16. Communicate – TLC: Talk, Laugh, Cry

A Gift of Grace

17. Reach out to family, friends, support groups

18. Make a Plan
    - Involve family
    - Have an intervention if needed – at doctor's office or hospital
    - Involve police by writing to secure a warrant – especially to be sure he gets to the intervention

19. Do what you love to do!
    - Perhaps it is baking for others and feeding your soul from their appreciation.
    - Maybe it is skiing, gardening or entertaining.

20. Know when to just let go!
    You raised your kids, modeling your beliefs and values. By age twelve your influence isn't as strong as that of their peers. Kids will make mistakes as they learn about themselves. But, they have had the opportunity to create a path for their life's journey, eventually they "come back" to embrace the lessons you taught them about basic beliefs and family values.

21. Do what you need to do to get the desired results
    Write letters to the judge. We needed letters at two different times to get Edward admitted to the psychiatric ward. The contents must indicate that he is injurious to himself and/or injurious to others. This is a heartbreaking ordeal, but you need to be strong in your resolve and hope for the best results.

Lessons I Learned

Afterword

The three petals of the Iris represent **courage, wisdom** and **hope** or **faith, hope** and **courage**. "Les Irises," Vincent van Gogh's historic artwork, was painted in the garden of the asylum at St. Remy in the south of France. It is now believed that what van Gogh suffered was schizophrenia. His painting, "Les Irises," sold for more than $50 million in 1987. The Iris features prominently in many Schizophrenia Society's public awareness and fund raising events.

To believe your own thoughts, to believe that what is true for you in your private heart is true for all men --- that is genius.

Ralph Waldo Emerson

****

Edward showed a life of promise from his first year of school to his graduation from UWC. He received a full scholarship to the University of Toronto, won their book prize and was named National Scholar. He fell out of university and into the "school of hard knocks" learning what it takes to live with a brain disease, schizophrenia, addictions, homelessness and HIV. His family has

A Gift of Grace

shown him love and that has allowed him to heal, enabling him to shine his brilliance once again. He came home to build a life to enjoy the present and the future.

Edward and his family have a message of resilience and the power of love.

EYE OF THE STORM

Edward K. Weatherly, 2004

About the Author

Beatrice Weatherly is a gifted educator and a courageous woman with a message of "you can achieve anything if you truly believe." This is a message her parents taught her and her five siblings during an amazing childhood growing up "in the house in the coulee" just south of Hughenden.

She models the unconditional love and acceptance she learned from her mother and challenges others to dream big just as her father inspired her to do. Bea realized her dream of becoming a teacher when she graduated from the University of Alberta with a Bachelor of Education degree and began teaching in the Provost area. Reflecting her parents' positive outlook, she encouraged her students to be all they could be. Shortly after she started teaching, Bea married and soon had her own three children to guide toward setting their sights high and dedicating themselves to reach their lofty goals. This teacher and principal made a significant difference to her students' lives and education, as well as being an amazing mother to Nicole, Shelley and Edward.

A Gift of Grace

Slowly cracks began breaking through the idyllic life. Bea became stronger through resolving many challenges, such as recovering from breast cancer, leaving unhealthy relationships, striking out on her own, embracing the "coming out" of her son and one daughter, all the while experiencing the roller coaster ride of her son's struggle with schizophrenia complicated by addictions. What she learned during this time, she incorporates in her book, *A Gift of Grace: A Mother's Journey Through Her Son's Schizophrenia.* As a mental health advocate, her goal is to remove the stigma of mental illness, addictions, homosexuality and homelessness to create a world of peace.

Retired from teaching elementary school students, Bea Weatherly retains the passion for education, which she now does through writing, speaking and life coaching. Meanwhile, she and two of her children, Nicole and Edward, formed a company called IDEGO Multimedia whose mission is to raise awareness and understanding of diverse social issues within the context of art.

For more about Bea, visit www.beaweatherly.com

About the Author

WATCH FOR EDWARD'S BOOK!

Watch for Edward Weatherly's soon to be released book

Making Sense of Crazy

Edward, a gifted musician and artist, went through the dark to show us the light. See life from Edward's eyes and his brilliant brain confused by mental illness. At the lowest point with multiple addictions, homelessness and insanity, he envisioned Hell and it frightened him. Throughout his life he kept journals, notebooks and scrapbooks interpreting the world as he experienced it. In this book he chronicles his arduous path from living hell to healthy recovery.

Edward is a courageous young man sharing his story with the BIG message:

★ Live your truth

★ Love yourself and others

★ Be tolerant of those who suffer mental illness because it could be you or a loved one who is the 1% of the population afflicted with schizophrenia or mental disease

★ Don't judge until you have walked in my shoes…

"The ones who are crazy enough to think they can change the world are the ones who do." Steve Jobs, CEO & co-founder, Apple Computer, Inc.

Mental Illness Awareness Week

Bea Weatherly, CEO of Upside Publishing (www.beaweatherly.com), is sponsoring **Mental Illness Awareness Week** (www.miaw.ca). Copies of *A Gift of Grace, A Mother's Journey Through Her Son's Schizophrenia* will be distributed to senior political, business and healthcare leaders at the 2008 *Mental Illness Awareness Week* during the Sixth Annual Champions of Mental Health Awards which take place on October 7, 2008 in the Great Hall of the National Gallery of Canada in Ottawa.

This event will bring together members of the Canadian Alliance on Mental Illness and Mental Health (CAMIMH), a network of politicians, business leaders, sponsors and other stakeholders, to celebrate individuals and organizations who have made outstanding contributions to the advancement of the mental health agenda in Canada.

Bea Weatherly and Edward Weatherly will attend this event and Edward has been selected as part of the *Faces Campaign*. His face and biography are posted on the MIAW website (www.miaw.ca).

20% of Canadians are affected by mental illness, either directly or have a loved one with mental illness. Stigma prevents millions of Canadians who have mental illness from receiving the help they so desperately need. Through the *Faces Campaign*, Mental Illness Awareness Week is working to change that. The "faces" are people, such as Edward, from every walk of life. Through their courage they are bringing mental illness out of the shadows and into the light of the world for all to see. The "faces" open the eyes of Canadians to the reality of mental illness. Their stories, including Edward's, show there is hope and proof "that through proper diagnosis, treatment and awareness, people with mental illnesses can live productive and fulfilling lives" (MIAW).

Mental Illness Awareness Week (www.miaw.ca) works continuously to bring new faces forward every year and to spread a message of hope for those afflicted with this disease.

Bea Weatherly, CEO, and *Upside Publishing and Productions* gratefully acknowledge Janssen-Ortho for its sponsorship of *A Gift of Grace, A Mother's Journey Through Her Son's Schizophrenia.*

A Gift of Grace

If you want to become a sponsor of the next edition of this book or a sponsor of Edward's book, please contact our office at:

Upside Publishing and Productions
Suite A, 3639 Sierra Morena Rd SW
Calgary Alberta
T3H 3A7

E-mail Bea Weatherly at
beaweatherly@shaw.ca

Give the Gift of
Extraordinary Books

This form has been included for your convenience in ordering additional copies of *A Gift of Grace: A Mother's Journey Through Her Son's Schizophrenia*

Please send me the following (for shipment to Canadian or US addresses)

_____ copies at @ $29.95 CDN each = _____ ___

Shipping & Handling: 1 copy at $8.00 CDN each = _____ ___

Additional copies _____ at $5.00 CDN each = _____ ___

Total (please remit in Canadian funds) = _____ ___

Please ship to:

Name: _____

Address - Street: _____

City: _____ Prov/State: _____

Postal/Zip Code: _____

Additional contact information (optional)

Phone: (___)_____ Fax: (___)_____ E-mail: _____

Method of payment: ❑ cheque ❑ money order

Send payment and order form to:

Upside Publishing and Productions
Suite A, 3639 Sierra Morena Rd SW
Calgary, Alberta Canada T3H 3A7